Roseates
and
Rectories

The birding biography of
The Revd FRANCIS LINLEY BLATHWAYT

Dr Trevor Kerry

Published in 2005 for:
Pintail Publications
TK Consultancy (Lincoln) Ltd
15 Lady Bower Close
North Hykeham
Lincoln LN6 8EX

by:
Tucann Books
19 High Street
Heighington
Lincoln LN4 1RG

ISBN 1 873257 58 9

Photographs: roseate terns (front cover) by kind permission of Paul Hackett. F.L. bird-watching (back cover), and the two images of F.L. on page 206 supplied by Lucy Morrill. The picture of F.L. on page 207 is courtesy of the Dorset County Museum.

CONTENTS

THIS BOOK AND HOW TO USE IT

This book will appeal to all those who have an interest in local birding and/or in local history. Birders will find it interesting because it traces aspects of the development of modern birding, supports the attraction of watching a local 'patch', and examines some of the changes in bird distribution that have taken place over the last hundred years. Local historians will, it is hoped, enjoy the gradual accumulation of evidence and matters of context that have allowed a re-assessment of the Revd Francis Linley Blathwayt, its subject.

Many readers may wish to ignore the bracketed note numbers in the text of each chapter, and may read the text straight through as a narrative; it is designed to be used in this way. Alternatively, the notes provide a commentary on items of interest, evidence for judgements made, and a source of reference for those who might like to pursue any specific issue further.

ACKNOWLEDGEMENTS

My thanks are due to a number of people who have assisted this research. To my wife, Dr Carolle Kerry, as always, for humouring my obsessions; but also for her help in gathering some of the diary data, especially Appendix 3, and searching the Lincolnshire and BTO archives with me.

To Mrs Lucy Morrill, F.L.'s grand-daughter, for generous help in providing photographs and papers from the family archive, and for being patient in answering my many queries.

To the Dorset County Museum at Dorchester, especially to Dr Jenny Cripps and her team, for organising access to the notebooks of Francis Linley Blathwayt and for supplying photographs. Their co-operation was exemplary. To Carole Showell and the British Trust for Ornithology for excellent, efficient and concerned access to the library. These sources were invaluable, and the individuals named deserve special thanks.

To Mary Blathwayt, a distant relative of F.L., for suggestions and early interest in the project. To Mrs Gillian Blathwayt, whose late husband, Christopher Blathwayt MC, was a nephew of F.L., for her contacts with me.

To the Bishop Grosseteste College Library, who accelerated the early work by finding Crockford entries. To Emma Jones of the University of Lincoln Learning Resources Library, who obtained many of the articles written by Francis. To Mr Ian Macalpine-Leny of The Old Rectory, Doddington, who provided a note about F.L.'s bat-spotting. To Norman Rosser of Malvern College, archivist, for data about F.L.'s school days. To Dr Gordon Jackson and his wife, for providing information about former occupants of their property. To the editor of the Chipping Sodbury Gazette, for printing a request for information. To Mrs Christiana Poole, who responded to my newspaper enquiry in order to send me invaluable information about Francis and Marjorie Blathwayt and their children. To the Rector of St Peter's, Dyrham, for passing on a request for help; and especially to Mrs Linda Hitchings for detailed responses to this. Mrs Pat Churchman supplied a photograph of F.L. at the porch of Dyrham church.

To the wardens of All Saints' Church, Lincoln, for access to papers relating to F.L. To Christopher J. Salmon of Exeter, who sent extended notes, cuttings and photographs of F.L.'s time in Dyrham.

None of the above named are responsible for any short-comings or inaccuracies in the text.

INTRODUCTION

The purpose of this book is to describe the life and achievement of the Revd Francis Linley Blathwayt, with particular reference to his contribution to birding in Lincolnshire.

Francis, who seems always to have signed himself F.L.Blathwayt, belonged to a wealthy and influential family and became one of that quintessentially English tradition – the parson-naturalist.

His interest was mainly in the growing study of ornithology, as opposed to other branches of natural history, which was a young and developing science. Young, despite the fact that birds had been studied systematically by others and had been a subject for English literary allusions since before the year 1000 (1). Developing, because this was a period of 'great debates' in the study of birds: debates about the merits of conservation as against shooting, the advantages of observation over collecting, and about the still controversial theory of evolution – to identify only a few issues that stirred passions.

To summarise his life: F.L. Blathwayt was a child of the Raj but moved to England for his schooling; he followed a traditional path to Oxbridge and into Holy Orders; he held curacies in Lincoln city; he took the cure of souls at the parish church at Doddington in Lincolnshire; during his time there he studied and published details of the birds of Lincolnshire; later, he moved to the Dorset living of Melbury; here he continued life-long birding with a series of papers, mostly relating to the birdlife of the Dorset area. He ended his days at Dyrham, Gloucestershire (2).

Stated baldly, it would seem a quiet and relatively uneventful life, a life bounded by the offices of the Anglican Church and by forays into the field to study his beloved birds. But this simple chronology is, it will be maintained, deceptive. For, history itself is more than a table of events, and the biography of a man more than the mere catalogue of his doings.

In this book are drawn together such threads as can be gleaned about the man – his family, surroundings, beliefs, actions, attitudes, personality. There are wider themes, too, drawn from that contextual history: about the economics, concerns, events, achievements and failures of the times in which he lived. Then, finally, more specific information is interwoven concerning the social, cultural and scientific development of the study of birds and the role of birding. The result might be called a 'birding biography'.

Francis Linley Blathwayt was both unique and archetypal: bird man, man of the people (albeit on a limited stage), man of letters, man of his time. He represents the backbone of English traditional society in his own age, yet is a fresh cog in the great new scientific machine that was beginning to drive forward innovative intellectual activity.

His is not the story of a great man; few can aspire to greatness. But it is the story of a concerned man, an enquiring man, a man of curiosity, and a man of integrity and achievement – characteristics to which all men and women can aspire.

NOTES TO THE INTRODUCTION

1.   James Fisher in *The Shell Bird Book* (1973edn) London: Ebury Press and Michael Joseph, p 43 quotes the Anglo-Saxon Exeter Book, where, in a passage called The Seafarer, there is an evocative section which is thought to date from 675A.D. about the birds of Bass Rock. But the tradition of writing about birds goes back much further in international literature, for example to the Georgics of Virgil, where the main concern is with nature as a tool of the farmer (cf. the lovely reference to 'the talkative martin [that] hangs her nest under the rafters' – book 4 line 307 in the C. Day Lewis translation, 1943, published by Readers' Union, London); and even (and more whimsically) to the Old Testament (cf. doves in The Song of Solomon, or the role of the raven in the story of Noah's Flood). Homer was obsessed with the symbolism of some birds, such as the halcyon or kingfisher. Depictions of birds go back many thousands of years before literature as such, mainly in the contexts of the hunt on the one hand, or of religious mythology on the other.

2.   In F.L.'s day the village of Dyrham was in Wiltshire accordng to his notepaper.

CHAPTER 1
THE BLATHWAYT FAMILY HISTORY

I first met the Revd F.L. Blathwayt when we were both thirty-five years old.

It was 1977. At the time, I was organising warden for a group of volunteers who were carrying out census work on the wildlife of an area of Lincoln city called Hartsholme Park, within walking distance of where I then lived. To try to put the area, and census work on its birds, in context I was undertaking an historical survey using sources such as the *Transactions of the Lincolnshire Naturalists' Union*, the annual publication of that body.

One of the items I unearthed in the pages of *Transactions* was an article by the Revd F.L. Blathwayt. It told of the irruption of crossbills into the park. The article held my attention, and I thought about it many times subsequently. It was published in 1910, when the Revd F.L. Blathwayt was aged thirty-five. The vision of this young Edwardian clergyman treading the same paths that I trod through Hartsholme at the same time of life intrigued me, but the terrible trio of career, family and busy-ness kept us apart. Somewhere in the back of my mind, though, was an intention to meet with him again.

Nearly thirty years later I glimpsed the Revd F. L. Blathwayt once more in the course of my birding. This book is the result.

•

Francis Linley Blathwayt (1875-1953), like many clergy of his time, came from the échelons of the landed gentry. He was born in India. The family was entirely typical of its social class, in that the professions of soldier and clergyman recurred through the male lines, and foreign service was common-place (1).

The family seat at Dyrham, Gloucestershire, was occupied by Blathwayts almost continuously from 1688, and re-built from 1692 onwards. The house had its doldrums, as we shall see; but was rescued and remained in the family until it passed to the National Trust in 1956.

At the time of the 1881 Census Captain George William Blathwayt (1824-1899) would have been the owner. But a house at Hurstpierpoint, Wickham Hill Lodge, seems also to have been a family residence of the period, in fact the English home to the children of Francis' uncle, Lt Col Linley Blathwayt, who was in the Bengal Staff Corps, an Indian army regiment (2). It seems probable that this arrangement was one of convenience so that Mary Bathwayt (born 1879), and presumably, later, William Blathwayt (born 1882), children of Lt Col Linley and his wife, could be schooled in England. Francis, living a short distance away at 61 Grafton Road, Broadwater, would have had a similar experience since we must assume that his own father, too, was still in India at that date, where he served as a member of the Indian Civil Service (3).

Like all Census data, the 1881 Census lists all persons present on the day that it was conducted (4). The list for Wickham Hill Lodge names Lt Col Linley Blathwayt, head of the house. His daughter Mary is there. Francis' family home in Broadwater was shared with Charles H. (i.e. Hugh) Blathwayt (born 1876 in India), and Henry W. (i.e. Wynter) Blathwayt (born about 1877 in India) – his younger brothers. Also recorded at Broadwater are : Anne Linley Blathwayt, Lt Col Linley Blathwayt's mother and Francis' grandmother, the most senior family member; and Anne S (presumably Anne Sophia, daughter of the Revd George Blathwayt and Isabella Pye), Francis' great aunt.

Broadwater itself 'was the original nucleus of Worthing, and the main street still has a village street air, rather than [being] taken aback by the suburban shopping centre it has become. Pleasant cottages N of the church in Broadwater Street East' – that is how Nairn and Pevsner described it in 1965 (5).

To trace Francis Blathwayt's origins we need to work backwards in time. Francis was the son of Charles George Blathwayt (born 1841), the younger brother of Lt Col Linley Blathwayt (born 1839). Charles George was married twice, first to Alice Mary Fowler, Francis' mother, and then to Georgina Mary Weeks. Francis was sent to England, in about 1879, following his mother's death.

Francis' grandfather, Charles George's father, was also Charles: the Revd Charles Blathwayt (1800-1874), Rector of Langridge, Somerset. The Revd Charles married Anne Linley Rose, from whom the recurrent family

10

name Linley was taken. He had two sisters (Frances and Anne Sophia, Francis' great aunts), and a brother (Lt Col George William Blathwayt, 1797-1871, who fought at the Battle of Waterloo). He in turn is noted as being 19th in direct descent from Henry II, and in direct descent from Gundred, daughter of William the Conqueror (6).

The Revd Charles' father was also a clergyman, the Revd George William Blathwayt (1759-1806). We now come to a most inconsiderate period in the Blathwayt saga during which each successive father and son were named William! So, George William was the son of William Blathwayt III, the son of William Blathwayt II, who was the son of William Blathwayt (c 1649-1717) and Mary Wynter Blathwayt (1650-1691). This William Blathwayt founded the Dyrham Park home of the family and was Secretary of State for War to King William III. Thus William Blathwayt was Francis' great-great-great-great-grandfather.

This brief sweep back in time shows Francis Linley Blathwayt descended from, and at the heart of, the English upper class but, typically, also committed to the Established Church throughout the family line. These two factors were to shape his life, though they were not the only influences on an existence that was more modest than might have been expected under the circumstances. It is to this part of the story that we can now turn.

•

Fox-Davies lists the armorials for the Blathwayt family (7):

Per sable or and sable, two bendlets engrailed counter-changed. Mantling sable and or. Crest on a wreath of the colours, on a rock proper, an eagle rising sable, winged or, charged on the breast with two bendlets or. Motto – virtute et veritate.

The eagle was a Blathwayt emblem. When Lt Col Linley Blathwayt moved his branch family to Batheaston in the early 1900s a stone eagle was also found on the gate-post to the house there – and the residence was called Eagle House. The stone eagle became associated with a range of fables from across the country of stones coming to life (8):

Quinn … also tracked down a stone eagle on Eagle House at Batheaston which picks up a stone cup and flies to fill it from the river nearby.

Today, the stone eagle sits on the roof-line of the house – a rather stylised

11

bird. Maybe the eagle caught the attention of the young Francis and began his attraction with birding. However that might be, the Blathwayt motto – *through integrity and truth* – is one that seems ideally suited to this clergyman of scientific persuasion, and he must have been familiar with it. It sums up the old aristocracy, too, where commitment to public service and to the servants and others dependent on them for labour and sustenance was often considerable.

It was only towards the later part of his life that Francis Linley Blathwayt began to live on the Dyrham estate (see below). As we have seen, his early childhood was located in India. He was born at Ahmednuggar on the 11th July 1875, but by the age of about five he had moved to the Broadwater district of Sussex. He was schooled at Malvern College, Worcestershire. Malvern had not long been established (1865), but it nestled among the Malvern Hills and must have been a comforting location to a young would-be birder. At this date Francis' family home is given as Walney House, Aylestone Hill, Hereford, by the records held at Malvern College for 1890. Malvern College had a strong natural history society even in these early days.

From here F.L. went to study at Oxford, possibly in 1894, at Hertford College, graduating as a Bachelor of Arts in 1899. Malvernians had a strong old-boy network there. The *Malvernian* journal for March 1898 contains this entry:

The Oxford Old Malvernian Club is flourishing. A most successful evening was spent in Wahl's rooms at Balliol, when Wahl, Costley-White and Blathwayt were at home to members of the Club. (9)

The Hertford College's current web-site is proud in announcing that its alumni have included some who have risen in government or public service, as well as 'scientists, writers, musicians, explorers and scholars'. Francis would have been aware that the College had hosted such luminaries as John Donne, the metaphysical poet; Jonathan Swift, author of Gulliver's Travels; Thomas Hobbes, the political analyst; and Bishop John Wilkins, one of the founders of the Royal Society. Again, the Malvern College records list his stay in Oxford, adding that he was 'reading for Indian Woods and Forests' (10). Francis was already a birder: for his first ornithological paper was published while he was an undergraduate.

From Oxford, Francis, in preparation for becoming ordained as a Church of England clergyman, trained for a year at the Lincoln Theological College, becoming ordained in 1900, and being assigned to the church of St Swithin in Lincoln city. His next appointment was to another city church (11), but then he became the Rector of Doddington – a village some six miles distant in the same Diocese. Here he remained from 1909 until 1916, before moving to the Dorset parish of Melbury Osmond with Melbury Sampford, again a rural living (in the gift of the Earl of Ilchester) (12) that consumed his energies for a further thirteen years. In 1929, at the comparatively late age of fifty-four he took up residence and cure of souls in the Rectory of the little church on the family estate at Dyrham Park, where he remained for the rest of his days, though he retained his birding connections with Dorset rather than in his county of residence, Gloucestershire.

It was quite late in the research for this text that I came across a photograph of the man himself (13), a head-and-shoulders portrait. Coming face-to-face with someone I had grown to know so well, but whom I could not visualise, was a strange experience. The image is a formal portrait: he wears a dark suit and clerical collar – exactly as one would expect. Everything else about him is unexpected.

The suit appears quite modern, single-breasted; and the cut of the collar has a touch of contemporary Italian sharpness about it. The face that looks out over the intervening decades is set above a long neck, emphasised by the crispness of the dog-collar. It is a modern face. Francis might just have emerged from the Unisex Hair Salon in today's Lincoln High Street, for the cut is neat and short – military, almost. Even the side-burns are cut short and high. His hairline recedes quite sharply, a wide peak of skull appearing between the two sides of the parting, and a touch of early grey just beginning to creep towards the left temple.

One might describe the face as well-chiselled. It is oval. Imagine the smooth, white egg of a wood pigeon, the larger end as the skull and the smaller as the chin, and the likeness is remarkable. In semi-profile, his left ear is made obvious by the receding hairline even though it is not large. The eyes are widely spaced, clear, open, honest, unblinking. An aquiline nose is reminiscent of Michaelangelo's David, nostrils slightly flared, suggesting to the observer the alertness of a wild animal. A wide mouth neither droops in serious mode, nor lifts in a smile, but emphasises the strong curve of the jaw. This face sits above a frame that is quite spare – athletic rather than powerful.

This is Francis Linley Blathwayt in about 1918. It contrasts in some ways with what one might have imagined from the evidence. In the Dyrham Park *Guidebook* (14) Captain George Blathwayt, pictured around 1880, though a fairly distant relative, is quite different. Older, he is more portly, short and stocky. But he is also a maverick. Unusually for the time, he wears a crumpled tweed jacket over a waist-coat of light colour, and a very pale bowler hat – the precise colour is not discernible in the monochrome image. His stance is studiedly casual, the body-language full of swagger, the features rounded and squat, and the face plays a self-satisfied smile as he lords it over the family on the garden steps below him. F.L. is quite different!

Though Francis Linley came late to Dyrham Park, and as Rector only not as owner, there is a sense in which his roots were always there. So it is opportune to consider a short history of the family seat, using National Trust guides to the house, especially Kenworthy-Brown's (15).

•

Dyrham Park featured significantly in the life of F.L. because of his occupation of the church on the estate. We have seen that William Blathwayt (1649-1717) married Mary Wynter (1650-1691) and thereby acquired the house at Dyrham Park, which he immediately felt needed to be replaced or re-built. The following paragraphs tell the story of the house chronologically. Thus it was that William set about putting a new façade onto the previously Tudor-style manor house. He was sceptical about the cost of this enterprise, employing an unknown architect, a Huguenot, Samuel Hauduroy, to whom he paid just ten pounds for the trouble.

The main house was completed in 1694. The proportions are very attractive: there are two storeys, thirteen window-lights wide in total. Each window is five panes deep; but the third floor is truncated in height and has a complementary row of windows just two panes deep, a ploy which holds the balance of the appearance perfectly. The main door is flanked by classical columns. An eagle sits in stone on the pinnacle above the centre of the building on the East front, placed there in 1705 above the family motto. William Blathwayt earned a considerable income as a senior civil servant, a competent one; a perk of the role was to be able to use the services of an architect from the Office of Works, and he chose William Talman, Sir Christopher Wren's deputy. The style of the house is said to ape a Genoese Palace with overtones from Versailles, and Talman was also connected with work at no less a site than Hampton Court Palace (16).

The West front was once the entrance. Now it faces the garden. An Italianate double stairway bordered by stone banister rails runs down to the lawn. There is a single-storey'd gallery on either side of the central core of the house, and one of these provides a covered walk to the village church of which Francis was, eventually, the Rector.

A new stable block was added in 1698, with stalls for twenty-six horses. There were also utilities here: 'nurseries, kitchens and offices, brewery, laundry, coach houses, with rooms and garrets for the staff.' A greenhouse or orangery hides the view of the stables from the house, and would double as a place for nurturing tender plants but also, when empty, as a garden house for the family. There is another carved motto here, translated as: 'observe moderation, keep the end in view, follow the law of nature' – a fitting motto for a naturalist! (17).

A vast garden was integral to the design of Dyrham Park from the beginning, probably the brain-child of George London, but largely put into effect by the head gardener, Hurnall. Exotic plants were brought in, in the manner of the time. The natural slopes of the site were landscaped into the design. Natural springs in the Park were utilised through a dam in the lake to provide fountains, and there were water-courses and ponds. These gardens have had a chequered history of decay and restoration, as well as falling victim to natural disasters such as Dutch Elm Disease. Yew trees were planted under the church about a hundred years ago and 'shaped into buttresses around 1900', so they would have been there and quite mature in this form in Francis' time as Rector.

The house and the Blathwayt line owe much to the entrepreneurial streak that William possessed. As a Dutch speaker he was useful to King William III; and he was a good administrator who kept away from the boundary of politics. His marriage to a mature lady (she was thirty-six) brought three children in quick succession (William II, John and Anne; a fourth died in infancy); but Mary died after just five years of their companionship. During the reign of Queen Anne, William became the victim of politicking, and resigned most of his offices – quite a blow to someone who had earned the substantial sum of £2000 a year. Kenworthy-Browne assesses his nature thus: serious, pedantic, reluctant to adjust to new ideas, fond of entertaining and cultured conversation, a lover of music and literature, a musician and collector of books. Some of these traits may have been passed on to his successors such as Francis.

Ownership of the house passed from William to his son, William II (d

1742), and then to William III (d 1787) and William IV (d 1806). At this point a skeleton in the family closet meant that the house became the property of William Crane, the child of William IV's sister Penelope, who ran away with a poor man, Jeremiah Crane. The couple gave up their child to William IV, and thus he inherited Dyrham, and chose also to take the Blathwayt name. Colonel George William Blathwayt took up ownership in due course followed by his son and namesake, Captain George William. On his death in 1899, the year that Francis left Oxford, the house passed to George William's brother, the Revd Wynter Thomas Blathwayt. Wynter Thomas lived only until 1909, when Robert Wynter (d 1936) succeeded him; he was the owner when Francis moved to be Rector of the Dyrham church in 1929. However, the ownership of Dyrham Park was to be short-lived in the modern world for the Blathwayt line. Between 1938 and 1946 the house was let to Lady Islington, who carried out some re-decoration; and during the years of the second World War part of the house was used as a hospital. Christopher George Wynter Blathwayt, M.C., renounced ownership, though it passed to his brother. Christopher died in 1990. During his period, in 1953, Francis died, still in post as the Rector of the little church in the garden. The family was already aware that it could not maintain the property adequately and just three years after Francis' death the house was taken over by the National Trust on behalf of the nation.

•

While the history of the family seat and the relatively distant (to Francis and to us) Blathwayt past is of interest as a context for our narrative, better light might be shed on Francis by examining what we know of some of the family members closest geographically and in age to his own situation. Three have particular interest: Lt Col Linley Blathwayt, his uncle; and his two cousins Mary and William, Colonel Linley's children (18).

It would be easy to assume the caricature of Linley Blathwayt as a crusty old soldier aloof from his stay-at-home contemporaries and severe with his family. Nothing would seem to be further from the truth. My first encounter with Linley came about in an odd way. Two elderly and slightly battered volumes caught the eye at an Antiques Fair: they were bound in blue rexine and the front covers were embossed in gold with a detailed and intricate flower pattern. But what was most interesting was that the spine announced that they were the products of the Selborne Society (19). No naturalist can pass by a reference to the great Gilbert White of Selborne without a second look.

One of the volumes was dated 1898 (20). Among the Treasurer's pleas to secure increased membership in the face of the Society's debt, and *the Answers to Correspondents* [gloriously quaint: *Beatrice Banks – We do not believe that animals are skinned alive for the manufacture of gloves*] (21), was a letter from Lt. Col. Linley Blathwayt F.L.S. of Eagle House, Batheaston, Bath.

It was clear that by this time Linley Blathwayt had moved his family to the Batheaston home, which was to become a somewhat famous venue in a few short years. For the moment, his pre-occupation was with the less contentious 'Earwig and Worm', as he scribbled this note to the editor:

In answer to your correspondent, who in the July number of NATURE NOTES says he saw a black earwig attack and kill an earthworm, and asks 'whether earthworms form part of the earwig's diet' I should think it very improbable, the earwig being, as a rule, a vegetarian, feeding on the petals and other parts of flowers, and on fruits and leaves, though it sometimes consumes animal *débris* as well. The fact, however, that your correspondent calls it a *black earwig* leads me to believe that the insect in question was not an earwig at all, but one of the larger beetles of the *Staphylinidae*…(22)

So the Colonel, pensioned off from Indian service, had discovered a modest but attractive property, Eagle House, reasonably close to the family seat, and was living an active life among the bugs. That such an assessment is substantially accurate was confirmed when following up some of Francis Linley's ornithological writing. In the Victoria History of Somerset (23) not only does Francis contribute the section on birds, but the Colonel is responsible for no less than seven entries about insect groups (24). This collaboration took place ready for publication in 1906; but in 1916 Francis moved to the Rectory of Melbury a short distance from Batheaston. Though Colonel Linley survived only three more years, they were for that time relatively near neighbours.

Two clues in this story to date lead to more understanding of this old soldier: his occupation of Eagle House, and the use of the word 'vegetarian' in the letter quoted above. To begin with Eagle House: quite recently a number of Blathwayt papers were archived to the local Record Office in Gloucester. Among these was the diary of Mary Blathwayt, unmarried daughter of Colonel Linley. Born in 1879, she was Francis' close contemporary. They would have known one another as children when they were resident close by one another at 61 Grafton Road and Wickham Hill Lodge respectively, as well as being cousins.

For a number of years, by about 1910, Mary had been entertaining members of the suffragette movement at Eagle House, and she and her mother Emily were active supporters. Indeed, Batheaston had become quite notorious for this connection. Colonel Linley Blathwayt, far from being scandalised, seemed to revel in the fact. Interesting evidence for this comes from photographs that he took of various members of the movement at Batheaston.

The suffragette movement was extremely controversial and divisive at the time, and still is among its historical analysts. It was illegal and dangerous. Even the mild-mannered Oxford Illustrated History of England describes it in these terms:

The WSPU [as Emmeline Pankhurst's movement was called] increasingly advocated violence against both property and individual politicians, as well as inflicting through imprisonment and hunger strikes considerable hardship and even death upon its members (25)

Hannam (26) selects three photographs which Colonel Linley took. They are of reasonable technical quality, so he must have been a fairly accomplished artist in this still-new medium. In each picture the women are simply but smartly dressed, and their hair is carefully coiffured; ordinary women engaged in high politics. The subject matter is of tree planting in the garden at Batheaston. Each tree bears a prominent label which signifies its genus and its planter.

Hannam indicates an interesting background to the pictures:

Colonel Linley's photographs provide us with less familiar images [i.e. than the conflict images of the national press]. In the first picture Annie Kenney watches Teresa Garnett plant a tree. Annie Kenney, a former mill worker, was an organiser for the WSPU in the West Country and was a key figure for the Blathwayt family. They found her to be a charismatic personality and Mary lived with her for several months in Bristol to help with organising work. Annie was a frequent visitor to Eagle House, where she had her own room, and the suffragette field was named after her. Teresa Garnett was very active from 1909, when in that year she attacked Winston Churchill with a riding whip in Bristol and went to prison for disturbing the peace. (27)

The Colonel's support for this disruptive movement might, on the face of it, seem surprising enough. But the story does not stop at creating a commemorative woodland (28). The Observer newspaper (29) ran a feature on Mary Blathwayt's diary, concentrating on the elements that concerned the relations between the women. Citing the work of Professor Martin Pugh (30) of the Liverpool John Moores University, it claimed:

Christabel was the most classically beautiful of the Pankhurst daughters and was the focus of rash 'crushes' across the [suffragette] movement. Pugh now believes she was briefly involved with Mary Blathwayt who, in her turn, was probably supplanted by Annie Kenney, a working class activist from Oldham... Many of the short-lived sexual couplings referred to in the diary took place in the Blathwayt family's Eagle House home in Batheaston, near Bath...Mary writes matter-of-fact lines such as, "Annie slept with someone else again last night," or "There was someone else in Annie's bed this morning," said Pugh. 'But it is all done with no moral opprobrium for the act itself.'

Pugh's construction of the diaries is hotly contested by Purvis (31), who questions Pugh's 'use and interpretation of evidence.' But this surprising political connection leads to another discovery – not scandalous or momentous in any way – but unusual for the time: many suffragettes were vegetarians and were treated at the Blathwayts' home at Eagle House to their vegetarian choices. The Blathwayt diaries record, for example, that Marion Wallace Dunlop (a hunger striker) and Florence Haig (who was imprisoned on various occasions):

...like so many of them never eat meat, and not much animal food at all (32)

An entry for 27th February 1911 records that Mr and Mrs Rogers came to lunch at Eagle House. Mr Rogers worked for the Men's League for Women's Suffrage, and Mrs Rogers:

...like so many suffrage people...did not eat the chicken, but she had vegetables, bread sauce, cream...

Leah Leneman records other references to this dietary habit in relation to meals at the Blathwayts'. Given the social standing of the Blathwayts, and the background of Lt Colonel Linley Blathwayt, it is a surprise to find him heading up a household that supports a revolutionary political view, welcomes the militant members of the movement, records their images for posterity, plants a garden to the cause, blinks at sexual irregularity, and panders to their culinary tastes. There is no evidence that he shared the vegetarianism of the suffragettes, but he clearly likes and supports them as people. He seems to have been not merely an expert bug-hunter but a man of unusual principle and unconventional view.

So where does Francis stand in relation to these revelations? It is incredibly difficult to judge from the extant evidence. But there is certainly no evidence of a rift with his uncle or Mary, even if he does not espouse the same causes with the same zeal. Francis and the Colonel work together on the shared project - the massive volumes comprising the *Victoria History of Somerset* - up to 1906. In 1916 Francis chose to move from the living at Doddington, Lincolnshire, to one a stone's throw from Batheaston, and to remain there beyond the death of the Colonel himself, for some thirteen years in total. In such small and closed communities their connections would have been transparent. Later, when Francis marries and a son is born to Francis and Marjorie, shortly before the move to Melbury, the boy is accorded the name Linley (33).

•

The other child of Colonel Linley is William, apparently less colourful than his sister. He is described as a 'minor poet', and some of his work appears in a 1926 volume, *Love and Stars* (34). This is a slim text, the pages often having more space than printing on them. The quality of the poetry leaves something to be desired. The Preface was composed at Batheaston in March 1926. The verses are a mixture of original items and translations, which William himself describes as 'paraphrases', and 'in no way literal'. The original work appears, at least to this author, as somewhat jéjeune.

There can be little doubt that William and Francis rubbed shoulders at Batheaston, though it is hard to see where their interests, tastes or personalities would have overlapped. If William's poetry is a mirror held up to the man, then the image is a slightly odd one. In a poem entitled 'Colours', for example, William's poetical review of 'nature's year' includes the paean to summer:

In summer time the roses are red
With wonderful depths of hue;
And fleecy clouds drift overhead
Till they melt away in the blue.

In another piece, oddly entitled 'World = Police' there is a cautionary tale that seems to suggest that, in the face of crime, it is good to have policemen on hand; but – just in case one is not available, the readers should 'keep your shoulders strong and square in case the sergeant isn't there.'

Nor is the poem called 'Religion and Science' a great help in illuminating any view of the world that Francis might have espoused, one suggests; though the statement:

A narrow mind will take a narrow view

might echo life in general at Batheaston, where minds were rather less than narrow for that era.

If Francis Linley has affinities with his family members at the Batheaston home, one suspects that it is with the entomologist, Lt Colonel Linley Blathwayt, above all. This connection will feature in a future chapter.

•

Thus we have had a first meeting with F.L., parson and naturalist, from a family of powerful and even colourful members, of aristocratic origin but living in relative obscurity for most of his life. He is, as far as we can see, educated and yet a man of simple taste, apparently true to the family motto – through integrity and truth. So we must take that image forward through the next three chapters, into the thought-worlds that he inhabited, before we go on to examine his unique contribution to natural science and to birding in particular.

NOTES TO CHAPTER 1

1. There are two guidebooks to Dyrham Park that provide 'simplified' i.e. incomplete genealogies, their main interest being in the line of Blathwayts who owned and occupied the family seat. The earlier text was written by John Kenworthy-Browne in 1981, though the copy in my possession is the 1999 edition, published by the National Trust. It is a relatively long and detailed account of the house, with some other data added. The more recent guide is the National Trust's *Dyrham Park* (undated), which is less detailed and more user-friendly but is designed mainly to move visitors through the rooms now on display.

2. The 1881 England Census (http://search.ancestry.co.uk) records Linley Blathwayt as born about 1840 in Langridge, Somerset, and residing at Wickham Hill Lodge, Hurstpierpoint, Sussex. His occupation is given as Lieutenant Colonel Bengal Staff Corps Retired List.

Of Roseates *and* Rectories

3.   This is recorded in the series 'The Presidents of the Lincolnshire Naturalists' Union', the entry for Rev. Francis Linley Blathwayt MA MBOU, written by someone whose initials only are shown (R.W.G. – but see chapter 12) in volume 5 of the *Transactions of the Lincolnshire Naturalists' Union*. Recruitment to the Indian Civil Service tended to be from Public School boys who were more likely to deal in factual events than big ideas and conceptual structures; and if Francis' father fell to this category then the characteristic might be a pre-courser to F.L.'s later pre-occupation with 'lists'.

4.   The fascinating detail comes from the web-site http://search.ancestry.co.uk.

5.   Nairn, I. and Pevsner, N. (1965) *Sussex* Harmondsworth: Penguin, p 390.

6.   There is a memorial to Lt Col George W Blathwayt on the High Street in Chipping Sodbury.

7.   Fox-Davies, A.C. (1970) *Armorial Families: A directory of gentlemen of coat-armour* London: David and Charles.

8.   'When Stones Go Wandering' by Jeremy Harte (2003), available at web-site: www.whitedragon.org.uk/articles

9.   Recorded by R.W.G. in *LNU Transactions* – see note 3. Additional information is taken from a letter and cuttings supplied by Norman Rosser (2005), archivist, Malvern College.

10.   www.hertford.ox.ac.uk is the web-site source for the College. Forestry has a long history at Oxford. Roger Mills' article '100 years of forestry information from Oxford' can be found on www.sconul/ac.uk/pubs_stats/new and contains this statement: 'The story of forestry in Oxford begins with the Royal Indian Engineering College at Coopers Hill, Windsor, a training college for the Indian civil service, which established a school of forestry in 1871.' This would link Francis' studies with his father's occupation.

11.   More detail about Francis' appointments can be found in a later chapter.

12.   Recorded by R.W.G. in *LNU Transactions* – see note 3.

13.   The current Rector of Doddington kindly put me in touch with the owner of the Rectory (now a private house) in the village, who supplied the photocopy of the R.W.G. article, already referenced, in which the picture appears. It was taken in the period 1916-1918. The Rectory's owner, Ian Macalpine-Leny, added the Revd Francis Blathwayt: 'The only other thing I know about him…is that he had the first Lincolnshire record of a Whiskered Bat here at the Rectory.' (Personal communication 14.04.05).

14.   National Trust (undated), p 2.

15.   In this I have followed the earlier of the two guidebooks in the main, Kenworthy-Browne (1999), which is more detailed but less concerned with the present room-displays. Because of boundary changes the house is now in Gloucestershire, though in F.L.'s time he records the Rectory as being in Dyrham, Wiltshire.

16.   Yarwood, D. (1967) *The Architecture of England* London: Batsford, 2nd edition, p 245.

17.   The Latin is: *servare modum, finemque tueri, naturamque sequi* from Lucan's *Pharsalia*. The word Dyrham means 'deer park' according to Foss, A. (1980) *Country House Treasures* London: BCA.

18.   Francis' own brothers do not feature very much in the extant sources. Henry Wynter Blathwayt (b 1877) died in 1917, killed in action in Cambrai. He had two sons Justin Robert Wynter (b. 1913), and Christopher George Wynter (1912-1990), who won a Military Cross in the second World War. What we know of Christopher shows him following in the family's military tradition in the King's Royal Rifle Corps. He was a member of a Jedburgh team, special forces dropped behind enemy lines to operate in uniform. He belonged to a cell that included Captain P. Carron de la Carriere and Sergeant N. Wood. The code name for this group was Gilbert, and Christopher's *nom de guerre* was P. Charron. He married Gillian Butcher. Justin Robert Winter was born in 1913 and married Cecily Mary Moore (née Fegan).

19.   The Selborne Society, founded in 1885 to commemorate the eighteenth century naturalist Gilbert White, of Selborne in Hampshire, was originally a national organisation. Its aims were to continue the traditions of this pioneer of environmental study by correspondence between members about their observations of natural history. Today's Selborne Society was originally the Brent Valley branch of the national Society. The present group continues the work of its founders, observing and recording wildlife in part of west London and managing and conserving Perivale Wood Local Nature Reserve as the Gilbert White Memorial.

20.   *Nature Notes, the Selborne Society's Magazine,* volume IX, London: John Bale and Son.

21.   Op. cit. pp 161 and 160 respectively.

22.   Op. cit. p 178.

23.   William Page (1906) *The Victoria History of the Counties of England: A History of Somerset in Five Volumes* Volume I.

24.   Orthoptera, Neuroptera, Hymenoptera, Coleoptera, Diptera and Hemiptera, plus an introductory section. His qualifications are listed now as F.L.S., F.E.S.

25.   Morgan, K.O., (1984) Oxford: Oxford University Press, p 519.

26.   Dr June Hannam, 'Suffragette photographs' The Regional History Centre at the University of the West of England, accessed on web-site file://A:\blathwayt\hannam.htm on 09.04.05.

27.   The suffragette field was an area of the garden at Batheaston, also known as Annie's Arboretum.

28.   Hannam records that the suffragette field was bulldozed in 1960 to make way for a housing estate.

29.   *The Observer,* Sunday June 11th, 2000, 'Diary reveals lesbian love trysts of suffragette leaders' by Vanessa Thorpe and Alec Marsh.

30.   Martin Pugh's (2001) *The Pankhursts* London: Penguin, is the source of the controversy. The rebuttal can be found in Purvis, J. (2003) 'Emmeline Pankhurst: a biographical interpretation' *Women's History Review* (12) 1, 73-102. The intention here is merely to present both sides of a case that is often seared by more heat than light.

31.   Purvis, J. (2003) 'Emmeline Pankhurst: a biographical interpretation' *Women's History Review* (12) 1, 73-102.

32. These details are taken from an article by Leah Leneman, 'The Awakened Instinct: vegetarianism and the women's suffrage movement in Britain', (1997) *Women's History Review* (6) 2, p 273.

33. The child was called Linley Dennys, following a Blathwayt tradition of using the mother's unmarried surname as a forename. He was born in Dorset on 28.07.16, and lived to the age of 86. An outline of his career can be pieced together from Crockford's Clerical Directory and from the web-site of Queen's College, Cambridge (www.quuns.cam.ac.uk/Queens/Record/2003/Deaths/html). He attended Queen's from Eastbourne College, reading Agriculture. He gained a BA in 1938, and proceeded to MA in 1944. He was reportedly 'a keen oarsman and, in spite of his slight stature, progressed from a place in the College third boat in his first year to rowing stroke in the first boat in the Lents in his final year'. After graduation, he undertook theological training at Wells. He was ordained deacon in 1940, priest in 1941. He served curacies at St John the Baptist, Halifax, from 1940 and Christ Church, Tynemouth, from 1945. He was then Vicar of Bywell from 1948, of St Peter, Monkseaton, from 1956 and of Shalbourne with Ham, Wiltshire from 1959. He moved to Scotland in 1966 as Rector of Ballachulish and Rector of Glencoe, Diocese of Argyll and the Isles. He returned in 1969 to the Salisbury Diocese as Rector of Gussage St Michael and Gussage All Saints. In 1971 he became Rector of Corscombe and Priest-in-charge of St Quintin, Frome, with Evershot and Melbury Bubb. He was Team Rector of Melbury from 1979. Concurrently with these posts he was Rural Dean of Beaminster, Dorset, from 1975 and Canon and Prebendary of Salisbury Cathedral from 1979 until his retirement to Allendale, Hexham, in 1981. Both Francis and Linley are recorded on the List of Rectors in Melbury church. F.L. was Rector of Melbury Osmund with Melbury Sampford – the latter being a chapel on the estate of the Earl of Ilchester; Linley, some years down the line, was team Rector in an age when parishes were beginning to be held in plurality. His daughter, Lucy, has supported this research.

34. London: Sir Isaac Pitman; a collection of original and translated verses. The flyleaf credits William Blathwayt with three other volumes: *The Garden of Sleep*, *Castles*, and *The Ginko Tree*. *Love and Stars* has minimal content, and 'minor' poet is perhaps a flattering description. Much of the original verse started its life in local newspapers, notably *The Bristol Times and Mirror* and *The Bath Chronicle and Herald*.

CHAPTER 2
NATURE IN THE GRAND DESIGN
contemporary issues in science and religion

To someone of the current generation, especially one who rarely darkens the door of a place of worship, it is hard to convey the immediacy of the kinds of debate that would have afforded moments of soul-searching to Frances Linley and the many parson-naturalists of his generation or of the previous fifty years. For the momentous events of 1859 surrounding the publication of the work of Charles Darwin (1), had caused a rift in the staid world of the churches like no other for centuries; and it was not easy to resolve the resulting problems of thought and belief.

In a nutshell, we all know that Darwin used the detailed notes of natural history gathered during his voyages with the *Beagle* to attempt to make sense of the fact that animals, birds and other living things seemed to change or to have changed in quite specific directions over time. This process of adaptation needed a theory, and the theory was that of evolution. Adaptation through evolution and 'natural selection' explained why the owl had acute vision through forward-facing eyes, why the wagtail signals with its tail, and why the Galapagos finches had learned to use twigs as tools to prise food out of crevices.

But the theory of evolution came into conflict with the literal interpretation of the scriptures. Every time that F.L. and his fellow parsons stood at the lectern to read from Genesis, the story of the seven days of creation came into conflict with the Darwinian science and, like as not, with their own. Of course, the two accounts of nature could be held in tension provided there was no overt challenge. But the temper of the times was that the more Protestant and Non-conformist wings of Christianity, even the more fundamentalist elements within the Church of England itself, held that scripture was literally true in every particular and that those who did not agree were, in a very real sense, heretics (2). The integrity of the bible as the unchangeable word of God was not merely sacrosanct, but it was incumbent on the fundamentalist to expose those who held it in any less regard. So F.L. was, like all those who were involved with both science and religion in his generation, caught up in the debate, however reluctantly and implicitly.

Of Roseates *and* Rectories

The problems to resolve the riddle of the relation between science and religion were complicated, and required both theological and scientific understandings.

On the face of it, the bible is full of 'nature' – allusions to natural phenomena. But if we break those allusions down, it quickly becomes apparent that they are not entirely consistent between the Old and the New Testaments. The Old Testament was the book of the Jewish faith from which Christianity had itself emerged. The Old Testament Jews saw nature as a gift of God, and part of the heritage that He had given them, as the chosen people. They believed they were given the Promised Land precisely because it was ' a land flowing with milk and honey' i.e. a naturally harmonious and bountiful land (3). For the early Jew, the harmony and bounty of nature were an essential ingredient of God's land, a gift to, and the heritage of, God's people on earth. This was because its creation had been His; and because His chosen people were the recipients of the benefits of that creation. The Old Testament is full of wonderful and poetic passages inspired by nature.

But if early Old Testament religion was one of physical benefits, the religion of the New Testament was not. Yes, of course, natural events and even details appear in the New Testament: 'Are not two sparrows sold for a farthing, and yet your Heavenly Father cares (even) for them?' (4). But the new 'Promised Land' is a spiritual land disassociated from geographical space; and the bliss of heaven is not worldly comfort born out of natural plenty but future, other-worldly salvation: 'In my Father's house there are many resting places, and I go to prepare a place for you.' (5).

However, if F.L. and his fellow Anglicans were aware of these contradictions as they read through the daily portions of the scriptures while saying their offices each morning and evening, they nevertheless had to face an awkward fact: that the Church had adopted both the Old and the New Testaments as its scriptures, so saddling itself with a dilemma. While the scientists among the clergy and educated laity could hold a Darwinian view over against a fairly literally interpreted New Testament, when it came to the Old Testament the paths of literalism and science diverged irreconcilably (6). While the clergy-scientists could accept, even embrace, the Old Testament view of God as creator and deity of the natural world, they could not rationalise nature as being literally created to a seven-day timetable as described in Genesis. Genesis did not fit the scientific and observable facts, and it had another in-built difficulty: it meant that nature as we know it was created out of nothing – *ex nihilo*, as the theologians put it (7).

So, Sunday by Sunday, as F.L. climbed into his pulpit to expound the word of God, he would have been faced with the pastoral dilemma of presenting a scientific view of the world or a literal one. Some of his predecessors and contemporaries tried to fudge the edges of this dilemma, and their thinking has a spurious logic to it.

Take, for example, the story of the Flood. It was possible to treat this as a myth or an allegory: people strayed from the way of the deity; the deity resolved to wipe out their wickedness by drowning them all in a deluge; before he did so, he decided in his mercy to save the remnant of the righteous. Since the chosen method of destruction was water, the righteous were warned to escape by boat under the leadership of the most charismatic of their number. The bible recounts this tale, and names the hero as Noah, explaining the survival of the rest of the natural world with the famous 'two-by-two' account of animals in the Ark.

The story itself is essentially implausible both in broad principle and in detail. It works as an allegory but not as a piece of factual history. Indeed the same story appears across the world in almost every primitive religion. Yet, the Christian tradition regarded the bible as the word of God, and thus totally true. For the Protestant wing of the church, truth meant only one thing: literal truth. If the bible said God spoke to Noah, then he addressed him in contemporary Hebrew. If he gave him the measurements of a boat then the boat was exactly that size. If the story says every species in nature was represented by a male and female example and packed into these few square metres, then they were. The duration of the voyage, the sending out of the raven and every detail is to be regarded as literal and factual truth. To question the bible on any detail was to question the word of God Himself and the veracity of the holy book (8).

For many clergy of the post-Darwinian era, the only get-out clause from this moral dilemma of biblical interpretation was to show, in some way, that both the text of the bible and the events of natural history were true and that they coincided. Thus Armstrong (9) relates the story of a number of clergy who tried to hold that the literal and the scientific accounts supported one another, confirmed each other's world-view. For anyone doubtful of the power and significance of this problem, the example of the Revd William Brown Galloway serves as a warning against scepticism or complacency. This is his story:

Galloway trained as a theologian at Durham University and held a succession of urban ministries in London; he lived until he was ninety-two, overlapping Francis Linley in date (1811-1903). He was a geologist, though apparently tending more to theoretical models than fieldwork. In his musings upon the underlying chalk and flint of Lincolnshire and eastern Britain generally, from Yorkshire south to East Anglia, he concluded that these had been formed in dry conditions; that is, not under the Flood. But, he suggested, their origin was meteoric and that, as a result of having 'fallen upon the earth at one time' (10) they had suddenly shifted the balance of the earth. Since the waters of the oceans had no time to adjust gradually, the result was a deluge – in other words the Flood – resulting from 'such a change of axis'. So that was fine: evidence from the natural world that supports, even 'proves', a theory of the Flood which can then be accepted quite literally.

If this approach didn't work, then there was an alternative: it could be claimed that the scientific data told the story they did merely because science had not advanced far enough to reveal the missing links between itself and the Mosaic account in Genesis. This was a good rationalisation because it meant you could hold the two views without even having to work as hard as Galloway to reconcile them! Alternatively, the 'days' of Genesis could be re-translated as 'periods of time (of unspecified length)' (11).

We of our largely secular and technological time should not doubt that these intellectual struggles, even if they might appear at times slightly bizarre to us, were nevertheless crucial at the time, and of great import. Reputations could be broken on them, livelihoods lost, credibilities shattered. It was critical not to say the wrong thing in the wrong place or at the wrong time. F.L. would have known this; even in the early 1900s, during his ministries in Lincoln and Doddington, the dilemmas would have stalked him in his dual roles as clergyman and scientist. Fundamentalists control many areas of America to this day; and in some states it is illegal to present alternatives, in schools for example, to the literal accounts of biblical creation, of the universal parentage of humankind from Adam and Eve, of the Flood, and so on (12). It is not necessary to look far under the skin of Non-conformity in England to find exactly the same views right now in the 21st century.

Partly as a spin-off from this scientific debate and partly as a result of independent theological scholarship, another force was gaining ground in the churches from 1900 onwards. This related to the treatment, by theologians, of the biblical text itself. Once regarded as an organic whole, the modernising theologians of the early 20th century now began to understand that the bible itself had – to put not too fine a point on it – evolved! (For example, there are actually two Creation stories in Genesis, the earlier one in chapter 2, and the later one in chapter 1).

F.L. would have been aware that the bible texts were dependent upon ancient manuscripts. These often existed in forms that were not in any sense 'original'; they were not the first copies ever made. Instead, manuscripts that formed the bible (both his and ours) had been handed down, transcribed by monks, translated from one language to another, had their errors 'corrected' and new errors imported by later copyists, and so on. Thus was being born the 'science' of biblical criticism. For anyone unfamiliar with the process, a brief explanation and example is appropriate.

There are four 'gospels' – Matthew, Mark, Luke and John. They purport to tell the story of the life of the man Jesus and to present him as divine. So take the simple expedient of cutting up a text of each gospel and placing side-by-side the four accounts of each incident recorded in them: the birth story, a parable or two, a miracle, or the events leading up to the death of Jesus. Let's assume that the text is in the original language of the manuscripts, Greek, so that the similarities and differences in the four accounts of each incident are more easily spotted. Several puzzles immediately emerge (13).

First, not every incident is common to all four accounts: so why are some included and some omitted?

Second, where there is an overlap between incidents (most often between the first three authors), the accounts are often similar in principle but differ in detail. What is the significance of the matters of detail?

Third, where there are agreements in the case of the first three writers, they are often closer than is accounted for by mere oral tradition. How can this be explained?

Fourth, why is the Gospel of John so consistently 'different' from the others?

While not wishing to over-simplify the processes, nor the explanations, about these phenomena, a brief account is called for; and it goes like this. The likelihood is that the written accounts of the life of Jesus were all composed several decades after his death and usually written down by people who were not there (even if they had access to people who were). In the case of the first three gospels (collectively known as the Synoptics i.e. they have similar view of events), they appear to depend on a single source for *some* of their material (14). Where there are differences between the first three writers we have no viable alternative often but to trace them to particular beliefs and values about Jesus; for example, in the birth story Matthew (whose account is strongly Jewish in flavour) wants to create a genealogy of Jesus that takes him back to Abraham, the father of the Jewish people. Mark, by contrast, wants to link Jesus with the fulfilment of Judaism (and perhaps some level of sectarianism) (15) by beginning with Jesus' baptism by John. Luke, more concerned than Matthew with the Graeco-Roman audience, puts Jesus in this latter context and draws his portrait as a messianic figure.

To complicate the picture, the fourth writer, John, presents Jesus entirely differently, using miracles as 'signs' of his power and status, and composing a picture of Jesus as the pre-existent Word of God – an altogether more philosophical view.

So the emergent science of biblical criticism, then, must deal with a New Testament that comes not as a secure text and with built-in levels of interpretation that can be peeled off, over time, in onion layers, to take us back as far as possible (some would say, not far enough) to the 'original' story. The same principles extend also into the Old Testament; and this same criticism comes to recognise such truths as that the Old Testament was composed over a long period of time, is made up of disparate books that happen to have been bound into a collection in relatively recent times, that its language and manuscripts are not without conflicts and queries, that each element has a literary genre (saga, myth, history, law) that must be separately interpreted and contextualised – and so on.

For F.L. and his generation of clergy, this new science of biblical criticism, though not without some precedent, was essentially an emerging intellectual process and one that was gathering momentum in the universities and theological colleges. In Lincoln, the high church influence of Bishop King probably did much to allay criticism away from those who were neither fundamentalists nor rejecters of the new critical approaches (16). But it should be noted that in Lincoln city a Church Association had been formed by the Protestant faction to fight off woolliness in relation to the bible and its interpretation, and to oppose what they saw as back-sliding into ritual practices. This was in 1900, just as F.L. took up his post at St Swithin's in the city.

There was one other important complicating factor that led from these first two issues – literalism and biblical criticism. That was the implication that one's stance on these two factors might have for one's view of the authority of the bible.

If, as a scientist, F.L. or any of his contemporaries questioned the literal interpretation of the bible on the basis of scientific evidence, then – almost, it seemed to the literalists, by definition – the authority of the bible was destroyed. If, as an exponent of the critical approach to the bible, F.L. or any of his contemporaries tried to weaken – as the literalists saw it – the truth of the bible by explaining its compilation and meaning in historical and literary terms, then again the authority of the bible was in question. To espouse *both* of these approaches was tantamount to absolute heresy.

Nor, as has been suggested, is the debate dead. The great commentary on the bible known as Peake's commentary was composed in the 1920s (17). It was at the forefront of biblical criticism when it was completely revised and re-written in the light of modern critical knowledge in the 1960s (18). However, the then Archbishop of Canterbury (19) had considerable difficulty in contributing its lead article on the authority of scripture. The Archbishop puts the issue in these terms:

If a man is compelled as the price of his intellectual integrity to reject the literal belief in the creation of the world in six days, and in the story of Adam and Eve and the inerrancy of the biblical narratives as a whole, is he thereby involved in rejecting the divine authority of the bible?

It is not possible for an Archbishop to answer in the affirmative, and Ramsey goes on to build a three-fold case for the bible's continued place as authoritative sacred scripture (20). He argues first that no words are adequate to contain the reality of God: the scriptures are true because they recount the symbolic story of God's intervention into human affairs, not because they are accurate in every detail of history – indeed 'the discrepancies in some of the narratives make the acceptance of them all as factually correct to be virtually impossible' (21). Then he shifts the conceptual nature of the question and inquires instead whether the scriptures hold authority because they are inspired. He concludes that they are; though the degrees of inspiration do, nevertheless, represent varying 'degrees of significance' of the material for us today (22). Finally, he suggests scriptures have authority because they are 'revelation'. 'Here modern critical studies have led to an emphasis on revelation as being a process, and upon the disparity of its phases' (23). So, the biblical content is reliable in part, inspired differentially, and holds revelations of God which are variable in dimension.

Thus the solution to the question of biblical authority has blurred edges that no literalist could accept. It has to be pointed out by Ramsey, as leader of the Anglican Church, that faith should not blind the reader of the bible to 'the spirit of enquiry', nor should enquiry rule out a response of faith. In synthesising the two 'the reader of the bible has the church to guide him' (24). And at that moment, at that very fragment in time, the whole edifice of the argument collapses – because we have to ask: which church, or which faction of which church? The fundamentalists and literalists? Or the liberal school of biblical criticism? The reader is back at the beginning. Question unresolved. Unresolved for us. Unresolved for F.L. and his generation. The key difference is that, for us, the consequences for the individual from choosing an inappropriate set of beliefs in the contemporary context is no longer a matter for major public concern or ecclesiastical censure.

This chapter has singled out for examination three key theological themes in the intellectual ether that surrounded the Church of England at the moment when Francis Blathwayt was ministering in Lincoln and Doddington. Before leaving theology behind, these themes must be challenged by a question. That question is: Does all this theological debate matter, in real terms, to ordinary Christians then and now? The answer must be that it did matter at the time, for it stirred passions we would reserve today for a major royal event or a Cup Final. It mattered for the parson in the early 1900s. It is important to take the matter seriously, for – as a scientist – we know that it is likely that F.L. would have held views that were being broadly labelled liberal not literal.

To illustrate the point let us visit the Annual Church Congress which met in Cambridge on 27th September 1910, a year after F.L. took up the post of Rector of Doddington-with-Whisby. The most significant item on the agenda was a book that had just been written by Albert Schweitzer (25). Schweitzer collected all the books about the Gospel story written by all the modern biblical critics. He tells a marvellous story about how he piled them around his living space for months on end during his studies for his own new book (26). We can fast-forward the story of this mammoth scholarship, and concern ourselves with the outcome rather than the process.

Schweitzer's purpose was to try to use biblical scholarship to get as close as possible to the man Jesus and his history, to pare away through form criticism and other means the glosses and interpretations in the story until he found the heart of it, its central essence – what we called earlier the 'onion layers'. He concluded that the primitive form of the story compels a belief that Jesus was a prophet not the messiah. He had a messianic consciousness, but it was misplaced. He expected the end of the world in a Second Coming and that it would be soon. When it didn't materialise, he tried to force the issue through his own crucifixion. But it was a miscalculation that went horribly wrong. If one can paraphrase Schweitzer, the 'last word' from the Cross ('It is finished'), is not a cry of triumph ('I have brought it to fulfilment') but one of despair ('I've blown it!') (27).

A scientific approach to the scriptures through biblical criticism was thus calling into question not only simple theology but simplistic faith. For the first time, the Church was having to grapple with the issue that sophisticated scientific man might apply that new understanding to religion. Could the Church cope? The theologian Sanday summed it up like this (28):

...the Saviour of mankind extends his arms towards the cultivated modern man just as much as he does towards the simple believer...I believe the cultivated modern man can enter the Church of Christ with his head erect...I believe he can afford to say what he really thinks - provided only that his fellow Christians of more traditional types are willing to greet him with the sympathetic intelligence he deserves, and do not turn towards him the cold shoulder of suspicion and denunciation.

The problem was that, in most cases, the more traditional types weren't willing, and they didn't share the 'cultivated modern man's' intelligence. But the story of the rise of the cultivated modern churchman, breathing the rarified air of Darwinism, Biblical Criticism, Liberalism, and finally Christology Revisited does represent the world of 1910 when F.L. translated from Lincoln city to the rural delights of Doddington. They are his intellectual and theological context, and he could not have escaped from his any more than we, in a modern world, can escape from ours. They were 'interesting times'.

The question now is whether there is any tangible evidence of where F.L. stood on these issues?

•

We know that F.L. was appointed to the church of St Swithin in Lincoln in 1900 by Bishop King. King was a high churchman, and the parish of St Swithin was a high church living (even into modern times). So clearly Francis was not a literalist in theological terms or he would not have received such an appointment.

It was fortuitous that the next Bishop, Edward Lee Hicks, was a relative high churchman and a liberal. His diaries give us a huge insight into his activity but less into his interests. Some things, however, are clear. Neville, in a fine book on the man (29) concludes that, when promoted to the House of Lords, the debates he turned up to hear were concerned with 'wartime reprisals, conscientious objectors, electoral reform and women's suffrage.' These were clearly his major concerns into old age – he was seventy-three at this time; and his diaries reveal concern for the worker, too. Neville documents the bishop as a competent theologian, and one who was prepared to engage in debate about biblical criticism. He also refused to be bound by literalist interpretations of the bible, refused merely to look back for old patterns rather than reach forward for new and reforming ones (30).

Hicks' diaries show him as committed to episcopal duties, far-travelled in the diocese, and sometimes very acerbic about his clergy. He was not a scientist, but the rare passages in his diaries that stray from pastoral matters often deal with natural phenomena: an appreciation of nature (31). There is only one direct reference to F.L., a Bird Dinner at which Hicks entertained a group of clergy and ornithologists (described in the next chapter). Hicks' verdict on this was one of great approval. Silence in the *Diaries* on the issue of the parish of Doddington suggests he felt Francis at least a safe pair of hands. The general approval of Hicks, both direct and indirect, is only circumstantial evidence that the men shared views; but it is evidence of a sort.

Evidence of F.L.'s pastoral and theological views is intensely difficult to come by; a key source that is missing is a collection of parish magazines for Doddington in the period 1909-1916. What is clear (and we shall return to the matter at a later stage) is that nowhere in his writing about the birds of Lincolnshire does he draw into the works any whisper of the debate between science and religion, nor indeed any reference whatsoever to creation and its origins or any sermonising of any kind. The absence is so striking as to be, of itself, notable. The explanation which is offered, tentatively, here is that he is taking every care to separate the two matters so as not to be drawn into an argument and thus cause offence (32).

NOTES TO CHAPTER 2

1.   The terrible struggle that Darwin himself experienced between accepted biblical faith and the evidence of his scientific discoveries prevented the publication of the latter for many years. He was not really prepared for the controversies that followed his revelations, or the odium that was poured on him in some quarters. An account of these events is to be found in Desmond, A. and Moore, J. (1991) *Darwin* London: Michael Joseph. Such was the feeling against him that Bishop Wilberforce swore to 'smash Darwin', but with the support of no less than T.H. Huxley he held the day (Pekin, L.B. 1937 *Darwin* London: Hogarth Press, p 48).

2.   Darwin found it difficult to be drawn on the subject of science and theology because of the intense opposition of sections of the church. Desmond and Moore (p 603) quote his view that the question of the existence of God is 'beyond the scope of man's intellect.' He tried to escape the issue by advocating the view that 'freedom of thought is best promoted by the gradual illumination of men's minds, which follows from the advance of science' (op. cit. p 645). Though Darwin died in 1892, the controversy did not go away. Desmond and Moore note that, immediately on Darwin's death, Canon Alfred Barry was advocating the view that Natural Selection 'was by no means alien to the Christian religion' provided it was understood correctly, with selection acting 'under the Divine intelligence' (p 671).

3.   Joshua 5 v 6. Portions of the Old Testament, such as the psalms, many of which are very ancient in origin, are full of imagery that promotes bountiful nature as a feature of the status accorded by God to his Chosen People, the Jews. The issue is well discussed in a paper by John Austin Baker 'Biblical Attitudes to Nature' (in Montefiore, H. ed. 1975 *Man and Nature* London: Collins, pp 87-109).

4.   Matthew 10 v 29 and Luke 12 v 16. Birders might note that the Hebrew word really indicates any small passerine and is not species specific.

5.   John 14 v 2. By the time of this fourth, and latest, Gospel it cannot reasonably be doubted that the text reflects the views, concerns and interpretations of the early church (probably an intellectual branch of it, at that) and not the literal words and doings of Jesus. This Gospel is often labelled 'the spiritual gospel' because of the particular glosses that it accords to events and sayings. It is a sophisticated 'production', written by an educated mind steeped in knowledge as diverse as synagogue lectionaries, Jewish symbolism and Hellenistic philosophy. It is a synthesising force within its contemporary setting, able both to label Jesus as the Logos ('word' or 'utterance') of God – a Greek concept – and promote him as a figure who not only fulfils, but supersedes, Judaism - the symbolism of the rending of the Temple veil is timed to coincide with the time of the crucifixion. Interestingly, Baker, in the paper cited earlier, attributes the New Testament's lack of concern for nature in religion to the more urban environment of its composition; but this theory, while it has some merit, may be rather weak as the main explanation. A more plausible option is that the earliest Christians, taking a 'messianic' view of Jesus, did not expect to wait long after Jesus' death for the Second Coming (or whatever description one chooses for the momentous intervention of the deity into human affairs). Unlike us, their concern was for salvation in the short term not ecological issues in the long term!

6.   This is because the challenge of the New Testament is the challenge of the 'gospel', i.e. the 'good news' of Christ. It 'takes as read' the Old Testament natural theology, accepting God's creation but also the flawed universe, and sets out how God decided to redeem it. The New Testament is concerned with the process of redemption and salvation through Jesus and his sacrifice on the Cross: its dilemma is that of faith – whether Jesus is, or is not, divine. That question and its answer do not fundamentally overlap or conflict with a particular scientific world-view. It is only after one has answered the challenge of the Gospel that one becomes enmeshed in the requirements of the Church, the formal and organisational fellowship and administrative base of Christians. At that point, and not before, the new believer is presented with a raft of other items of faith, which includes demands on how one views the scriptures and how they are interpreted.

7.   Montefiore, H. (1975) *Man and Nature* London: Collins, makes an interesting point. While most religions, ancient and modern, have a creation myth, in the Old Testament version the difference is that it is assumed that creation is tied, as historical fact, to the remaining events of Hebrew history. The Hebrew word *'barah'* used to denote the act of creating is, at least in extant literature, used only with God as a subject; and it implies not only action but relationship, i.e. to humankind. Two theories of physics might be seen to argue against a single act of a divinely instigated creation – the view that chance played a role in the evolution of human beings, and the view that the universe will ultimately run out of energy and die. The refutation of these views depends on accepting that the universe has a purpose (spiritual in

nature) beyond the physical, and that forms of knowledge may include scientific knowledge but are not exhausted by it ('On the alleged incompatibility between Christianity and science', Mary Hesse, in Montefiore, op.cit. pp 121-131).

8.   An example of fundamentalist approaches to science in the UK can be found in the *Evangelical Times.* David J. Tyler 'Neanderthal', an article in the February edition for 2001, also on www.evangelical-times.org/articles. This article reviews discoveries of Neanderthal bones, and attempts to locate the discoveries within a (literal) biblical context. The following extract gives the flavour: 'Locating Neanderthals in the biblical framework of history is not that difficult to do. There is no evidence for an anthropologically universal deluge after the Neanderthals, so they must have lived post-Flood. Neanderthals probably lived in the span of time between the Noachian Deluge and the dispersal of people from the Tower of Babel. We infer that some descendants of Noah did not stay with the majority, but wandered off to live as hunter/gatherer tribes in other parts of the wild and inhospitable Earth.' The Rt Revd Dr Anthony Russell draws attention to the conflict of OT and NT perceptions, and says that the modern backlash is to diminish the 'dominion' of humanity over creation in what he calls 'an almost pre-Darwinian view of the natural world' (2004 'The Priesthood of Creation: the Hulsean Sermon 2004' *Rural Theology* 2 (2) 119-125).

9.   The account in Armstrong, R. (2000) *The English Parson-Naturalist* Leominster: Greenwing, can be found on pp 123-132. Much of the section deals with the issue of literal interpretation at dates earlier than F.L. (earlier even than Darwin), but is interesting in showing how persistent this view is in the Christian tradition.

10.   Galloway, W.B. (1888) *Science and Geology in Relation to the Universal Deluge* London: Samson Low, pp 3, 41.

11.   The Revd Samuel Kinns produced a volume entitled *Moses and Geology: or, Harmony of the Bible with Science* (1992) London: Cassell, in which he attempted to demonstrate that the various stages of creation outlined in Genesis could be reconciled with known geological phenomena.

12.   Maidment, R. and Mitchell, J. (2000) *The United States in the 20th Century* (2nd edn) London: Hodder & Stoughton/Open University, p 30, review the split in American society between the 'people who follow the orthodox tendency...(e.g. the final authority of scripture...) and ...[those with] a tendency to resymbolise historic faiths according to the prevailing assumptions of contemporary life...' In some States it is illegal to teach other than the literal interpretation of the bible in every detail.

13.   This was the language of the extant manuscripts, but not, of course, of the participants in the stories which they told. Jesus would have spoken the everyday version of the Hebrew language known as Aramaic.

14.   This common material was given the code-letter Q, which was the first letter of the German word indicating a source. The source Q was thought to consist of the earliest material in the Gospels, and the hypothesis is that it existed, possibly in written form, but is now lost except for these recoverable remnants. Q contains some basic narrative material, but is also concerned with Jesus' teaching.

15.   This is a highly contentious area, and one which cannot be explored in this space. However, it is worth saying that John the Baptist, whose unusual appearance and distinctive actions are described vividly in the New Testament gospels, looks to some biblical scholars like a member of a sect such as the Essenes. Various sectarian groups existed in Judaism, were often militantly opposed to the Roman occupation of Israel, and lived an ascetic life preaching eschatological downfall for the world. Literature such as the Dead Sea Scrolls throws light on these groups, but many modern theologians have tried hard to distance Jesus from them.

16. Sir Francis Hill (1974) *Victorian Lincoln* Cambridge: Cambridge University Press, pp 244-7.

17. J.H.B. Peake D.D. was the original editor of this tome.

18. Matthew Black and H.H. Rowley edited the 1962 edition of *Peake's Commentary on the Bible*, which was published by Thomas Nelson of London and became the *vade mecum* of all biblical scholars.

19. 'The Authority of the Bible' in Peake (1962 edn; pp 1-7) was written by the Rt Rev Arthur Michael Ramsey D.D., an academic theologian as well as Primate.

20. Ramsey, op.cit. p 5 section 9b.

21. Ramsey, op.cit. p 6 para 10a.

22. Ramsey, op.cit. p 6 para 10b.

23. Ramsey, op.cit. p 7 para 10d.

24. Ramsey, op.cit. p 7 para 11b.

25. *The Quest of the Historical Jesus* (1910; also in various later editions) London: A & C Black; translated by W. Montgomery. See also note 32 below.

26. Schweitzer, A. (1933) *My Life and Thought* London: Allen and Unwin, translated by C. T. Campion, p 58: 'For many a month all the people who visited me had to thread their way across the room along paths which ran between heaps of books.'

27. The ambiguity is there in the original Greek – the translation 'It is finished' is effectively value-free: it can mean either 'finished and completed', or 'finished and unsuccessful'. The interpretation that Schweitzer put on this saying did not bring into question, for him, a life spent in the service of God, and in imitation of Jesus, in the mission field. Commitment was not dulled by biblical interpretation.

28. Quoted in Lloyd, R. (1965) *The Church of England 1900-1965* London: SCM Press, p 90.

29. Neville, G. (1998) *Radical Churchman: Edward Lee Hicks and the New Liberalism* Oxford: Clarendon.

30. Neville, G. (1998) op. cit. chapter 13, pp 271-292

31. Neville, G. (1993) *The Diaries of Edward Lee Hicks Bishop of Lincoln 1910-1919* Lincoln Record Society: The Boydell Press includes the following references: 17th January 1913 (lunched with H.J. Roby and) 'he showed us round his beautiful garden'; 5th February 1913 'the day was quite lovely with sunshine and mild wind'; 26th July 1913 at Withern 'pretty green country with fine trees, esp. elms'; and even an appreciation of skylark song (5th February 1913 'singing merrily' at Canwick) and golden pheasants (27th March 1912). Hicks was a member of the Lincolnshire Naturalists' Union.

32. As a final aside it is worth noting that the *Lincoln Diocesan Magazine* of the period 1908-1916 offered annual opportunities to the local clergy to study and listen to foremost theological speakers at Oxford and Cambridge. Anyone to wished, would have been able to immerse himself in these debates.

CHAPTER 3
FRANCIS LINLEY IN LINCOLNSHIRE

When F.L. took over the living of St Peter at Doddington, six miles from the centre of Lincoln city, with its towering Norman cathedral and smaller, fairytale castle, he became the incumbent of a rural parish that embraced also the village of Whisby, one mile to the south. It was 1909, Victoria had been dead for just eight years, and the Edwardian era was beginning to feel its way to a greater freedom and social expansiveness.

During this period he was to write a collection of papers about the birds of Lincolnshire that have been quoted into modern times despite the fact that the pursuit of knowledge of birds has moved on at a vast pace and that scientific data about birds has proliferated out of all recognition. These works and their significance are described and discussed in later chapters. Here, it is our purpose to set the scene, to place F.L. in his Lincolnshire context and to provide a rounded picture of Francis the man, to augment that of the Revd F.L. Blathwayt, parson, author and naturalist.

The modest church of St Peter, Doddington, is described by Pevsner as 'a very remarkable building, Gothic...except for the west tower, which still has all the Strawberry Hill prettiness' (1). It is set adjacent to, and forward of, the lawn of the Late Tudor Doddington Hall. Even in the 1970s Pevsner (2) can write: 'To come across Doddington [Hall] in the remote Lincolnshire fields is a surprise.' The interior of the church is tiny, the flags of the floor a little sunken and uneven, and the whole edifice quite intimate.

Doddington today is a parish of just 300 souls (3), and Doddington with Whisby had a population recorded as 232 individuals (4) in 1901; clearly, not much changed between then and F.L.'s arrival in 1909. Even this modest total, though, was an expansion on the 1801 Census figure of 189 (5). Today, Lincoln's western bypass is just a mile away; but then the old road to Lincoln passed through unbroken agricultural land.

Only with the take-over of Pevsner's 'remote fields' for aerodromes in World War II did the attrition of the surrounding countryside gather any momentum. If Doddington seems like a 'place out of time' today - with its grand house, estate cottages and workers, and complete lack of facilities - it must have been even more isolated at the turn of the 20th century.

Today's village consists of a cluster of houses at a bend in the road, which may have replaced or augmented earlier buildings (6), and a line of estate cottages at right-angles to the churchyard, which border the drive to the Hall. In all other particulars Doddington stands divorced from anything but its own land and fields. Besides Doddington Hall and associated cottages, and the little church, the handful of remaining (mainly red brick) properties now incorporate the old school. The Rectory once occupied by Francis is almost hidden behind trees; the original shell of the house is modest. A small new development of executive houses is being constructed adjacent to this Rectory plot.

There was no church building at Whisby; so each of these two settlements which formed Francis' living was tiny even by Lincolnshire standards. Doddington Hall itself was, as now, in the hands of the Jarvis family, and remains, as then, the centre and dominant feature of the village community (7).

Kelly's Directory for 1895 paints an interesting picture. As well as a picturesque description of the location of the village (8), it records a railway station at Thorpe on the Midland Railway branch-line to Nottingham, and that a new station – 'Doddington and Harby' would shortly be constructed by the Derbyshire and East Coast Railway on a line running from Chesterfield to Sutton-on-Sea. The railway may well have had a bearing on F.L.'s ability to travel in order to go birding, though he does not seem to have used this 'Dukeries line' to study the birds of Derbyshire. The railway has long gone, though the track itself can be traced.

Nevertheless, this small parish, during a seven-year residence in which Francis was (as we shall recount later) to write many of his early papers about birds, was not his first encounter with Lincolnshire. For he had moved (as we have noted in the Introduction) to the countryside after a spell as curate of the church of St Swithin (also spelled Swithun),

Lincoln, and then as curate at All Saints, Lincoln. Having graduated from Hertford College, Oxford, in 1899, he undertook his theological training in Lincoln, becoming ordained in 1900, and served as deacon at St Swithin's, Lincoln; during this curacy he was made priest in 1901 as well as gaining his MA degree (1902). He moved to All Saints from 1904 until 1909 (9). The move is noted in various ways in the records, but one has to look closely to discover that he moved to this second curacy alongside his first vicar, so clearly they had established team-working and a rapport. Crockford's Clerical Directory for 1900 lists F.L.'s address as 178 Monks Road. Later, he moved to 5 Monks Leys Terrace (10). The licences for his status as curate are extant in the Lincoln Archives Office; he paid the sum of ten shillings for one, and has 'corrected' the clerk's entry on it to indicate that his place of residence (at the time the family home must have moved to Saltaire, Weston-super-Mare) is NOT in the county of Dorset but of Somerset. His story is bound by his ministry as curate and priest, therefore, both to the village and to the city.

We have seen that it would be false to visualise F.L. in his black clergy garb in the same way that one often perceives old photographs of Victorian and Edwardian worthies, making the assumption from our own perspective that they represent something 'old-fashioned' or reactionary. The probability is that F.L. would have considered himself a 'modern' man. It is fascinating to reflect that the church of St Swithin in Free School Lane was relatively new, having not been completed until 1887. It was tall-spired with a cathedral-like interior, where the presence of the deity seemed as remote as the distant altar. It was built over an ancient Roman site, and much of the immediate area is even today under-mined by the remains of Roman constructions. All Saints Church in Monks Road, though adjacent to the ruined Monks Abbey, was not built until after Francis arrived in the city, in fact in 1903 just a year before he moved there as priest. It was more tangible in its dimensions and more personal in its ambience; red brick not stone; and one imagines that he thought of his ministry there in very modern terms.

The fact, however, that from his accession to Doddington in 1909 until he died in 1953 he remained a rural clergyman may convey a message about his feelings concerning his time as a city dweller and town parson. It is worth noting in passing that, while F.L. possessed some of the essential qualities that opened the door to a bishopric in the Church of England, he did not fulfil all the accepted criteria; nor does his ambition seem to have stretched to this promoted office (11). The climate of the time did not favour as bishop anyone whose most obvious inclination was to be a scientist; and as we have seen – coincidentally or not – the scientist-priests were on the cusp of a difficult theological dilemma about the debate between Creationism and Evolution that may have been deemed disturbing to good order in the Church (12).

Nor would revulsion from city life surprise, as a review of Lincoln's recent past, as perceived by F.L., would confirm. Sir Francis Hill (13) asserts that the city was 'modern' by 1850 on the grounds that the railway had arrived – indeed the main road into the centre was already plagued by its two level crossings even at that date (14) – and that 2,500 men were employed in the crucial noise, heat and dirt of the iron industry. Today's visitor might be beguiled by the tourist shops around the Castle and Cathedral, and by the renovation in the University area adjacent to the Brayford Pool. But one guidebook captures the spirit of Lincoln city at F.L.'s time:

It is only when you enter the city that disappointment assails you: the town grew enormously in the 19th century and much of it is grim and sordid – dreary streets of ugly red houses spread everywhere. Half is 'above hill', half 'below hill'. From the top you look down on factories and chimneys and a haze of smoke…(15)

Doddington in this era must have contrasted starkly with the city, where the rivers flooded and housing was poor. Typhus and cholera were common in the city. Throughout the early 1800s debate and inertia (16) ran side-by-side and achieved little improvement in the water supply. The Council was so inept and badly attended there were complaints to government. Richard Carline had created a reservoir in Prial Brook and by 1848 water was being pumped to houses. But in 1867 the water was condemned as unfit. Controversy, rather than action, continued until the 1870s. A local man, H K Hebb was appointed clerk to the urban sanitary authority and deputy town clerk, serving until 1902. Under his guidance the new Urban Sanitary Authority bought the waterworks and the gasworks, inaugurated the sewage scheme and launched the electricity undertaking. F.L.'s first living coincided with this development, and his church at St Swithin's was a short stone's throw from the filthy river.

Throughout the late Victorian era, the poorer workers of Lincoln had scratched an existence in insanitary stews alongside this river. Then, in 1904-1905, a typhoid outbreak overtook the city (17). Francis was priest at All Saints at this time. He would have witnessed the squalor and the loss of life; doubtless he ministered to the victims and their families in their misery. But it should not be assumed that the citizens were mere victims of political incompetence. Hill notes that 'a refuse destructor was set up in 1911', but in the city people still resisted moves to distance pig sties from their houses! (18). Furthermore, the Royal Commission on Canals and Waterways found, in 1906, that despite the burgeoning railways there was a strong traffic by water through Torksey Lock (which needed better upkeep) from companies in Lincoln: glue-works, iron and wood manufacturers. No doubt these industries made the rich even more wealthy, but added to the overall pollution of the city.

All this sickness and squalor, alongside considerable unemployment, had made Lincoln less of a sleepy backwater in political terms, and more of a hot-bed of civil unrest and industrial action. At the end of the 1800s it was not unknown for there to be riots in the streets; and on occasion the city constabulary had to be augmented by policemen drawn from the countryside and even by troops (19). Many of the problems stemmed from the erosion of agricultural jobs with the consequent move into the towns; but the towns and cities in turn were experiencing a down-turn in fortunes. They were thus filled with the discontent of unemployment and poverty egged on by growing unionisation. This was the era of Booth and of Rowntree, and the recognition of poverty as a social phenomenon. Thus discontent lingered on until 1911 in Lincoln, and F.L. may have considered himself well out of the firing line as he visited his metaphorical flocks in the little villages of Doddington and Whisby.

However, the trends were not all negative. Sir Daniel Hall noted in 1910-2 that the farms on the Lincoln heath were all let and there was demand for them (20). Wool from Lincoln and its surrounding areas was highly sought after and in 1895 Lincoln Red shorthorn cattle became a registered breed. The Corn Exchange and Markets Company made its largest profit to date in 1905. A Bishop of Lincoln, Edward Hicks who acceded in 1910, is recorded, however, as observing two reasons to be sceptical of this new world: that the new breed of local farmers was a 'smaller sort and mostly Methodists', and in the fens they were essentially businessmen, who managed money well but had replaced the old families (21). Anglicanism and the influence of birth were perceived as beginning to wane.

Culturally, though, Lincoln city was a backwater, for the 'old world' had bred inertia rather than progressivism. The Lincoln Training College for schoolmistresses had, it is true, been established in two phases in the 1840s and the late 1860s (22). But, in an age when the educated doctor, schoolmaster, parson or squire would have acquired considerable 'collections' of things geological, oological or entomological, as well as a substantial library, the city could not manage either a library or a museum for public use. Sir Reginald Blomfield built the public library in 1906, while F.L. was engaged at All Saints, but the same architect's Usher Gallery had to wait until 1927. For an Oxford graduate such as F.L., this must have seemed like intellectual nihilism. Schooling for young people in the city was poorly provided for, though there is a record of a school at Doddington, having been built in 1851, with an average attendance of 25 pupils (23).

If the young Blathwayt, starting his city-centre ministry at the age of 26, and moving over the next nine years from a young church building to a new one, felt any deep missionary zeal, then he would have been acutely conscious that his chosen Anglicanism did not have things all its own way in the hearts of Lincolnians. Despite the brooding presence of the cathedral, it is possible to establish that there was a strong pulse of Non-conformity running through the veins of city and county. In the outlying areas one has only to remember the Pilgrim Fathers to confirm this tradition; and even today, if it looks at all, many a hamlet looks to a chapel rather than a church as its predominant building.

In 1903 - just as F.L. was about to move to All Saints - a count of church attendances by the *Lincoln Leader* newspaper (24) established that there were, on a particular Sunday, 7,103 Anglican attendances in the city, and 9,046 Non-conformist. At St Swithin's on 14th March 1903, towards the end of F.L.'s curacy there, 262 women and 377 men attended during the day, a total of 639 souls from a parish population of around ten thousand. At the All Saints mission where he would shortly minister (for the church itself was not completed, one recalls, until some time later that year) 36 women and 75 men turned up for services – a lower number than for any one of the Non-conformist places of worship run by the Congregationalists, Free Methodists, Primitive Methodists, or Baptists with the one exception of the Portland Place Mission in Coultham Street (104 attendees). Non-conformity was growing while Anglicanism was losing its hold.

Leaving aside the strong Non-conformist tradition itself, two specific factors probably contributed to this state of affairs in Lincoln. The first was that, while the cathedral itself had a presence in the city that has endured for centuries, it was then (as it has often been into modern times) a source also of controversy. Though the cathedral is presided over by the Dean, the Bishop of Lincoln (one of the largest and most influential church dioceses) had a seat or 'palace' next door and would often have been in the cathedral and identified with its activities. The Bishop of F.L.'s time was Edward King, appointed in 1885, a man saintly enough to be spoken about in hushed tones even by today's adherents. He had a good brain, having been professor of pastoral theology at Oxford, F.L.'s *alma mater*. Unfortunately, he also attracted controversy. He wore a mitre – the first time this head-dress had been seen in the cathedral since the Reformation; and he was, in his practices, sufficiently 'high church' and ritualistic to antagonise the more Protestant elements in the county.

King remained in post throughout F.L.'s time in the city. Indeed there was even a legal action taken against the bishop's ritualism by the Church Association – an action that took years to resolve and which ended with King being indicted on two counts. It was not until a year after Francis moved to Doddington that King died and was replaced by Edward Lee Hicks, who moved from an appointment as canon of Manchester Cathedral. Hicks was a facilitator and worker with the Non-conformists, who espoused the temperance cause. So the period was one of relative turmoil at the head of Lincoln's Anglican hierarchy, a situation mirrored powerfully also in more modern times (25).

If these controversies damaged the work of ordinary parish clergy at the turn of the 20th century, then there was a more worrying and long-term trend at work: secularisation. When F.L. moved from the city to Doddington it was estimated that fifty per cent of city folk never attended a church service of any kind: the tip of an ice-berg that was to grow inexorably. In Doddington the situation was likely to have been less extreme because of the power of village tradition and the influence of the estate and its leading family.

Controversy in the church and social unrest in the streets, then, were not strangers to Francis Blathwayt in his ministry in Lincoln city; and some of this turmoil was down to the closely allied debates that surrounded matters political, at both national and local levels. However proud and patriotic one might be of what might be termed the 'Victorian successes of Empire' – the Boer War, for example, lasted from 1899 to 1902 – these emotions had to be balanced against the 'primary and secondary poverty' of up to thirty per cent of the population of cities across the nation (26).

Liberalism had, in the late Victorian age, been the voice of the workers; but at the beginning of the 20th century the movement was weak in the country as a whole (27) and during F.L.'s time in Lincoln the country had been dominated by Unionist policies. The Labour Party was formed in 1906, and the Liberals managed to galvanise a series of popular discontents: including opposition to tariffs on food. These issues won them the national vote in 1906. One result was that, between 1907 and 1914, there was a series of important national reforms, the reverberations of which would have been felt in the city. Free school meals were introduced in 1907; the first old-age pensions in 1908; a young Winston Churchill established Labour Exchanges in 1909; and Lloyd George promoted the National Insurance Bill of 1911. In the same year Lloyd George also established a form of 'super tax' on the rich, largely to pay for a class of warship, the Dreadnought, in the face of German arms growth: a portent of things to come.

So it was that, in Lincoln, Charles Henry Roberts, the Liberal candidate, was also successful at the 1906 election. A former Fellow of Exeter College, Oxford, Roberts appealed to the Non-conformist vote and the temperance cause. When, four years later, Winston Churchill spoke locally in his support, he gained another (albeit narrow) majority. This time he had also taken under his wing the sympathisers with women's suffrage following the establishment in 1903 of Emily Pankhurst's Women's Social and Political Union. There is no evidence either way of F.L.'s political leanings. His origins among the ranks of the landed gentry, his relative wealth, and his position in society, may have swayed him to the Unionist cause; but we know of his ministry in the poorer areas of Lincoln at this time of social awakening, and of his family connection with the suffragettes – both of which may have moved his allegiance into the Liberal camp.

Francis Blathwayt's ministry to the city of Lincoln lasted from his twenty-sixth year until his thirty-fifth. Then came his investiture as the incumbent of 'Doddington-Pigot with Whisby', as Crockford's records it. From a city that was vibrant with social problems if somewhat tardy in embracing the changes of the Edwardian era, F.L. was translated to the role of rural parson – a role he was to play for another forty-five years until the end of his comparatively long life.

It would be extremely easy to caricature this life, to cross-reference it to the many such parsons whose small-world comings and goings are recorded so frequently in the fiction of the time (28). Indeed, it is tempting to do so in order to augment the limited data that we have about daily life in the Rectory at Doddington. But it is better to stick to the facts, and to what might be reasonably inferred from secure knowledge of life in the countryside at this time.

It can be reasonably suggested that Francis had a social circle that had some degree of influence – both social influence and an influence within the growing pastime and science of birding. We know this because of a fascinating entry in the diary of the Bishop (Hicks) himself (29). It reads:

Bird Dinner at 7.45. Peacock of Cadney, Blathwayt of Doddington, Proudfoot of North Somercotes, A S Wright of Spridlington, Miss Brewster of South Kelsey, Miss Mary Gibbons of Holton Park: all to meet Warde Fowler: also Miss Boyd's brother, Arnold Boyd. A very successful dinner. (30)

The mention of Warde Fowler is interesting and provokes an extended reference to him by another ornithologist of note, J.K. Stanford (31):

In 1912 I paid a visit to Kingham, cycling over before breakfast, to meet Professor Warde-Fowler of Lincoln College. He was famous among the ornithologists of those days for having found the marsh-warbler for the first time in England. He had done this by recognising its song, a song richer and more varied than that of the reed-warblers in the same osier beds. Most birdwatchers of normal hearing would have been proud of this achievement, but to me it was positively uncanny. For the professor, as well as his sister, was, I speedily found at breakfast, as deaf as any beetle. Even by roaring down his ear-trumpet, I had the greatest difficulty in carrying on any sort of conversation at the table. But undergraduates at Lincoln told me Warde-Fowler could recognise the note of almost any bird except the cuckoo, which too closely resembled the human voice!...This encounter with the deaf professor set me wondering, as I have often done since, how many other rare warblers may breed from year to year undetected, and even unsuspected, by anybody, in the lush undergrowth of summer England.

The other intriguing facet of Bishop Hicks' dinner is that it included two lady birders. For women to be let into such a circle was, of itself, something of a social revolution (32) that may signal a liberalism uncharacteristic of the times. Certainly the existence of such an event implies that F.L. had birding contacts around and beyond the county (he mentions 'friends' who supply information – see chapter 8); and he had birding companions on some of his forays (chapter 9).

Travelling to places of bird-watching interest would have presented choices to F.L.: to take the train to the nearest station, to cycle, to travel on horse-back, to ride in a horse-drawn vehicle or to walk. At Oxford, F.L. had won cups for running and jumping, and so we have to assume he was fit, and that he would have chosen to walk in many cases. Evidence from his diaries and from his obituary indicates that he walked and cycled throughout his long and active life (33). Dress was (to our eyes) relatively formal: hat, collar and tie, dark suit, waist-coat and watch-chain, overcoat for inclement weather, leather gloves, stout boots, and almost certainly a dog-collar to denote his office. Gordon Winter's (34) evocative collection of photographs of the period show the street scenes and village affairs that F.L. would have witnessed: the killing of the family pig; the Lincoln horse-fair; the uniformed postman wheeling a hand-cart on his rounds; the first motor bus to reach Caistor; and a passing gig carrying the doctor on his rounds.

Social contact would clearly have included invitations to the Hall at Doddington, to the Bishop's Palace, and to the homes of other birders as well as his routine visits to villagers in Doddington and Whisby. Since it is clear from his scientific reports on birds that he was familiar with Hartsholme, on the outskirts of Lincoln city, it seems possible that he would have known the family of Lord Liverpool – the owner from 1910 (35).

However, in the years of the Doddington incumbency, we have to assume a degree of calm and genteel socialising. There would have been tea on the lawn at the Rectory for invited guests; a rather sombre affair with a side-table or two transported onto the grass and covered with a lace cloth, some folding chairs, the best china, and cake to be shared. The fine weather would allow a boater over a formal suit for the men, and a similar straw hat atop a long, wide-skirted dress and shawl for the ladies (36).

F.L., as Rector, was a manager of the school at Doddington (37). His connection with the school is documented in the Log Book, which is kept at the Lincoln Archive Office. The first occasion on which his name appears (21st May 1909) it is incorrectly spelled: Blaithwayt. Thereafter the Log builds a picture of someone who is assiduous in his duties, recording numerous visits until the end of 1916, often twice or even three visits a week. He gives instruction in religious education to the children, which is regularly inspected by the Diocesan Inspector. He gains glowing reports, as in the entry for 10th June 1910:

Nothing could give greater satisfaction than the work done in this little school. The answers among the juniors were all that could be desired, and those of the seniors who had been at the school for more than a year showed in their answers that great pains had been taken in Religious Instruction. (38)

Sometimes, F.L.'s school visits are accompanied by Mr Jarvis from the Hall. Sometimes, the previous Rector returns for a visit: the Revd Cole. Mrs Blathwayt (Marjorie May Dennys, whom he married in 1910 in the St Thomas district of Devon) (39) features for the first time on 14th February 1913. Later, she becomes more involved with the school, visiting with Mrs Jarvis, or to give singing lessons (13th June 1913), or to invite the children to the Rectory for a singing lesson (18th July 1913).

The Log is not very detailed, is bald even for its genre; few insights are gained from it into the life of the community except that one child had a tree branch fall on her, which broke her leg; or that the annual potato picking shut the school; or, once that the school closed for a Grand Bazaar (7th July 1911) in the village; or once that the Rector gave special permission for secular lessons to begin at nine in the morning in order that the children could finish early and go to see the Meet (27th February 1914). Between visits to teach the scriptures, F.L. examined the registers and signed them off as correct – a regular chore of the managers.

F.L.'s involvement with the managers increased over time. When he first puts entries into the log he signs himself simply: F.L. Blathwayt (Manager); later he becomes the Correspondent. Then, in 1914, things begin to disintegrate as the head mistress endures a long illness until, at the end of that year, F.L. writes:

I enter, with much regret, the sad fact that Jane Price died on Saturday, Nov. 28th, at 3.30p.m. F.L.Blathwayt. (40)

The entry is short, factual, clipped, though doubtless sincere, for he had worked with the head mistress on a regular basis, and she had assiduously recorded his many visits as if she valued the support. But the school found it hard to recruit a replacement head, and was given over to the temporary control of various incumbents. A number of routine entries are made in F.L.'s hand and clearly he is helping to keep the school on an even keel. From 1916 the style of the Log changes, and F.L.'s visits are not individually recorded, though clearly they continued, the Diocesan Inspector was still content, and the registers were still signed off. The final relevant entry is as follows:

The Rev F.L. Blathwayt paid his farewell visit to the school on Tuesday morning and spoke a few words to the children.

The entry is dated 17th November 1916. England is embroiled in a costly war. Francis and Marjorie are about to take up the living at Melbury, Dorset, closer to the family seat, and to the family of Colonel Linley Blathwayt at Batheaston. F.L. is completing a final paper on the birds of Lincolnshire. By now they have a daughter, and a very young son. Things are in a state of flux.

The school Log gives us a mere speck of insight into Francis Blathwayt and his world at Doddington. His wife is passably musical – a typical female accomplishment of the time. He carries out his duties more regularly and attentively than was required. He had some care for the scriptures and for the education of the children in them. He seems to have been an able teacher, one that could get results by the standards of the time, but his educational interests do not spill out beyond religious education. He takes an increasing responsibility for the affairs of the school; but the record of his dealings with Miss Price and Miss Barnes (assistant teacher) show sympathy rather than compassion. He makes his entries in the Log with a hand that starts small, and becomes smaller over time. The writing is right-sloped, the letters minimalist: the bar on the 't', for example, almost imperceptible. In 1916, when he is making regular notes in the Log, the entries are crammed together. When he finally leaves he speaks 'a few words' only to the children; nothing remains of what he said nor of its tenor.

But if there were social and political controversies at work in the Lincoln area during F.L.'s time there, and if there were biblical debates about critical approaches to the scriptures in the wider context of the Anglican Church that might exercise F.L.'s ministry and beliefs, even the quiet world of natural history was not free of its schisms. As a birder, F.L. would have been only too aware of these; and before examining Francis Blathwayt's own contribution to birding, it is necessary first to establish this context, too.

NOTES TO CHAPTER 3

1.   Pevsner, N. and Harris, J, (1978 edn) *Lincolnshire* Harmondsworth: Penguin, p 514. The authors date the church as built by Thomas and William Lumby in 1771-5, with probable Victorian alterations, though the font is Early English.

2.   Pevsner and Harris (op.cit. p 515) attribute the Hall to Robert Smithson, who was also engaged in building Worksop Manor, Wollaton, and Hardwick Hall: 'it was built between 1593 and 1600 for Thomas Taylor, the Bishop of Lincoln's Recorder.'

3.   In 1991 the population of Doddington was 303 based on data obtained from www.askjeeves.co.uk .

4.   This is the number listed in Mills, D.R. (ed) 1989 *Twentieth Century Lincolnshire: History of Lincolnshire vol XII* Lincoln: History of Lincolnshire Committee. The figure had risen only to 325 by 1971 according to the same source.

5.   *Doddington: the prospect of a village 1560-1830* is the title of a small pamphlet about the village that resulted in 1977 from a study by history students of Bishop Grosseteste College, Lincoln, led by their tutor, Ian Beckwith. The roneo item is housed in the College Library and contains some fascinating day-to-day detail of life in early Doddington, though before Francis Blathwayt's era.

6.   The earliest of these were described as 'wattle-and-daub hovels' in the *Guide to Doddington Hall* (1986, no page numbers).

7.   Mr and Mrs Anthony Jarvis took over the Hall in 1975 which 'forms the focal point of a small rural community in which farming and forestry both play their part in providing a wide range of employment.' *Guide to Doddington Hall* (1986).

8.   Kelly's Directory (1895) describes Doddington in these words: 'a parish, township and

small village, on an elevation commanding an extensive view over fine picturesque country, and bounded to the west by the county of Nottingham' (p 150). Among the twelve commercial workers listed, apart from the gardener to G.E. Jarvis at Doddington Hall and his joiner, there was a blacksmith and the remainder were farmers.

9.   These data are available from Crockford's Clerical Directory and were taken from the 1936 edition. This names F.L.'s Oxford College, lists his degree as BA, and records that he is 'Can. Scho.' or from the Schola Cancellarii at Lincoln (Lincoln Theological College, as it was later known). As an Oxford graduate, when dressed for services, he would have been entitled to wear 'the hood of his degree' – of black stuff, in traditional simple shape, and lined with white fur. Doubtless this would have marked him out as an educated man. Alternatively, as a 'Can.Scho.' he might have sometimes worn a full-shaped hood of black stuff (i.e. not silk) the cowl lined with 3 inches of peacock blue silk, according to Charles Franklyn (1969) *Academical Dress,* a privately printed volume. On becoming MA, F.L. would probably have adopted the hood of the master's degree – a simple shaped black hood lined with 'blood crimson' silk (Franklyn, op.cit. p 99). Francis was paid the sum of £120 per annum in quarterly instalments for his curacy at St Swithin's; with a rise to £150 when he took the post at All Saints.

10.   These addresses still exist. The house in Monks Road is a tall red-brick affair; that in Monks Leys Terrace is reached down a narrow footpath that is squeezed between the house and the Arboretum. F.L. could have looked out of this latter property directly over the trees and lawns of the Arboretum and, indeed, though the sightings are rather limited (as they would be today) some bird records in F.L.'s diary do refer to this location. The Arboretum itself had a Victorian bandstand, a small lake, a maze, a massive stone lion and snaking paths through the shrubs. It fell into dis-repair and was recently restored, an account of which by Steffie Shield ('A winter walk in the Arboretum') can be found in *Lincolnshire Life* magazine dated December 2004. The Arboretum was designed by Edward Milner (1819-1894) who had previously designed Hartsholme Hall in Lincoln. The church of All Saints, just opposite the Arboretum still, in 2005, advertises its Holy Communion services as Said Mass and Sung Mass, sustaining its 'high' church status.

11.   In a seminal article in the *British Journal of Sociology,* (1969 (20) 3, pp 295- 310) 'The social and educational background of Anglican bishops', D.H.J. Morgan argued that four criteria held true in the vast majority of cases of clergy promoted to the bishopric of the Church of England between 1860 and 1960: a public school education, attendance at either Oxford or Cambridge, connections to the landed gentry, and training for the priesthood at one of four favoured theological colleges (Cuddesdon, Ridley, Westcott and Wells). In this last respect, F.L. fell short.

12.   Paul Welsby, writing in 1962, (in *Prism* 'Ecclesiastical Appointments 1942 – 1961' (6) 5, p 23) notes that only two bishops had a scientific training even at that time.

13.   Sir Francis Hill wrote the definitive statement about Victorian Lincoln in his book of the same name (1974, Cambridge: Cambridge University Press).

14.   The double level crossings were not removed until about 1994 when that serving St Mark's was removed to allow the St Mark's Shopping Centre to be constructed. The crossing for Central Station remains.

15.   Yates, J. and Thorold, H. (1965) *Shell Guide: Lincolnshire* London: Faber and Faber, p 92, so describe the city, despite its having 'one of the great sights of Europe' i.e. Lincoln cathedral.

16.   Hill notes that Lincolnshire's elected Councillors were unable or unwilling to carry out their duties effectively. This might come as no surprise to a modern electorate since, in 2005, the government's Audit Commission judged that Lincolnshire County Council was 'inadequate

Of Roseates *and* Rectories

at a political, managerial and community level' and that, despite this damning judgement was as yet 'in denial' (Lewis Lloyd 'Innuendoes, half-truths and elections' published in *The Source Public Management Journal* at www.sourceuk.net 31.03.05; Chris Willey 'Report blasts weak council' *Lincoln Chronicle* 17.03.05 p 1).

17. A painting about the typhoid outbreak was recently sold in the city. The outbreak began in December 1904 and by the following March 118 people had died and there were over 1,000 confirmed cases. There was a rumour that the Councillors were receiving their own water supplies from outside the city. A local artist, A.E.White, painted a cartoon-style picture in which the Councillors are being boiled in a huge pot by devils, while Death looks on, and the caption reads: Why not boil them for ten minutes in their own water? A report of the proposed sale appears in Mike Lyon (2005) 'Painting which so nearly caused a riot' *Lincolnshire Chronicle* 2nd June 2005 p 2. A brief history of the typhoid outbreak can be found on www.bbc.co.uk/legacies/heritage/england/lincolnshire/article_1.shtml; there is a postcard that depicts men, women and children queuing for clean water. The women wear heavy dresses, capes and hats, the men heavy boots and flat caps; they carry wooden or metal buckets or watering cans. It is, unsurprisingly, a dejected group with the body-language of depressed resignation.

18. Hill, op.cit. p 240.

19. Hill mentions rowdy behaviour in the city in a number of places, e.g. pp 34, 207, 297.

20. Sir Daniel Hall (1914) *A Pilgrimage of British Farming 1910-1912* pp 97, 98.

21. Bishop Hicks' comments are quoted by Hill (op.cit. page 217) from the former's *Diary* 28.09.14, and 21.11.15

22. It survives today as Bishop Grosseteste College having had several incarnations as a teacher training institution, and now also as a college awarding degrees of the University of Leicester. A history of the College can be found in Zebedee, D.H.J. (1962) *Lincoln Training College* Lincoln: Keyworth Fry.

23. Kelly's Directory for 1895 lists this school, adding that it was supported by George Eden Jarvis Esq., and the Rector. At the time the mistress was Miss Mary Barker. The school no longer exists, but seems to have been formed into two red-brick cottages still labelled no.1 and no.2 School House.

24. The figures quoted here are extracted from the Appendices to Hill's work.

25. It is not the intention to raise the sordid saga of the wrangles at Lincoln cathedral in this text. It was widely report throughout the late 1980s onwards in the local and national papers. There were two strands in the story, one concerning the sub-Dean, Canon Rex Davis, and alleged financial irregularities; the other relating to the Dean, Brandon Jackson, and some putative dealings with a female verger. Two bishops had the onerous task of trying to sort the matters out and neither really succeeded. Lincoln has been unfortunate, over the years, in having a superb cathedral but variable calibre among its senior officers.

26. Seebohm Rowntree (1901) *Poverty: A study of Town Life;* and Charles Booth (1889-1903 in 33 volumes) *Life and Labour of the People in London.*

27. H.C.G. Matthew's chapter on 'The Liberal Age' in Kenneth Morgan (1984) *The Oxford Illustrated History of Britain* Oxford: Oxford University Press (pages 463-522) captures the essence of the time.

28.   For example, F.E. Christmas (1950) *The Parson in English Literature* Gloucester: Alan Sutton Publishing, gives a fascinating account through extracts from major authors. While doubtless based on reality, these accounts are nevertheless not biographical and are often tongue-in-cheek.

29.   From Graham Neville (1993) *The Diaries of Edward Lee Hicks, Bishop of Lincoln 1910-19* Lincoln: Lincoln Record Office, item 441. Entry for Feb 9 1914.

30.   The 'Peacock' listed may have been M. Peacock author of *The Birds of North-West Lindsey* which appeared in instalments: *The Naturalist* 1902 pp 197-204, 1906 pp 42-47, 1908 pp 272-277, and 399-402. This Peacock was, it must be assumed, related to the vicar of Cadney, the Revd Edward Adrian Woodruffe-Peacock (1858-1922), himself a rather eccentric, or perhaps, individualistic and colourful botanist who contributed to *The Naturalist, The Transactions of the Lincolnshire Naturalists' Union* and *The Journal of Botany*. It is very possible that it refers to Woodruffe-Peacock himself. Woodruffe Peacock's brief biography appears in Patrick Armstrong's (2000) work *The English Parson-Naturalist* Leominster: Greenwing, pp 57-59 and 62-63. Hicks' Diaries contain various references to him (entries 177, 441, 831, 916 and 1154) e.g. 'he is a born and trained naturalist', an expert on the effect of turnips on farming, who was pipped to the post to be first to discover bilberry in Lincolnshire by Dr Claye. But he allowed his Rectory to fall into ruination, much to Bishop Hicks' chagrin. E. Elder (1993) records more about this unusual family, experts on Lincolnshire dialect, in 'The Peacocks of North-West Lincolnshire: Collectors and Recorders of Lincolnshire Dialect from c. 1850 –1920 – part II' in *Lincolnshire History and Archaeology* (28) pp 44-57.

31.   J.K.Stanford (1954)   *A Bewilderment of Birds*   London: Rupert Hart-Davies, p 53. This book, as well as containing excellent accounts of birding in this country and overseas, is immensely humorous about such activities as attending birding conferences. A good read. The author was part of a birding circle that included many of the luminaries of the 20th century such as C.B. Ticehurst, with whom he co-authored *The Birds of Burma*. Nevertheless the accreditation of the first English marsh warbler to Warde-Fowler is not without a touch of ambiguity. According to Holloway the first record was at Alresford Great Pond in 1863 (i.e. some 49 years earlier than the date of this dinner (Holloway, S. 1996 *The Historical Atlas of Breeding Birds in Britain and Ireland 1875-1900* London: Poyser). W. Warde-Fowler's account of the marsh warbler was published in 1906 ('The marsh warbler: a breeding record of fourteen years' *The Zoologist* (10) 401-409). Presumably this is the source of the reference in Witherby's *Handbook:* 'chief alarm- or scalding-notes are a chirring, higher pitched and less grating than sedge-warbler's (W. Warde-Fowler)' - Witherby, H.F., Jourdain, F.C.R., Ticehurst, N.F. and Tucker, B.W. (1938) *The Handbook of British Birds* London: H.F. & G. Witherby, page 50.

32.   Stephen Moss (2004) *A Bird in the Bush: a social history of birdwatching* London: Aurum Press devotes a chapter to women in birdwatching. Despite the fact that women were involved in the setting up of the Royal Society for the Protection of Birds, remarkably few women have been involved in birding until modern times, except for a few spouses of famous birders, and of some of our clergy-naturalists (see Armstrong, op. cit. p 53). They are still frequently excluded from the unofficial 'clubs' of those birders who claim the description 'twitchers'.

33.   The information comes from two sources. First, notes supplied by the Revd Linley Blathwayt, F.L.'s son, to Dorset County Museum, Dorchester, to which the museum kindly allowed access. Second, F.L.'s obituary notice by Dr K. B. Rooke, which is discussed at length in the final chapter of this book.

34.   Winter, G. (1972) *A Country Camera 1844-1914* Newton Abbot: David and Charles. The scenes referred to appear on pp 14 (1905), 89 (1905), 95 (1905), 109 (1906) and 34 (1905).

35.   The Hartsholme connection is pursued later in the book.

36.   The general flavour is conveyed by Winter op.cit. p 32 and in numerous unpublished cabinet photographs and lantern slide pictures of the time.

37.   The Forster Act of 1870 had provided public elementary schools, but the 1902 Balfour Education Act created Local Education Authorities, and thus had a profound effect on the structure of education nationally. Controversially, these LEAs now had the power to 'control secular teaching in denominational schools…Denominational instruction was to be provided in LEA schools. There was to be no religious discrimination in publicly provided schools.' Farrell, in Farrell, M., Kerry, T. and Kerry, C. (1995) *Blackwell Handbook of Education* Oxford: Basil Blackwell p 298.

38.   The Diocesan Inspector in this case was the Revd T. Hamilton, who also visited the school on 26th April 1911 and was equally impressed. Thereafter the inspector changed to the Revd C. Richmond Poole, who is inclined to be less effusive, but always concludes that overall the work is 'quite good' or 'good' (entries for 21st May 1913, 3rd July 1914, 28th June 1916).

39.   The marriage is on record in the Civil Registration Index available via www.ancestry.co.uk; Marjorie was born in 1887, also a daughter of the Raj, and is recorded in the 1901 Census as living in Eastbourne. She died in 1976 aged 89. Some aspects of her life were recorded by her sister, Joyce Dennys (1984 *And then there was one* Padstow: Tabb House). In the paperback version of this book there is a picture of Marjorie (between pp 4,5), a demure little girl with dark hair, standing in a long coat that has eight huge circular buttons in two lines down the front; she wears a vast velvet hat with what looks like a flower decoration. Facts taken from the book about Marjorie are, in outline, as follows. Born in India she received rudimentary home schooling and then was sent to Eastbourne Ladies' College; she was 'sweet' and conformist, a good pianist. Marjorie was sent back to India as part of the 'fishing fleet' looking for a husband, but she hated India and sought ways to return. When the parents retired she came back. The family moved later to Budleigh Salterton, Devon. While Joyce's story continues, Marjorie's is dismissed with the bald statement: 'Marjorie married a parson, one of the Blathwayts of Dyrham, and remained sweet and good to the end of her life' (p 90).

40.   This is the entry for 1st December 1914. It is succeeded by one regarding the assistant teacher on 4th of the month: 'Owing to the very serious illness, and death, of Jane Price, Miss [the entry appears to give instead the first name, but it is unreadable] Barnes (assistant teacher) had leave from the managers to be absent six days from her duties in this school.' The entry is made and signed by F.L.

CHAPTER 4
BIRDING IN F.L.'s DAY
debates, protection and growing interest

Just as the thinking in the Church of F.L.'s time was in a state of flux because of the controversies surrounding the scientific approach to biblical criticism, so there were controversies in the apparently peaceable world of birding. Nor were they any less vicious than the religious debates.

While the Royal Society for the Protection of Birds (RSPB) has over a million members today, it did not exist until 1889. Then, a group of women in Didsbury banded together to make common cause against the use of bird feathers and skins for making hats and adorning clothes. As F.L. was graduating, in 1899, the membership had risen to twenty thousand across some one hundred and fifty local groups (1). This movement was in response to a critical situation in both the United Kingdom and America, in which wild birds were disappearing in the face of a voracious clothing trade, so that many species had reached crisis point (2).

Part of the problem, too, was to be found among the birders themselves. Two approaches to birding were causing untold damage to bird populations: shooting and egg-collecting. Some of the most famous and revered names in the birding world followed one or both of these routes to birding fame, but even the ordinary 'bird lover' was apt to do the same – as the following note from the Selborne Society's magazine for 1899 shows (3):

Last month a kingfisher – the first I had ever seen – became a frequent visitor to my garden, which is situated nearly in the middle of town, and has an oval-shaped pond about 18 feet in length, in which there were about fifty goldfish. One morning at breakfast I was attracted by the brilliant colours of a strange bird perching in a tree, and intently watching the pond, and occasionally diving to the surface and picking up and gobbling something in gull-fashion, which I saw must be my goldfish. The bird was having his breakfast at the same time as myself. He came again for his dinner, and for three or four days in succession. I became anxious for my goldfish, and desperate enough to shoot the bird. I, however, did not want to injure his beautiful plumage, and used very fine shot. One of these only struck him, but it was in the eye, and that was enough. The bird is now stuffed, and for the next hundred years will, no doubt, be on view to anyone who wants to see a kingfisher. The query is how this bird should be so clever as to find out my pond and the goldfish therein.

The total unself-consciousness with which this story is told is amazing to a modern ear. Its author conveys, unwittingly, the farce of Victor Borge and the rapaciousness of a spoiled soccer star. A hundred years of looking at a skin is obviously worth more than to see the living being! But these events were not uncommon, they may even have been the norm. In an earlier section of the same volume (4) there is a clue to the mentality of shooting – the rarer the creature is, the more prestigious it becomes to shoot it:

A male and female pied oyster-catcher were shot yesterday morning by Mr J. Atkinson, of Barnet, in a field near Rickmansworth. These birds are the constant inhabitants of the seashore, and though nowhere plentiful, yet are widely distributed over the globe…It is not often, however, they are seen far inland…Those shot yesterday appeared to be fatigued as a result of an extra long flight. Shortly after this capture was also shot another very rare bird, the male scoter, black duck or black diver…

Members of the Selborne Society took a dim view of this kind of activity, and campaigned actively against it; as did the RSPB and the RSPCA along with a growing cadre of other wildlife organisations; but progress was slow. Even parson birders were not immune from the habit. Armstrong, for example, records the exploits of The Great Gun of Durham, one Canon Tristram; though he did become converted to the conservation cause later in life (5). One of the most famous naturalists to have been recruited to the RSPB's cause against shooting was W.H. Hudson, who wrote a pamphlet entitled *Osprey: or Egrets and Aigrettes,* which was sold at nine-pence a dozen as a way of spreading the word (6). Hudson campaigned furiously on the issue, as a brief extract from his *Adventures Among Birds* shows (7):

Going into Hampshire I was by-and-by at a spot which cannot be named owing to the fact that I was there in quest of a rare and elusive little bird. For we who desire to save our birds must keep the private collector in mind; that injurious person who is ever anxious to secure the very last British-killed specimen of any rare species…The law does not protect our birds and country from these robbers; they have too many respected representatives in the high places, on the benches of magistrates, in the houses of Parliament, and among important people generally…Those who break into our houses to steal our gold steal trash in comparison; while these, who are never sent to Portland or Dartmoor, are depriving the country with its millions of inhabitants of one of its best possessions – its lustrous wildlife.

Hudson's outburst at the protection afforded by position in society to such offenders is reinforced by an entry, again in the Selbornian (8), which records that a certain Captain George F. Whitmore was found guilty of killing gulls by shooting them from his yacht during the close season – for which crime he received a fine of two shillings and six pence. On which travesty the journal comments: 'No real punishment to an offender in Captain Whitmore's position.'

The problem with egg-collecting was that it was more insidious and more easily defensible than shooting. In a sense, once a bird was shot, it was dead; there was no going back and no argument that the act was terminal. Egg-collecting, however, could be defended because only one egg of a clutch, or an early clutch (when the bird would lay again) might be taken. This act could be passed off as 'harmless' 'science'. The cases of empty shells, though they may have a spurious interest because of the aesthetic value or their minor variations in colour and form, were generally, however, nothing more than trophies.

Some of the 'greatest' birders of F.L.'s age were, or had been, egg-collectors. Among these was the Revd Francis Charles Robert Jordain (1865-1943): he of the Witherby, Jourdain, Ticehurst and Tucker *Handbook* (9). Jourdain's collection was reckoned to be 'one of the largest and most scientifically useful', even if it was compiled 'After forty years of ransacking the most important West Palearctic habitats' (10). Many of the egg-collecting fraternity were persistent and self-justificatory, and collecting was harder to stamp out than shooting. So the early part of the twentieth century was riddled with controversy about what was and what was not legitimate in terms of 'collecting'.

The cult of collecting, especially the practice of shooting, was designed in part to test the waters of what was 'out there' in birding terms. By raking the coastal shrub-lands with shot during the migration season, and more or less obliterating everything that moved therein, it was possible to get a pretty good idea of what rare birds were about among the commoner species. Capturing scalps has always been a part of the birding process, witnessed today in the growth of the 'twitcher' network (11). Indeed, just as that movement has its extremists who are determined to score new birds at all costs, so there raged in F.L.'s day a controversy of huge proportions.

On the quiet, sea-swept beaches of the south-east of England around Hastings between the years 1892 and 1930 there appeared a most amazing procession of rare birds. Intrinsically, if one were to seek a haven for unusual species, especially at migration time, this evocative length of coast-line would be a place to look. When a rarity turned up here it would have the great advantage that some of the best ornithologists of the time were local worthies, who might be called upon at short notice to give a definitive opinion as to its identification. So the list of sightings grew, throughout F.L.'s time in Lincolnshire, and then during much of his Rectorship at Melbury. Though he is silent on the issue, he must have been aware of the debate. But as the catalogue expanded its sheer volume and quality began to be questioned, even though 'greats' of birding such as Ticehurst were among those providing identifications. Indeed, Witherby, with whom Ticehurst had collaborated on the *Handbook* was among the sceptics. It was not until after F.L.'s death that the matter was settled. Despite an ardent defence of the list of Hastings birds by someone as eminent as David Bannerman (12), the sceptics eventually won the day. Stephen Moss records (13):

The August 1962 edition of *British Birds* was entirely devoted to the repudiation of the Hastings Rarities. In all, 542 specimens and 43 sight records of almost 100 species, including no fewer than 16 species which had never occurred anywhere else in the country, were deleted from the 'British list'.

Nowhere does Francis allude to this controversy, though we know that he wrote for and read *British Birds*. But it stands far outside his intentions for personal and county birding. There were others in the county who agreed with his approach: observation backed up by documented research and personal testimony. In the President's address (14) to the Lincolnshire Naturalists' Union in 1910 it is suggested that both *Transactions* from past years and the pages of *The Naturalist* are full of Lincolnshire sightings: 'not all of it the dry bones of science, but replete with suggestions for the future, reminiscences of the past.' There is also a plea not to ignore the common-place: 'For it is the common species that are the dominant ones, and offer the most suggestive field for detailed observation.'

What will emerge in subsequent chapters is that there is almost never, in the work of Francis Blathwayt the suggestion that he personally collects eggs or shoots adult birds (15). His works are dependent on observation; and any recording is done through 'powerful glasses' (16), not by dealing death to the specimen or invading the nest. His concerns are with the distribution of birds, and with increasing that distribution by means of careful encouragement of species to nest. Here and there, there are laments that eggs have been stolen (not always for collections, but for food), and about the effect this has had on bird numbers; though he accepts, as we shall see, that some species are, effectively, farmed. But neither is he an emotional propagandist like Hudson; his concern is for the science of birding, and the conservation of species, and not primarily for the spurious actions of humans.

•

It was precisely this kind of interest in observation and distribution of birds, as recorded in chapter 1, that brought F.L. to my attention in 1977. I was involved with an area of about eighty acres known as Hartsholme Park, on the outskirts of Lincoln city. Something of the story of Hartsholme during the years 1975-1980 is in order at this point in our narrative. But it must wait a few more lines while I recount for you the observation of Francis Blathwayt that stopped me in my tracks, and which led, some years later, to this modest volume.

Though it is no longer true, and has not been the case for some years (17), in the early decades of the 20th century the annual bird report for the county of Lincolnshire was in the hands of the Lincolnshire Naturalists' Union. So, while engaged in active conservation and recording work for the Hartsholme area, it made sense to consult the back numbers of the

Of Roseates *and* Rectories

Transactions for historical records of birds in that location. This passage caught my eye:

The irruption of the crossbill as observed in Lincolnshire: ...Large parties inhabited the Fir Woods at Hartsholme, near Lincoln, from January to June 1910, and I myself many times saw them there in flocks of twenty or thirty birds, chiefly during the month of April. A few pairs probably nested during April and May in the woods, as a bird was seen carrying nesting materials into the fir trees and pairs were also observed apart from the flocks, the males being in song. The flocks departed during June or early July for N. Europe. One bird was picked up dead at Donna Nook, on the coast, 9 July 1910...*F.L. Blathwayt, Doddington Rectory.*

This kind of observation and recording so closely mirrored what I and others were trying to do in Hartsholme from 1975 onwards that I was intrigued by the entry dated more than sixty years before. It became clear to me that this clergyman might have watched more systematically in the vicinity, and I resolved to track down his other work. Thus came the revelation that he had been involved in birding in the Lincoln area from about 1900 until 1916, and the seed of this text was planted.

Hartsholme was especially important at that time since a group (18) had been established to try to preserve an important local wildlife resource which was under threat from building around its boundaries. The Park consisted of eighty-eight acres (some forty-plus hectares) of land, of which the major features were a lake, a tree-lined walk along the edge of the lake, an island in the middle of the lake, an avenue of yews, a long and narrow stream feeding the lake and edged with willow and alder (19), a small area of dry heath, and a tiny marshy area. From the park boundary it was possible to view, but not to gain legitimate access to, Swanholme gravel pits. Contiguous with the park was a derelict airfield (20), very boggy in winter, and a considerable area of birch and fir scrub. On the opposite side of the main Skellingthorpe road scrub gave way to farmland, with a couple of footpaths that led into Lincoln city close to the Lincoln-Nottingham railway line.

Members of EMBSC carried out five years of census work in the park, visiting on average twice weekly, and recording the bird-life. These records were summarised annually (21). In addition, the group also ran, for several years, a guided walk for members of the public each

Sunday morning throughout the year. This facility continued beyond the appointment of a Ranger service for the Park, set up by the Lincoln City Council. Volunteer wardens also surveyed, or caused to be surveyed, other wildlife than birds in the area (22); and they were active in advising the Council about management matters (23). As a result of this work, which was carried out without support from larger groups (24), the Park was confirmed in its Country Park status. While some of the contiguous habitats were lost (25), the main park area and the Swanholme gravel pits have been preserved and continue to encourage a good variety of local bird life.

Among the fascinating discoveries relating to Hartsholme was the revelation that the old stone steps leading down to the lake were the clue to a large house that had once stood on the site. The lake had been constructed in 1848 'as a reservoir for the water supply for Lincoln' (26) – neither a good nor a viable investment, as we have seen; for this was fed by the same Prial Drain that instigated the typhoid outbreak of 1904 onwards.

The Hall itself was started in 1862 by Joseph Shuttleworth, a local industrialist, and his son succeeded to the house; though it was soon in the hands of Nathaniel Clayton Cockborn. This last owner moved to Harmston Hall by 1900, and the house stood empty for a time, the period when F.L. was curate in Lincoln. By 1905, however, Colonel T.W.Harding was installed as owner – a moderniser who was adding the newly available electricity and other refinements – but he does not seem to have spent much time at the Hall. The sale of the Hall to Lord Liverpool, begun in 1906, was completed on 24th June 1908 after protracted negotiations about fittings to be included or excluded from the sale. Lord Liverpool set about enlarging the estate: unnecessary when it had been constructed, since the first owner was an industrialist in search of a home not a farmer in search of rents. In the park today there are a few remnants of these occupations (27). But it is at this point that the Hall has an intriguing connection to Doddington, F.L.'s parish.

A letter from another clergyman, the Revd A.R. Maddison, forges a link between Hartsholme and the Jarvis family in which Arthur Jarvis appears to be acting as some kind of broker:

My dear Arthur Jarvis of Doddington has just been in and asks me to write and tell you that Capt. Ellison of Boultham is willing to sell that bit of land between the railway and the back of Hartsholme. It is worthless as land but it is worth buying as someone else might someday build a house on it which would be disagreeable to you (28).

Lord Liverpool may well not have lived regularly in the Hall during F.L.'s time at Doddington, though it was staffed; he was otherwise occupied as Governor-General of New Zealand. What we do know is that from 1909 Francis Blathwayt is birding in the area, and continues to do so during his time at Doddington Rectory. His diaries reveal that the crossbill sighting triggered his first interest in the area and that afterwards he watched there from time to time. He records a male siskin there in 1911, the record being contained in the *Transactions* for that year (29). A visitor to the Park today can still see the old stable block (now an information centre and café), and the steps down to the lake. But the Hall itself is demolished (30), though it once had some nineteen bedrooms, as well as drawing rooms, gun room, library and all the usual servants' quarters. We can only speculate on the intelligence F.L. might have provided about the area to the Jarvis family as an incidental to his birding there.

•

So the direct connection between Hartsholme and Francis Blathwayt has been established, both through his birding and through his connection to the Jarvis family. Regrettably, F.L. did not, as far as we know, keep a systematic list of the birds of the Hartsholme area during the period of his visits (31). Mention of the siskin accords with observations by EMBSC during the late seventies; and even more recently this species would feed from the alder catkins adjacent to the boat-house during the winter. F.L.'s reference to the crossbill precisely reflects the habits of these birds, which irrupt following food availability and have adapted to breed in any month of the year if food is readily obtainable and in good supply (32). Birds of this species do turn up locally from time to time: small parties have been seen at Woodhall by the author; and one bird was recorded just a couple miles from Hartsholme, in Whisby (33), during 2004.

But the important issue rests with the report of the crossbills in 1910, which so closely linked with the work that EMBSC was carrying out at the time, and overlapped specifically in its tone and the desire for accurate recording of the area. The brief paragraph quoted from F.L. earlier in the chapter, demonstrates important qualities in a naturalist: an economy of words, accuracy of personal observation, an eye for detail, the ability to deduce and speculate, and a wish to place the observations in a context of time and place as well as to look for wider patterns. The full text of the note shows he was a researcher, too ('…the following is a short summary of all the published reports I have been able to find…').

These few lines seemed to capture the spirit of the man, but importantly, the spirit of the man as a birder. EMBSC tried to emulate these ambitions at Hartsholme, and in a very real sense F.L. inspired a 1970s contribution to the wildlife potential of Lincoln city. His interest in Hartsholme is examined in more detail in chapter 9.

In the preceding chapters, an attempt has been made to provide a scientific and historical context for Francis Linley Blathwayt with special reference to his time in, and contribution to, birding in Lincolnshire. The next chapter examines some of F.L.'s early published writing. These published articles, included in books and wildlife journals, help to build a portrait of Francis Linley Blathwayt, birder, and to point to the experience he brought to birding in Lincolnshire between 1900 and 1916.

NOTES TO CHAPTER 4

1.   The history of the RSPB can be found in Samstag, T. (1988) *For the Love of Birds* Sandy: RSPB. The 'Royal' title was added in 1904, while F.L. was serving as curate at All Saints, Lincoln.

2.   Stephen Moss tells this story in chapter 6 of *A Bird in the Bush* (2004) London: Aurum.

3.   This at the very moment when Queen Victoria herself was banning the use of plumes on military uniforms! The letter quoted is from J.H.Gartell of Penzance, p 43, and is headed (by the editor) 'Was there no alternative?' Volume X, 1899.

4.   Op. cit. p 19.

5.   Armstrong, P. (2000) *The English Parson-Naturalist* Leominster: Gracewing, pp 72-78 outline this activity among the clergy though, of course, it was rife in society as a whole. Aristocrats tended to pay handsomely to augment their collections as well as collecting in person, and the poor had an eye not only for a bird but also for a quick profit.

6.   Fisher, J. (1973 edn) *The Shell Bird Book* London: Ebury Press and Michael Joseph, p 139.

Of Roseates *and* Rectories

7.   The chapter 'In a Hampshire Village' begins with this passage. The book is the 1932 edition published in London by Dent, p 139. This chapter also has a brilliant description of a former and much decorated old soldier from the Empire who, now a park-keeper in the London parks, spends his days 'guarding a blackbird's nest from the wild, lawless little Afghans and Soudanese (sic) of the London slums.' Political correctness hadn't been discovered in Hudson's time.

8.   Volume IX, 1898, p 182.

9.   Witherby, H.F., Jourdain, F.C. R. , Ticehurst, N.F. and Tucker, B. (1938-41) *The Handbook of British Birds* (5 volumes) London: H.F. & G. Witherby – classic of identification until very recent times. There was also a less-known *Practical Handbook* compressed into three volumes.

10.   Mearns, B. and Mearns, R. (1988) *Biographies for Birdwatchers: The Lives of those Commemorated in Western Palearctic Bird Names* London: Academic Press. It may come as a surprise that *Bird Study,* the highly respected journal of the British Trust for Ornithology, volume 1 no. 1, March 1954, page 32, carries a note about a resolution to outlaw egg-collecting. An Extraordinary General Meeting of the Trust on 29th January of that year carried the following motion by an overwhelming majority: 'That the B.T.O. considers that egg-collecting, in the manner in which it is usually practised today in the British Isles, is not only without scientific justification but is a serious hindrance to field research in ornithology and, therefore, contrary to the aims and objects of the Trust.' That such a resolution should still be necessary half a century after the beginning of Blathwayt's work is surprising. That the Secretary of the BTO should emphasise that its primary purpose was not to 'protect birds but the members of the Trust who were studying their habits seriously' is something that today's ornithological organisations would probably feel was best forgotten.

11.   Moss, S. (2004) *A Bird in the Bush* London: Aurum; chapter 14 takes a detailed look at the twitching fraternity, with perhaps a touch more affection than many deserve.

12.   David Bannerman was an ornithologist of vast knowledge and with a huge range of contacts who had watched birds all over the world. His *Birds of the British Isles* Edinburgh & London: Oliver & Boyd, is a classic study in 12 volumes. Appendix III in volume XII is careful to guard against accepting *some* of the putative sightings, but anxious to defend the reputations of the many fine ornithologists who may have been duped.

13.   Moss, op.cit., p 216. It seems that fraud *may* have been committed by a taxidermist called Bristow, and the ornithologist Michael Nicholl. If there was a motive, other than fame, it was greed at the money to be made from stuffed specimens from wealthy collectors. Some of the skins may have been brought in to the country on the early refrigerated container ships, possibly via an elderly steward name Parkman. But these are speculative conclusions and the truth is unknown.

14.   The President's Address for 1909 in *LNU Transactions.*

15.   Lest anyone think that I am being economical with the truth at this point, it must be recorded that Blathwayt's note on crossbills ends with a single sentence in a free-standing paragraph. It runs: 'A specimen was obtained from Hartsholme for the Lincoln Museum.' Caution is urged against taking this statement as condoning the practice. A fact of life at the time was that many museums contained and displayed specimens (indeed, many still display them). Like egg-collecting this was seen as a 'scientific' and 'educational' activity. The sentence stands conspicuously alone, without comment, as a statement of factual accuracy. It will be argued later

that this literary ploy is one that F.L. uses when he wishes not to offend but distance himself from an event. There is also a record in the diaries (see chapter 9) that on one occasion a pair of stonechats was taken for museum use, and perhaps on another occasion a clutch of eggs.

16.   Powerful glasses are mentioned in many of F.L.'s articles and we shall expand on this theme later.

17.   In a later note to chapter 7 the removal of the County Bird List from the control of the LNU is discussed at some length.

18.   The group called itself EMBSC – East Midlands Bird Study and Conservation. Membership consisted of the author as organising warden for the Park; plus a number of young adults and teenagers – members of my own family, Michael Willey who put a lot of time and energy into the project, Richard Arden, Susan Jones, Bill Booth a local farmer, Tricia Brown who had expertise in botany and soils, Frank Dixon and his nephew who supported weekly guided walks, and Steve Russell who was tragically killed during this time by an uninsured driver while trying to turn into his home village. Arthur Gilpin, the well-known and pioneer bird photographer, was our Patron. A couple of other observers joined for short periods; and several non-members actively provided sightings.

19.   This stream was part of or connected to the Prial Drain, the watercourse that served the city so ill and was instrumental in the typhoid epidemic recorded earlier in the book. See note 26 below.

20.   Locally this was often referred to as Birchwood airfield, but strictly was Skellingthorpe airfield. Otter, P. (1999 edn) *Lincolnshire Airfields During the Second World War* Newbury: Countryside Books, p 210, describes it as 'built amid the gravel pits and birch trees three miles west of the city centre in 1941.' It was a heavy bomber base flying Hampdens, Manchesters and Lancasters. Most famous pilot was Leslie Manser VC, who gives his name to a local school. A photograph (op.cit. p 217) shows the fir woods clearly in the background of a group picture of RAF personnel at the base in 1945. The exploits of the RAF officers and men who served there are marked by a memorial in Birchwood Avenue, a stone's throw from Hartsholme Park.

21.   Annual Reports regarding birdlife in Hartsholme are as follows:

Hartsholme Park Nature Trail 1976, 1ˢᵗ Annual Report
Hartsholme Park 1977, 2ⁿᵈ Annual Report
Hartsholme Park 1978, 3ʳᵈ Annual Report
Hartsholme 1979, 4ᵗʰ Annual Report of the Nature Trail
Hartsholme Trail EMBSC Report 1980, no 5
All of these were privately published by EMBSC, Lincoln. Bound copies were donated to the Hartsholme Ranger Service and to the library of the British Trust for Ornithology. The group also produced:
Kerry, T. (1978) *An Historical Review of the Birds of Hartsholme and Lincoln* Lincoln: EMBSC.

22.   Non-bird related Reports included: Booth, P (1978) *Seed-producing plants at Hartsholme* Lincoln: EMBSC; and Kerry, T. (1979) 'Hartsholme: A model for devising and using a nature trail' *Journal of Biological Education* (13), 1, 32-40. Other surveys were included as part of the Annual Reports listed in note 21.

23.   The main Management Report was Kerry, T. (1979) *Management Possibilities of*

Of Roseates *and* Rectories

24. All the members of EMBSC were, at the time, members of the RSPB. The national organisation would not take on such a local project, and the then local RSPB group leader was not prepared to support a collection of young people running such an upstart project. Going it alone was the only option. The Official Opening of the park as a Country Park took place on 10th April 1979 (though it had been designated some years before) and was carried out by Mr R.J. Hookway, Director of the Countryside Commission (an invitation card is in my personal archive of the park). A number of wildlife groups became interested after EMBSC's intervention from 1975-1980, demonstrating perhaps that a little hindsight is a wonderful thing. Luckily, beyond Lincolnshire, the potential was noted even at the time, and the EMBSC archive contains a letter from the Acting Director of the British Trust for Ornithology dated 14th January 1976 which reads: 'The first annual report of the Hartsholme Park Nature Trail is a very ambitious achievement for so "young" a body and must, I am sure, give great satisfaction to all who have been involved with the preparation of it. Certainly the list of birds is an impressive one and indicates that you have a rich area to study.'

25. A visitor to the park today would note that most of the land adjacent to the area on the Birchwood side has been taken over for housing, indeed properties run very close to the boundary. Most of the Skellingthorpe airfield is also under housing; as are the birch/fir woods along the Skellingthorpe Road. Inevitably, this has had a deleterious effect on some species. For example, flocks of up to 70 redpolls have all but been extinguished; and the huge winter flocks of bramblings and other mixed finches, sometimes numbering 500 birds, have long since departed the airfield. Within the park itself the marshy area has been allowed to dry out because of the failure to control succession vegetation, so even the occasional woodcock has disappeared. Incorporating Swanholme has added some wildfowl species, the most notable being a considerable rise in gadwall numbers, and small groups of wintering goosanders.

26. Details about the Hall at Hartsholme here are taken from a roneo article by Laurence Elvin from the Fireside Magazine, a Lincoln Association for the Care of the Elderly publication, January 1965; and from Pacey, R. (2002) *Lost Lincolnshire Country Houses* Burgh le Marsh: Old Chapel Lane Books (volume 5). Another interesting text was compiled by the pupils of the All Saints CE Primary School at North Hykeham. Called *Memories of the Hartsholme Hall Estate* (undated), this records '1904: Fateful outbreak of typhoid in Lincoln leads to 243 deaths. Hartsholme Lake water suspected of being the source of the epidemic.'

27. For example, there are dog graves from the 1870s at one corner of the lake; and an obelisk set up by Lord Liverpool, as well as the boat house.

28. Pacey, op.cit. p 23, sourced from the Northamptonshire Record Office FS/118.

29. When, on behalf of the EMBSC, I began researching early records at Hartsholme in about 1976 and was beginning to collect my first data about F.L. Blathwayt, I had sought access to the complete set of *LNU Transactions* that were kept at the city's museum. The then curator discovered this and, disapproving of the organisation and its attempt to raise the profile of Hartsholme, banned me from access to these documents. The work was completed (but rather hurriedly) by the ploy of discovering his afternoon off, and approaching the junior staff during his absence! Just a small example of how introverted the birding world can be – wholly out of touch with Blathwayt's vision of pushing back the boundaries of knowledge. The current officer of the re-named The Collection, Lincoln, also broke an arrangement for me to view LNU *Transactions*, and the matter went to formal complaint; given such uphill struggles it is little wonder that this study has not appeared before!

30.   Later history demanded its conversion into barracks for troops during World War II. Thereafter it was in a poor state and the Local Authority, its new owners by this time, could not afford the upkeep. It was demolished rather than restored; though the boathouse remains beside the lake. When the lake was drained for remedial work during the 1970s much WWII .303 ammunition was dug up from the mud by schoolboys from the City School. Luckily, none of it exploded!

31.   EMBSC did, for the years 1975-1980, and it appears as Appendix 2. F.L.'s diaries record a number of visits to the area; the diaries are described in chapter 9.

32.   Desmond Nethersole-Thompson is the authority on the species: (1975) *Pine Crossbills* Berkhampsted: Poyser. See, for example, p 87 on breeding behaviour.

33.   It will be recalled that F.L. was Rector of Doddington-Pigot with Whisby. Whisby now has its own nature park, and this was the location of the sighting, by the assistant warden.

CHAPTER 5
EARLY WRITINGS

F.L. had begun serious birding with a view to publication before he left Oxford (1). His first recorded article was published in 1897, and by 1900 he had reached the dizzy heights of writing in the Zoologist. At the time of this latter article he was undergoing (or had just completed) training for ordination at Lincoln Theological College; he does not sign the piece 'The Revd'. This chapter examines F.L.'s early publications: 'A Visit to Lundy' (1900), and 'The Roseate Tern on the Farne Islands' (1902), along with a third piece, published in 1906 but dependent on earlier research: 'Birds' from the Victoria History of Somerset. The trio of items makes up a group of published writings that pre-date his work on the county of Lincolnshire, but in many respects they set the pattern for his distinctive style of bird recording.

Chapters 6,7 and 8 then look at the published material about birding in Lincolnshire, covering the period 1908-1916. Chapter 9 extracts data from F.L.'s bird diaries for this same Lincolnshire period (the diaries are now stored in the Dorset County Museum in Dorchester).

●

The Lundy article is interesting, because many of the Blathwayt characteristics are already embedded in it. Early on it states: 'I have not been able to find any attempt at a complete list of the avifauna of Lundy' (2). This signals a keen interest in listing, and in his wish always to examine the whole range of bird-life, past and present, in a location, not merely to engross himself in his own sightings.

The visit took place from the 5th to the 11th May 1900; he had intended to cross to the island on the 3rd, but the weather was too rough. So, at last – and we can imagine perhaps a touch of irritation as well as anticipation – he sets sail in *The Gannet,* a weekly mail boat out of Instow.

Immediately he makes an assessment of the terrain. Lundy, 'with the exception of the south-east corner', is of granite rising between 300 and 500 feet out of the sea, and measures about one mile by three-quarters. It lies in the Bristol Channel, some twelve miles off-shore. He notes the fantastical forms of the granite, and the composition of the scrub vegetation. His experience of the crossing leads him to reflect that of the few places to dock, the shingle beach at the south-east corner is the best, and that getting ashore 'with dry feet' is difficult when the wind is in the East; the voice of experience, one suspects! The higher, western cliffs are the best haunt of the sea-birds.

Unusually, the article has a touch of the travelogue about it, the only one of his whole collection that does. The closing paragraph gives the visitor this advice:

I would advise anyone interested in birds, who may chance to visit Lundy by excursion steamer, to spend the two or three hours allowed on land in exploring the coastline of the northern half of the island. It will have to be done hurriedly in the limited time at the tourist's disposal, as it takes about an hour to walk from the landing-place to the North Lighthouse. If time does not allow a visit to all the cliffs on the north-west side, where the Guillemots and Kittiwakes chiefly congregate, the visitor would do well to follow the rough track on the top of the island to the north end, where he may see the large colony of Puffins and Razorbills, which to the bird-lover is perhaps the most interesting sight which can be obtained on this picturesque island.

The passage is, it is suggested, unusual in the works of F.L. in so far as it conveys a kind of excitement, a boyish enthusiasm to share the sights of this wild place. But there are subtle nuances of language. He has spent a week as a birder and worked thoroughly over the location, yet the advice is for 'tourists' with a limited time-span. Nonetheless there is an effervescence about the passage that is less obvious elsewhere in the corpus.

Despite this, the article shows an enduring concern not for mere listing, but for compiling a 'complete' list in the name of science; and it follows the F.L. trait of seeking historical sources. Chanter's monograph of 1877 is cited; and a piece in *The Zoologist* by Mathew (3). Contemporary data are collected by word of mouth, and it is clear from the text that F.L. takes the opportunity to talk in detail with local people – a characteristic he is to repeat throughout much of his birding. So here, he reports that 'some years ago, it is said, a feud broke out between the Peregrines and Ravens on Lundy'; and the Revd H.G.Heaven, 'proprietor of the island', suggests to him that one or two hooded crows remained during the summer and he (Heaven) thought they interbred with carrion crows.

F.L. clearly made use of local intelligence in relation to his birding. That should not blind us to his critical references to people whose sympathies did not lie in that direction. The sting is in the tail of this quotation:

...the Chough (*Pyrrhocorax graculus*), formerly common, has now been quite exterminated. Their final disappearance is said to be due to the persecution they received from the men who some years ago were engaged in quarrying granite on the eastern side of the island...The price that may be obtained from the skins and eggs of these birds has done much towards banishing them from many of their former haunts...

So there are – in birding terms – good people and bad people; which is a shrewd enough perception even today.

The visit to Lundy was not random; it had a (scientific) focus: 'I was most anxious to find out whether the Gannet (*Sula bassana*) still nested on Lundy.' The mission is successful, though numbers of this species are small, 'in great danger of extermination.' There is a reason for this: 'the eggs have a market value of one shilling a piece.' The egg predation by humans was exacerbated by the blasting, reported earlier. F.L. took comfort that the colony of three or four pairs might survive because they 'seemed to have learned wisdom by experience, and have selected a place where only bold climbers could reach their nests' in contrast to former times when, he is informed by the islanders 'any child could take their eggs without danger.' So the purpose of the visit has been achieved, and an assessment of the population of gannets and its chances of survival made. In modern parlance, a research question has been formulated, the evidence collected and evaluated, and a conclusion reached.

A secondary purpose of the visit is to compile a 'list', as we have seen. This involves personal research through observation. A feature of F.L.'s reports about birding is the acute personal observation. The article is shot through with phrases that indicate this: 'three or four pairs which I saw this year', 'I frequently saw', 'I noticed', 'I only noticed a single bird', 'I noticed in particular', 'I was struck by' – and so on. But there is indirect evidence of this observation, and its sensitivity, too:

When I arrived, on May 5th, I was told that not all the birds had yet come in from the sea, but during my short stay they arrived daily in large numbers…On May 7th particularly, which was a fine warm day, I noticed the Puffins coming in from the sea to the island in a continuous stream.

This kind of careful, interpretative observation is to become a trademark of the man. In this article it is married to a fine turn of phrase in description:

The chief colony of the Puffins (*Fratercula arctica*) is at the northern end, where the birds burrow in the soft soil among a *débris* of huge granite boulders scattered about in wild confusion. The number of birds must be enormous, as, when one approaches the colony, all the rocks and the sea beneath appear to be covered with Puffins and Razorbills; while hundreds more are swinging round and round in a large circle, which extends some distance over the water…I had Puffins and Razorbills all around me, and some almost within arm's length. One Razorbill perched on the very stone which I had selected as a seat.

This is, to steal a modern phrase, a moment of awe and wonder. It is worth marking well. It is the point at which we might have expected, from a man of the cloth, an aside at least about creation and the Creator. There is none. Rather, the hand of science rests on the work; the note is about bird behaviour not about ultimate or theological questions.

The species he lists are often compared with their counterparts on the north Devon coast (though at this time Francis is ensconced in Lincolnshire; his visits may have been to see his future wife, Marjorie, whose family lived in Devon, though this is surmise). F.L. notes common buzzards, but they are unusually scarce in comparison to north Devon; the peregrine likewise. Furthermore, Francis is cautious not to go beyond the evidence of his own eyes, or of what can be confirmed. He 'identified' a list of small birds, and notes that the dunlins and golden plovers were 'in breeding plumage', but does not draw the conclusion that they were breeding on Lundy. The interbreeding of the hoodie and the carrion crow 'is in a measure confirmed' by apparently hybrid birds.

F.L. is even prepared to re-tell a story about the 'King Murr', a putative great auk; but when he does he stresses the reservations of the teller; and he concludes:

The story is interesting, though it cannot be said to prove that the Great Auk was ever an inhabitant of Lundy.

In this short article is encapsulated much of the F.L. Blathwayt that later study will reveal; a man of science, able to be a detached yet intimate observer, who places his observations in physical context, who can reproduce his sightings in terse yet insightful prose, and who collects information from historical and living sources but sifts its veracity. Yet this picture is tempered by an enthusiasm that permeates the pages, and by a need to convey the excitement of this unusual habitat. All of these traits will recur except this last, which is replaced by a restraint that masks the exuberance of this initial article.

•

By the time of the publication of 'The Roseate Tern on the Farne Islands' in 1902, F.L. had become the Revd F.L. He was taking hours out from the parish of St Swithin in Lincoln city to compose this note. The text is short: just two pages long. There is no evidence of a journey to discover the birds in question, and it is now very difficult to conjecture why F.L. should have chosen to write this item or why he chose the specific species about which to do so (a possible explanation is offered later in the chapter).

Short though it is, the article follows a Blathwayt approach by beginning from historical sources. He records the bird's documented first occurrence, by Dr McDougall in 1812 on islands in the Firth of Clyde (4). He also notes that it was reported in 1811 from the Farne Islands but that the date (given by Selby in the *Zoological Journal* volume II) is probably incorrect. Despite increasing by 1825, the species then declines, though keeps a toe-hold according to Gould (1873). F.L. asserts, but uncharacteristically without a quoted source, that a few pairs arrived again in May 1880; he would have been just five at the time. From 1888 a local Naturalists' Association kept track of sea birds and their protection on the Farnes, but the roseates probably drifted down to as few as a single pair (5).

This potted history forms the bulk of the item. He, typically, cites claim and counter-claim that the roseate tern may be persecuted 'by its larger congeners'; though he comes down on the side of persecution. So he concludes:

The [roseate tern] does not appear to be a very sociable species...among the thousands of sea-fowl which haunt the Farnes there can scarcely be many quiet spots where Roseate Terns could establish a colony without coming into contact with other birds.

What will emerge later is that F.L. has a particularly soft spot for the roseate tern; perhaps this article is the fruit of some research that he undertook before setting out to find the species in some now unknown location.

•

By 1906, with the publication of his essay on 'Birds' in volume one of the monumental *Victoria History of Somerset*, F.L. has matured measurably. We must assume that the research for this paper was carried out considerably earlier than its publication date; indeed the entry in this paper for the cormorant makes this point irrefutably:

I saw a pair on Steep Holm on April 20, 1900, and five together on June 25 of the present year (1901).

The essay itself falls into two sections: a review written in continuous prose, followed by a list of all the species ever recorded in the county. As well as being a substantial paper in its own right, it is also a work of considerable scholarship. F.L. did not write about Somerset birds before this, as far as can be discovered, nor afterwards. So how did he come to write this paper?

One can only conjecture that it was through the good offices of Lt Colonel Linley Blathwayt of Batheaston. Col Linley produced most of the material on insects in this volume of the *Victoria History*, and one can imagine the editor casting around for a writer on birds and the Colonel putting in a word for his nephew. If this were the case, then F.L. – with his usual attention to detail – did not let the family side down: through integrity and truth, as the motto has it. But he does wear his heart on his sleeve.

Of Roseates *and* Rectories

The opening salvo of the *Somerset* essay holds a tinge of regret:

It must be admitted however that in a county possessing about seventy miles of seaboard and such a variety of dale, moor and marsh, one would expect to find even a greater variety of birds than are at present known to occur.

It doesn't take too much imagination for anyone who has ever researched any topic to share F.L.'s frustration that, however hard one searches the sources and the contemporary situation, the evidence one would like simply fails to appear! (In this text it is the elusive Lincolnshire-based evidence for F.L.'s theological stance!). Nevertheless, he begins from his tried and tested base-line: the physical context of the county, which is 'diversified'; and he will pursue the paucity (as he sees it) of Somerset species with a hypothesis in due course. The contextual material, describing the habitats that can be met within the county, is pursued with very considerable thoroughness.

The first tranche of countryside is the hilly north-east, where he locates marsh warblers (6), three species of woodpecker, and hawfinches; and there are occasional golden orioles, too (7). The second area is also hilly, and includes the Quantocks, the Blackdown hills and the Brendon hills. F.L. is wary (important, in view of note 7) of asserting that golden plovers breed even though they are recorded in autumn and spring: 'the fact has yet to be established.' Among the more unusual species he records here are the ring ouzel and black grouse; the former still present in small numbers while the latter recently lost its foothold (8) in the Quantocks.

F.L.'s third division of the county includes 'the central area, which is coextensive with the rivers Perret, Brue and Axe' and is largely flat. Here are the Somerset levels with their extensive reed beds and peat bogs, and the handsome fern *Osmunda regalis*. Here, too, are lesser redpolls, snipe, and water rails as well as many duck species, among which Montagu's records of garganey are most interesting (9). Finally, there is the tranche of coastline where cliffs are low but there are sand dunes, ooze and 'bold headlands'. Because the cliffs are low they do not support sea bird colonies, but there are peregrines, and white wagtails on migration (10).

This background geography sets the scene for an assessment of the species that are decreasing or increasing. The former include all the larger birds of prey, of which the 'kite has vanished as a breeding species' (11). As we have noted before, F.L. is no fan of the gamekeeper: 'The sparrowhawk has in some districts been almost exterminated by the gamekeepers, and it is extremely doubtful whether any of the harriers or the chough can at the present time be claimed as breeding.'

In reviewing birds that are on the increase, F.L. hits on a problem that besets modern ornithologists, too:

Here however we are on somewhat dangerous ground, for it is not always easy to decide whether increase of observation on the part of naturalists or real extension of range on the part of the species is the true cause of the apparent or real increase in numbers.

This is a scientifically important insight (12). Increases, where they appear, affect a wide range of species: nightingale, reed warbler, lesser whitethroat, hawfinch, lesser redpoll, stock dove, sheld-duck and black-headed gull.

Having set the overall scene, F.L. reverts to his tested methods. First he consults sources, lamenting that there are few (13). Then he taps into the living voice of contemporary birders:

My thanks are also due to a number of gentlemen who have furnished me with local lists and notes from various parts of the country, and so have helped me in my attempt, unsuccessful though it may be, to draw up a complete and up to date list of the birds of Somerset.

The resulting County List consists of 258 species, with a brief comment on the status of each as far as it can be ascertained. But before looking at some aspects of the list itself, it is opportune to return to the opening essay and to examine these early pages for evidence of F.L.'s distinctive approaches. A good place to start might be with the problem that F.L. set himself: to explain the relative paucity of some species of birds in Somerset. He suggests two hypotheses which are not mutually exclusive:

...A peculiarity in the county list is that many species have been noticed on only one or two occasions. This feature, where not due to lack of observation, may perhaps be accounted for by the supposition that many migratory birds on their journey up and down the Bristol Channel do not as a rule stop either in Somerset or in the opposite counties of South Wales, but that an occasional straggler drops away from the line of migration...the absence of any important river which might serve as a flight-line to migrating birds is likely to modify the distribution of species in the county. It appears indeed that a stream of land birds enters the county by Bridgewater Bay and proceeds south-west...but there is no large river running through the county, for the Avon would only affect the northern district.

This is an important deduction (14). It has long been noted that birds follow the terrain using natural features, such as ranges of hills or the valleys of rivers, and most birders will have sat at spring migration time and seen the fresh influx of swallows and hobbies and other species working along the line of an estuary (15). But this theory does not satisfy F.L. on the vexed question of why so few coastal species favour the Somerset coast while apparently enjoying neighbouring areas. He laments the comparative lack of divers, guillemots, razorbills and terns. This requires a second explanation:

They all seek their prey in water...and the opaqueness of the water in the Bristol Channel, at any rate as far west as Minehead, cannot be said to offer them a tempting feeding-ground.

This is not his assessment alone, and F.L. credits it to Smith's *Birds of Somerset*. He returns to the issue later in the essay, noting that species such as the greater black-backs and some terns nest more readily on the Gower coast 'where the water is clearer.' In the list, the rarity of the osprey and, when it does turn up, its tendency to frequent ornamental waters, are attributed to the same cause.

This kind of observation and research combine to make F.L.'s bird reporting not only interesting to read but a source of significant importance. That same keen observation is evident in many places. In the County List he often remarks that a particular feature is asserted on the basis of what he himself has seen. For example, he records seeing for himself small flights of golden plover on Exmoor in August and September; he has counted up to 200 oystercatchers together on the Burnham mud-flats; he notes a pair of cormorants on Steep Holm, and five more some of which were young birds; he has noticed grasshopper warblers breeding behind Porlock Weir; and lesser whitethroats in the same area. These touches secure F.L.'s place as a field ornithologist; but there are more interesting observations, too, such as that of the whimbrel:

Common on the coast in spring but rarer in autumn. I have noticed them arrive as early as April 25, and seen them again on August 3. (16)

We have noted already, in passing, F.L.'s tendency to draw on knowledge of other areas to compare and contrast with the study location; and this paper is no exception since it calls on information he has gathered from Cornwall, Devon and the counties of South Wales. We have noted, too, his dissatisfaction with current knowledge and recording, witnessed as early as the second page of this paper, where he laments the lack of information about the breeding of golden plovers. Similarly, we have seen his effective use of written sources, and his willingness to consult other birders – but neither process is executed uncritically. Sometimes his caution has to be read from the semantics of the entry, as for the red-spotted blue-throat:

There is a specimen in the Albert Memorial Museum at Exeter, which is stated to have been obtained in Somerset in 1856.

In the same way, he treats information about a firecrest occurrence with a tinge of scepticism:

Mr H. St B. Goldsmith, formerly of Bridgwater, writes that a friend of his accurately described to him a firecrest...

But F.L. concludes that the occurrence 'must be regarded as doubtful.' Nevertheless, this does not prevent his judicious use of sources. He accepts three woodchat shrike records, one logged in *The Birds of Wiltshire,* one in the *Zoologist,* and one a bird recorded as shot according to the book *A Mendip Valley* (17). Despite his caution he concedes that the curlew sandpiper, an autumn migrant, is probably more common than supposed since it might easily be overlooked among the flocks of dunlins with which it characteristically associates.

We have seen that he aims a disapproving nod at shooters and other persecutors. This attitude surfaces again in individual entries in the

County List. Of the wood lark he complains 'it is getting scarcer than in former years, owing to the raids of bird-catchers.' The tawny owl is 'much persecuted', and so on. He does not indulge in the kinds of propagandist outbursts that Hudson espoused, but his dislike of the process is as evident for all its unemotional matter-of-factness.

There are two interests of F.L. that surface in this paper. The first concerns the roseate tern. While other entries in the County List are recounted in measured tones, that of the roseate is in a different *timbre*. It reads:

Accidental. Mr Sargent has an adult, shot at Clevedon in the year 1898. I have examined the specimen, and the beautiful rose tint on the breast, though considerably faded, is still apparent.

One can imagine the mixed feelings with which F.L. handled this specimen, victim of the bird-killer, yet – in all its faded glory – a thing of joy and admiration. Most birders have a 'favourite', sometimes a bird often seen but never tired of, sometimes a species long sought and not yet found. Clearly, the F.L. weakness resides in this tern (18). One can understand why; the harsh cry of this tiny, buoyant bundle of white feathers, that traverses huge areas of the world and lives its life in the teeth of violent oceans, makes most birders' stomachs churn with excitement.

He has another, more prosaic, interest, too: duck decoys. It is something that will recur in later chapters. There is a footnote to the essay which betrays more than a passing familiarity with the topic, and with the location of now disused decoys (19). The only operational one in Somerset in 1901, on King's Sedgemoor, is said to take 700 duck a year, mainly teal. In the list, by contrast with the opening essay, this decoy seems to be referred to as Walton decoy, and is said to trap a few pintail annually. Montagu also made a study of decoy trapping, and the entry in the County List for the wigeon suggests these were taken in substantial numbers in earlier years.

One feature of the introductory remarks to the *Victoria History's* County List is what we might now call an interdisciplinary approach to birding. F.L. records the discovery near Glastonbury, in 1892, of a Lake Village some 1900 years old. Bones found there had been examined

(20) and had been identified as belonging to pelicans, as well as duck, goshawk, white-tailed eagle, kite, barn owl, cormorant, bittern, coot and crane. F.L. describes the discovery as 'exceedingly interesting', and seems to revel in the historical reconstruction of Somerset at that time as 'a district of marsh and mere, haunted by flocks of pelicans and cranes, and in winter by swarms of wildfowl, which furnished the inhabitants of the pile-dwellings with food.'

These interests and enthusiasms are coupled to a sense of the unusual. The entry for the turtle dove on the County List, for example, records the finding, in 1900, of a nest 'consisting almost entirely of pieces of old rusty wire' (21). A bird not admitted to the County List is the purple gallinule, though F.L. regards it as worthwhile to tell the tale that one was 'caught by a sheep dog in the parish of Bagworth on August 25, 1875.' He is forced, though, to conclude it was an 'escape' from a private collection.

Nor is Francis afraid of voicing an opinion, for he is unhappy about including in the list the rock dove on the grounds:

It is impossible to say whether these records refer to the wild breed or only to escaped farmyard pigeons. I am strongly inclined to the opinion that the true wild rock dove is not to be found anywhere in the county of Somerset.

With that, it is confined to square brackets. The judgement is surprisingly modern (22).

So we come to a final feature of this important essay and list, and to the closing phrases of the essay itself. In the Blathwayt works recorded in this chapter – and we shall note later, throughout his corpus – there is virtually nothing that passes for humour. Here, in the last phrases of this paper, is the only example, mild as it is. He is explaining his criteria for including and excluding species from the County List that follows. He is concerned that some might find him inconsistent, perhaps for including the pheasant which was originally an introduced species, but excluding others such as the Canada goose. He remarks, with the use of a daring exclamation mark:

The line must be drawn somewhere, or we might find ourselves obliged to include in a local list escaped canaries or even parrots! (23)

•

Drawing together the threads of these three early articles in the Blathwayt corpus we can trace features that will recur in his later writing. These include a strong sense of place: an interest in the distribution of species. His work is driven by questions, and these are informed and tested by hypotheses in proper scientific manner. He draws on evidence, and that evidence comes from three sources: what has already been written; the observations of others; and his own sightings. In interpreting evidence he is cautious, and he weighs the possibilities with care. Often, the end-product of his work is a list – the most complete list he can compile for an area, be it larger or smaller.

F.L. records birds shot in the past as part of the evidence for distribution of species; but his condemnation of the work of game-keepers and other shooters in his more enlightened present is clear throughout his work. He has no qualms about more primitive people feeding off the flesh and eggs of birds in ancient lake villages; but is irritated by the egg-stealing from gannets in the contemporary world. His focus of concern is the bird, not the exigencies of the rural economy. In his day, however, the problem of persecution had not gone away, even though contemporary legislation had been substantially tightened over the laws of 1906 (24).

Two particular themes have emerged: a fascination with the roseate tern, and an almost antiquarian interest in duck decoys, current and disused. He was unable to pursue the former enthusiasm in Lincolnshire, as we shall see, since the bird is more or less absent. But there will be future references to duck decoys and to the men who ran them, and to what they may tell us about these species.

In terms of writing style, F.L. is always concerned for accuracy. The language is precise (he even gives heights of cliffs, for example, to the nearest foot on occasion), but that does not rob his writing of intimate description. From time to time in his published work there is an almost poetic quality driven on by his entrancement with the subjects of the writing, the birds themselves. This is a quality perhaps too rarely shown in the published works.

F.L. will reject any record he considers spurious or uncertain. This makes him a scientist; and his judgement is based on good evidence. Thus it is that the data he compiles have stood the test of time when viewed against modern knowledge.

In the earliest work – on the Farne Islands – there is an infectious enthusiasm that spills over into an inclusion of the reader into the experience; he advises on how to share in it. By the *Victoria History* paper this enthusiasm has changed its course somewhat: there is one fleeting attempt at humour, and the reporting of a few 'oddities' in bird-life, but that is all. Science in the form of objective reporting drives the writing.

We must note, too, an omission and file it in the memory for later assessment. Most parson-naturalists have, in their writings, a strong vein of moralising or of theology, an overt sense that nature belongs to God and that he has to be credited for it and lauded through it. This does not happen in F.L.'s early work. In a similar way, most modern birders have an emotional response to their quarry (25); the nearest F.L. comes to this is the restrained description of the roseate tern shot in 1898.

These, then, are the works of Francis Blathwayt dating for the most part, though not exclusively, before he became immersed in the pastoral work in Lincoln city and then in the rural parish of Doddington. They form the platform to his later birding, as we shall see in the chapter that follows.

NOTES TO CHAPTER 5

1.   A selected list of the writings of F.L. Blathwayt about birds is given in Appendix 1. I have been unable to track down the 1897 article.

2.   Many of the F.L. articles cited are quite short, and so I have not made reference to specific pages.

3.   I have not traced back all of these ancient sources; and F.L. does not adopt today's conventions by referencing in detail his sources. The article by the Revd Murray A. Mathew is to be found in *The Zoologist* for 1866, on p 100.

4.   Bruce Campbell (1977) *Birds of the Coast and Sea: Britain and Northern Europe* Newton Abbot: Readers' Union p 138 accepts the MacDougall sighting of the roseate tern as the first: 'On 12th July 1812, Dr MacDougall and some friends landed on a small island on Millport Bay, Great Cumbrae, where there was a large colony of terns. Certain birds, distinguished by the whiteness of their plumage and by the elegance of motion were "easily singled out by the sportsmen and dispatched". The victims of this minor holocaust were seen in the hand to have a rosy suffusion on the breast and the doctor secured immortality by sending one to

Of Roseates *and* Rectories

Colonel George Montagu, who named the species after him' i.e. *Sterna dougallii* The birds are distinctive because of the flight and their long tail streamers. Numbers of pairs fluctuate from year to year, and are more numerous in Ireland than on the mainland of Britain. It seems they are not merely victims of other tern species, as F.L. suggested, as they rob other terns of their food on occasion. The cover photo shows adult and immature roseates.

5.   Harrison, C. (1988) *The History of the Birds of Britain* London: Collins in association with Witherby, agrees that: 'it suffered a drastic reduction in the early nineteenth century' and was almost extinct by the end of it. Numbers then increased again, to about 3,500 in the 1960s. It now has breeding status in Orkney, the Moray Firth, Firth of Forth, eastern Northumberland, in Hampshire, Anglesey and Morecombe Bay. He records its first appearance as being confirmed by Montagu in 1813, so F.L.'s date seems to be in the right area. Harrison posits two issues that may affect numbers: first, that roseates are at the northern end of the breeding range in Britain and generally prefer warmer areas, and second that they may be persecuted by snaring in their wintering grounds, especially the coast of Ghana.

6.   An earlier chapter recorded his encounter at the Bird Dinner given by Bishop Hicks with Warde-Fowler, who was credited with seeing the first marsh warbler in England. This meeting was some eight years in the future when this paper was written. In modern times breeding of marsh warblers has been inconsistent, though they still occur in Somerset (last breeding 1961 according to Gibbons, D., Reid, J. and Chapman, R. (1993) *The New Atlas of Breeding Birds in Britain and Ireland 1988-1991* London: Poyser, p 332.)

7.   This last record is interesting. According to Holloway, S. (1996) *The Historical Atlas of Breeding Birds in Britain and Ireland 1875-1900* London: Poyser [henceforward referred to as *The Historical Atlas*], golden orioles had been recorded in the 19th century from Sussex, East Anglia, Devon, Dorset, Surrey, Kent, Essex and Hertfordshire. Holloway also notes that Smith, A. and Cornwallis, R. (1955) *The Birds of Lincolnshire* Lincoln: Lincolnshire Naturalists' Union, p 105, suggest Francis Blathwayt as the source of a report that these birds had been established in the north-west of Lincolnshire in the forty years prior to 1914; but they conclude 'there seems to be no adequate evidence and records of birds seen in this area in 1899 and 1900 are not very convincing.' *The New Atlas* does, however, record birds present in the breeding season – mostly in East Anglia – but also in the West Country. A relative of mine had a sighting of a male golden oriole from a train on the Lincoln to Gainsborough line in Lincolnshire during the 1980s, and while this does not establish breeding, orioles are pretty hard to mistake for anything else!

8.   *The New Atlas,* p 130.

9.   Harrison, in his *History of the Birds of Britain,* (1988, London: Collins/Witherby) notes that this species was discovered in 'Iron Age Somerset.'

10.   Simms, E. (1992) *Larks, Pipits and Wagtails* London: Collins New Naturalist, pp 280-282, suggests this movement involving birds moving through Wales and western Britain still obtains.

11.   F.L. would have approved of the re-introduction, in recent years, of the red kite across England. There are now areas of Wales around the Brecon Beacons, and of central England around Corby where the bird is met with regularly and where it breeds. Along some motorways (e.g. M 40) and in the vicinity of Princes Risborough, and even over the suburban gardens there, the species is now relatively common. Re-introduction is in hand in Yorkshire; in F.L.'s old haunts in Lincolnshire the bird now passages through.

12.   In modern birding, journal articles that report survey work sometimes use statistical analysis to 'adjust' for factors such as this. Field workers might be reasonably sceptical of such a course; and Francis' reservations hold as true now as then.

13.   He cites *The Birds of Somerset* by Cecil Smith, published in 1869; and 'A revised list of the birds of Somerset' by the Revd M.A. Mathew in *The Proceedings of the Somersetshire Archaeological and Natural History Society*, 1893.

14.   Sutton, A. (1988) *The Birds of Somerset* Somerset: Somerset Ornithological Society, is the key text for the county's birds. The situation described by F.L. has not, it would appear, changed markedly. The Bibliography (p 243) pays tribute to the work of Blathwayt's *Victoria County History* paper, finding it 'more important' than Mathew's *Revised List of the Birds of Somerset* (1893 paper in *The Proceedings of the Somerset Archaeological and Natural History Society*) and, by implication, than Lewis's (1955) *The Breeding Birds of Somerset and their Eggs*, Ilfracombe, since he was 'an egg-collector of the old school' despite being a good naturalist.

15.   Garth Christian in his book *Down the Long Wind* (1961, London: Newnes) notes this phenomenon in several places e.g. in relation to movements of flocks of finches that 'push along the narrow route between the Chiltern escarpment and the Berkshire Downs' (p 128). Other factors, such as climatic conditions, may also have an effect.

16.   Ogilvey, M. (1979) *The Birdwatcher's Guide to the Wetlands of Britain* London: Batsford, p 127, under the entry for the Bridgwater Bay National Nature Reserve, mentions 'A feature of the waders is an April-May build-up of whimbrel to form the largest flock in the country'. Sutton's *Birds of Somerset* (p 137) indicates 'the average first date, 1924-1965, was 26th April', which accords well with F.L.'s view – though since the date has drifted earlier.

17.   The bird was recorded in Cheddar Wood in T. Compton's book of the name, page 133. Sutton's *Birds of Somerset* records, in relation to woodchat shrikes, three single birds: in 1860, 1926 and 1974. Firecrests are first recorded (p 213) in 1924, with 'a further 21 up to 1966' and 'now almost annual.'

18.   Many birders have shared F.L.'s fascination with terns. The most fluent writer among these is probably the American ornithologist John L. Hay of the Cape Cod Museum of Wildlife. Hay's response to terns is more emotional than that of an English Edwardian parson: 'In the last analysis, I do not know terns, any more than I know myself. They keep leading me toward a number of questions to which I only receive tangential answers. Still, they have enlarged my sight, my aspiration, my grasp of the earth's great distances. What more do we need to know than that the truth does not lie in us alone, but with every other form of life, no matter how insignificant it may seem.' (Hay, J. 1991 *Bird of Light* New York: W.W. Norton, p 158). A later chapter in this text returns to the issue of F.L.'s emotional and spiritual attachment to birds. Sutton's County List gives only six records of roseates for Somerset, the first being in 1954, the last in 1984, with two each in May, June and September.

19.   Duck decoys are a recurrent theme of F.L. There is a survey of the old decoys of Lincolnshire in Lorand, S. and Atkin, K. (1988) *The Birds of Lincolnshire and South Humberside* Hawes: Leading Edge. Sutton's *Birds of Somerset* (p 22) claims there are 'remains of a number of old duck decoys' at Kings Sedge Moor.

20.   F.L. refers to an article in the *Ibis* (by C.W. Andrews, 7th series vol v no. 19).

21.   This record is contained in *Country Life* for August 11th 1900.

Of Roseates *and* Rectories

22.   *The New Atlas* recorders had the same problem, as the entry on rock dove and feral pigeon (p 232) shows: 'Its ancestor, the rock dove, is primarily a bird of coastal cliffs of the N and W of Britain, but hybridization between the two forms casts doubt of the genetic integrity of rock doves in all but the most isolated colonies.' Sutton's County List suggests 'there is no evidence to suggest that the rock dove has ever occurred in a truly wild state' in the county (p 170).

23.   How prophetic this statement turned out to be! The Canada goose and Egyptian goose do turn up in County Lists now. Canada geese are almost at plague proportions, and alongside feral grey-lags have reached a stage where their disturbance to other, less common, species is a nuisance. Egyptian geese are in smaller numbers, but blunder about our coasts and reservoirs in similar fashion. Escaped canaries are absent, but then the habit of keeping them in numbers has diminished and they have not turned feral. Ironically, ring-necked parakeets have, and can be found all over London south of the Thames as well as in the West Country, in Kent, Norfolk, and many other locations. Some birders hate them, others love them: they certainly add colour – and noise.

24.   The pages of the RSPB's magazine, *Birds*, are still, issue by issue, filled with stories of prosecutions for shooting, trapping and egg-stealing. Taking for food is not dead either. The *Telegraph Magazine* for 23rd April 2005 carried a tasteless (excuse the pun) piece about gulls eggs in which Dominic Prince argued they were 'a delicacy worth fighting for.' He went on to lament: 'Since the taking of wild birds' eggs is illegal, harvesting is strictly licensed by the Department for Environmental Food and Rural Affairs…To its supporters, picking eggs serves to control the gull population effectively and add a little cash to the rural economy, but to some it is highly controversial.' The piece had a flippant flavour to it: 'You don't eat gulls' eggs with bacon or put them in a sandwich with mayonnaise. Their translucent whites, reddish-yellow yolks and combined flavour of delicate fish and garden vegetables is (sic) best savoured alone.' Michel Roux Jr added some recipes for good measure.

25.   Max Nicholson (1931) *The Art of Birdwatching* London: The Sports and Pastimes Library, remarks: 'For those who practise it bird-watching is not a sport and a science, but also something near a religion.'

CHAPTER 6
LINCOLNSHIRE BIRDS
Scotton Common

A visitor to Scotton Common today would see but a remnant of what F.L. saw in 1908: a heath covered with yellow gorse, open grassland, and stands of birch and fir. It is tightly contained between boundary roads. To the west the common slips down onto the low, damp meadows of the Trent Valley bordering Nottinghamshire. In early summer yellow wagtails flit along the furrows of the cultivated fields and linnets forage among that modern citrine crop – oil-seed rape. A wheatear might flick its tail among the grasses of the heath, perhaps a late migrant still on the move. High in the blue ether swifts, too, are on their restless way. This is the context for F.L.'s first paper on birds of Lincolnshire.

In the previous chapter a picture has begun to emerge of the interests and style of Francis Blathwayt as a recorder and observer of birds. The chapter dealt with his earlier work, some carried out while he was a curate in Lincoln city and while he was still a very young man (twenty-five to thirty years of age). The papers that he wrote featured observations in locations outside the county of Lincolnshire.

In this chapter it is the intention to begin to discuss F.L.'s observations and records of Lincolnshire bird-life. He produced six substantial published papers about Lincolnshire birds (1) over the period 1906 to 1919, the last coming into print after he had left the county in 1916 to take up the post of Rector of Melbury, Dorset, though based on work carried out while he was resident in Lincoln and Doddington (2). This chapter deals with one paper only.

His first Lincolnshire paper, on the birds of Scotton Common, is in some ways the most interesting, though not the most important, of this county group. The diminished nature of the Common today is remarked upon by Lorand and Atkin, who report that the local Naturalists' Trust maintains thirty-six acres of 'old habitat' (3), which is tiny in ecological terms and under pressure. Today's visitor can expect, above all, to be disappointed by the variety of birds there; though the old dry heathland and the birch and pine do hold some species less common in other parts of the county, as will emerge.

F.L.'s paper is written in a style that is, in part at least, narrative. Clearly, he found his visits there a hundred years ago rewarding. The study contains insights into his birding, and into bird behaviour, that engage and absorb the reader. It retains the scientific detachment which is emerging as a feature of F.L.'s approach to birding, yet it - like the paper on the birds of Lundy described in the previous chapter - retains an enthusiasm which is infectious for the reader.

The Scotton Common paper is the result of seven years' work. This would encompass the seasons 1900-1906; so the visits there began when F.L. came to train at the Lincoln Theological College after leaving Oxford, and continued until the paper was published while he was a curate at All Saints, Monks Road. He calls the paper 'a sketch of the bird life of the Common as it exists at the beginning of the 20th century.' It is not, as he would perhaps have liked, an exhaustive list.

His first concern is for matters ecological: even for Francis, writing a hundred years ago, 'the ancient glory' of the area has departed and there is a diminishing list of species to be noted. While, some hundred years later, the miracle is that the Common still exists in some guise, no doubt he would be even more disappointed at its present state of attrition and at the changes wrought to the habitat since his death. F.L. has a 'feel' for the demise of habitat and this is one of the features that marks him out as entirely 'modern' in his approach.

As in other papers, in order to gather information he relies on three sources: his own eyes, word of mouth from other birders, and historical i.e. documented records. A Mr F. M. Burton from Gainsborough has sent F.L. notes on the birds of the district forty years previously; the late, and very eminent, John Cordeaux (4), made written records of the Birds of the Humber District; and there are skins from the area to be studied in the Lincoln Museum. He begins his survey with the historical data.

Among late lamented birds are stone curlews; ruffs and dunlins are also recorded as nesters during the nineteenth century (5). While short-eared owls still visit in autumn and winter during F.L.'s time, the birds have disappeared as a breeding species. A pair of bitterns, shot in the middle of the nineteenth century, were on view in Francis' era in the Lincoln Museum. Other rarities of the past included Pallas' sand-grouse and Selavonian (sic) grebe.

F.L. himself admits that his expeditions to the Common were spring and summer affairs; since he is likely to have cycled there (perhaps sometimes taking a train as far as Gainsborough), this is not unexpected. The paper is 'the result of personal observation' and 'careful notes have been kept.' Among the species of small birds, the warblers feature quite strongly: willow, sedge, reed and grasshopper warblers are noted. He still uses the old nomenclature for the willow warbler (willow wren). Reed warblers were discovered by listening for their songs. Most elusive of the warblers is the grasshopper warbler, and this was apparently recorded only once: a fact sufficiently significant to merit a specific date – 27th May 1901.

Of the chats, F.L. seems to suggest that the stonechat ('one or two pairs') is the less frequent and the whinchat the more so. This would surprise a modern birder in the area. However, Lorand and Atkin confirm that whinchats were once frequent in the county, and that it was intensive farming that spelled their demise (6). Wheatears are also recorded, though these, too, seem far less frequent than even two decades ago (7).

Lesser redpolls are another species that F.L. implies are frequent among the birch scrub at Scotton, as indeed they were throughout suitable wooded areas until very recently. These, too, have largely departed (8). Long-eared owls may be no more frequent now than then; but as they are generally very elusive it is hard to make an accurate assessment. F.L. also noted the presence of nightjars:

On a summer's evening, about the time of the year when the little blue flower *Pinguicula* may be looked for on the Common, the curious rattling cry of the nightjar may often be heard, but it takes a very careful search to enable one to find the eggs, looking like two flints on a bare patch among the heather (9).

This record has all the hallmarks of hard-won personal experience. One wonders whether, after encounters with nightjars, F.L. still had to cycle back to Doddington! Certainly this species does not seem to have held its own in recent decades, though small numbers still survive in the most suitable habitats. Part of the problem seems to be that the birds prefer trees of a certain age to surround the clearings where they hunt; as the woods mature or are cut, the birds have to move on and it may not always be possible to find suitable replacement habitat. Occasional birds turn up away from the main haunts, and it may be that some are overlooked simply because they are nocturnal and cryptic (10).

We have noted before that F.L. has a keen interest in duck decoys and an interest in ducks. It comes as no surprise, then, that he inventories the duck species of the Common. There are mallard, teal, shoveler, sheld-duck, wigeon and pochard, he says. Clearly he has spent time with these ducks. He has been drawn away from nests by the 'broken wing trick' of the shoveler duck and admired the superb plumage of the drake. He has listened to the 'pretty whistling notes' of the drake teal. He has logged dates for the wigeon, the earliest being 28th April, but believes that they do not stay to breed. Pochard have been noted only in March (11). But his most intimate encounter is with the sheld-ducks:

In April three or four pairs of sheld-ducks usually appear on the ponds and much chattering and squabbling takes place. Not more than one or perhaps two pairs remain to breed. The eggs are laid at the end of a burrow in the sand among the heather, and the young are hatched out about the middle of June. On June 22nd, 1903, I saw a pair with four ducklings of a few days old on one of the ponds. These latter were exceedingly active little creatures, diving very cleverly and staying a long time beneath the water. I caught one of them with great difficulty, and on being released it immediately dived, and I could watch it for some time travelling at a good pace not far below the surface, and paddling vigorously with its webbed feet. The parent birds showed great anxiety until I moved away, the female being particularly demonstrative and flying close up to me while I was standing in the water.

This stunning passage reveals more about the man than about the ducks. Here, perhaps for the first time, we trace the curiosity that drives him. He is prepared to get a soaking in the cause of science, and he notes with great perceptiveness the actions of both chick and parent bird. This kind of writing puts him close to the inquisitiveness of a Gilbert White, and proximate to the writing of Julian Huxley (12). It reveals, unintentionally perhaps for someone usually so restrained, how he spent the long hours of loneliness in wild places studying the birds.

Scotton also played host to coot and moorhen, little grebe and snipe, and the lapwing. According to F.L.'s account the lapwings' eggs were 'harvested' by a keeper. Presumably this individual took early clutches and/or part clutches to keep the birds laying; 'gathering about 250 in a season'. F.L. reports this as a fact, without judgement. The process does not seem to harm the birds since 'at the end of July, young and old birds are seen about the common in large flocks.' Sharrock's *Atlas* (13) reported nationally some decrease in southern counties' breeding by the 1970s, probably due to changes in farming practice; but also increases in the northern counties attributed to climate change.

But it is with the snipe that F.L. comes into his own again as a naturalist. At the turn of the twentieth century the cause of 'drumming' in the snipe was still an issue of considerable debate. F.L. sets out to settle the matter, and to do so transcribes a passage from his field-notes. It is a fine sequence and is quoted here in full:

Scotton Common April 28th , 1904. Snipe very excited, and were continually circling over the marsh, uttering sharp cries of 'chip-chip' or 'drumming.' I watched the latter process carefully through my prism glasses. Just before the noise is heard the bird may be seen to spread out its tail like a fan, the outer feathers on each side standing well apart from the rest. The bird then takes a head-long dive towards the ground, and the wings, and I think the tail feathers also, vibrate rapidly while the sound is produced. The wings do not touch the tail feathers during the process, I am practically sure of this. The noise which is peculiarly like the bleat of a goat is certainly produced by the action of the bird's wing and tail feathers upon the air, during the slanting downward flight, and as it is very rarely heard except in the breeding season, it is probably of the nature of a signal either to mate or young.

To a modern ear, this debate that F.L. is having, through his notebook, with himself and fellow birders may seem rather odd. But it certainly was not at the time. Brian Vesey-Fitzgerald, FLS, the distinguished former editor of *The Field* was documenting the controversy in 1953 (14), when it was still, remarkably, unresolved. But this is a good example of what marks out F.L. not as a simple birder, still less as a mere list-maker, but as a naturalist of some distinction.

So what of other birds of the area, which all-of-a-piece still do not satisfy F.L. as a 'complete list'? There are breeding sedge warblers, meadow pipits, linnets and skylarks. There are handsome reed buntings, the males with their clerical collars, perhaps reflecting the image of F.L. himself. There are green and great spotted woodpeckers, but they are not common. Kestrels, by contrast, are frequently seen hunting for mice and lizards. Wood pigeons and stock doves breed in the drier areas; and redshanks in the wetter ones. F.L. has a specially soft spot for the green sandpiper:

These little birds as they dart away with shrill alarm notes, showing their conspicuous white upper tail-coverts during flight, always fill me with interest. No absolute proof exists that the species has bred in Britain, so the two or three seen yearly on the Common are probably hatched somewhere in the land of the midnight sun, and are spending a week or two by the ponds on their way to a warmer winter home. Naturalists tell us that they lay their eggs in old nests of thrushes, jays and other birds, at elevations reaching to thirty-five feet from the ground, a curious spot indeed in which to expect to find the eggs of a wading bird.

Once again F.L. has hit an important birding target about which to raise questions. The description of the retreating bird is apposite; every birder has witnessed this distinctive behaviour. Green sandpipers certainly turn up in Lincolnshire every year, usually during the autumn migration period (15). There is still 'no absolute proof' of breeding, though the possibility has sparked extensive debate over the years (16). Among the 'naturalists' who record (later than the date of this paper, of course) the unexpected nesting sites are Witherby and his co-authors of the *Handbook* (17). What F.L. manages to do is to encapsulate in a few lines a whole world of birding knowledge, and this is a mark of his intellect and of his sound grasp of the subject. If it frustrates, then it is because the reader is thus made aware of his or her own short-comings; and if F.L. has a fault, it is the error of assuming too much in the reader out of humility for his own erudition.

The final bird species singled out for attention at Scotton is the black-headed gull (18). To the unwary reader this might seem like an odd choice for a key subject, but F.L. is aware that Lincolnshire hosts three gulleries where this species breeds. He believes that local naturalists 'should be thankful' for this fact and expounds the theme.

As always Francis is keen to set the context. The Common holds a large colony of about one thousand pairs but they are sub-divided into three main groups. The largest of these occupies 'a shallow irregular piece of water of small extent, on one side of which is a thick growth of bracken.' Here the nests are 'fairly substantial structures.' The birds begin to arrive from the coast in about March – he believes some come from the mudflats of the Humber. Initially, they do what one would expect winter gulls to do; they follow the plough. F.L. also thinks that they eat toads; he found 'partially devoured toads' around the ponds, but did not see the gulls actually killing or eating them.

Egg-laying is usually an April affair, and the eggs vary widely in colour. There are usually three to a nest. F.L. conjectures that the six he found in one nest belonged to two different females. The young leave the nest as soon as they are fledged, and the colony is deserted by the end of July. These, then, are the bare facts of the case. The experience is something more searing:

Anyone visiting a large colony of these gulls for the first time will not easily forget the occasion. The whirling wings above, the incessant almost deafening screams and laughing notes of the birds, and the numerous downy chicks floating on the water or crouching among the reeds, all help to form a lasting impression on the mind...Some of the birds are very bold if the young are handled, and more than once a screaming parent has swooped down upon me and struck me sharply on the back of my head.

Again, the last passage is an exact and accurate piece of description. F.L. is a man whose writing, economical though it is, captures the essence of the moment even within the determination to report scientifically. Furthermore, in assessing F.L.'s competence as a naturalist, it may be thought that his expertise is confined to birds. While there is no doubt that it was birds that motivated and drove him, the present paper shows that he noticed other natural phenomena, too. We have mentioned in passing the reference to the coincidence of the nightjar season to the appearance of the butterwort. There is another incidental passage in the paper that has an almost poetic quality:

Towards the end of July, when clusters of yellow stars of the Bog Asphodel gleam in the swampy places and the purple heads of the Plume

Thistle (*C. Pratensis*), nod in the breeze, and the first Marsh Gentian is opening its bright blue corolla to the early autumn sun, a handsome little stranger, the green sandpiper, invariably puts in an appearance...

As a piece of context this is a gem among writing. It has survived a century without looking stylistically dated. It demonstrates F.L.'s ability as a botanist; and also his acute observation of plants as well as birds. The construction of the passage is, as a piece of literature, quite superior to the style he uses in the 'listing' papers of which – at other times – he is so fond. It leaves the reader longing for more (19). This extra sensitivity should be borne in mind later, when we come to assess F.L.'s overall contribution to Lincolnshire natural history.

And so we come to the final issue raised by this paper. This is directly the issue of the means by which birds are observed, and indirectly the matter of accuracy in recording. Earlier, attention was drawn to F.L.'s insistence that he made personal observations and kept careful notes; he did not rely on single visits; and, while he trusted his own eyes, he was prepared to consult with written records and other birders to augment his knowledge. But one of the things that singles out his observations is that he carried them out with the aid of 'my prism glasses', which he describes at other times as 'powerful.' Early bird-watchers had used telescopes, at that time large, cumbersome draw-tube scopes which were fine when used with static subjects but less adaptable to birding.

Moss describes (20) how the breakthrough in binocular technology came in 1854 when the Italian, Ignatio Porro, 'registered a patent for a compact prismatic system.' In 1894 Ernst Abbe collaborated with Carl Zeiss, in Jena, to produce the first really effective field glasses which sold at £6. 10s. Similar glasses were soon manufactured in England, too. These glasses eventually led to the adoption of sight records as evidence of rare birds, and avoided the need to obliterate the very specimens one observed by shooting them as evidence. Foremost in this movement for sight records were H.F. Witherby, and the Revd F.C.R. Jourdain – a name that has cropped up before in this book.

We do not know what the parishioners of Monks Road, Lincoln, or of Doddington village made of the young parson setting off on a bicycle with a pair of new-fangled binoculars round his neck. Hero or eccentric, one wonders? We do know that another parson-naturalist was alleged to have switched his attention from birds to plants because his parishioners, seeing him depart the vicarage with his glasses, thought he was off to the races (21). One suspects Francis Blathwayt went out of his way to make clear what he was doing; after all, the family motto was 'integrity and truth.'

Over the next few years, F.L. must have been a regular figure, cycling and walking to collect data about the county's birds. He began to visit his favoured birding 'patches' more often; he studied the status of chosen species like the heron and the black-headed gull in the county; and he became immersed in the business of the Lincolnshire Naturalists' Union. The resulting papers are described in the next chapter.

NOTES TO CHAPTER 6

1.   These titles are as follows: 'Notes on the birds which inhabit Scotton Common' 1906, *Transactions of the Lincolnshire Naturalists' Union;* 'Notes on the birds of a ballast pit' 1908, *Transactions;* 'Lincolnshire heronries' 1908, *The Zoologist;* 'Lincolnshire gulleries' 1909, *The Zoologist;* 'The birds of Lincolnshire' 1914, *Transactions;* 'The birds of Lincolnshire, past, present and future' 1919, *Transactions.*

2.   These six papers do not exhaust the work of F.L. on Lincolnshire birds. His notebooks, which are described in chapter 9, show that he was extremely active in the quiet and unassuming work of documenting the bird-life of Lincolnshire and adding to knowledge of bird behaviour in general throughout the period of his living in Lincoln city (1900-1909) and in the nearby village of Doddington (1909-1916). See also Appendix 1.

3.   Lorand, S. and Atkin, K. (1989) *The Birds of Lincolnshire and South Humberside* Hawes: Leading Edge, p 13.

4.   John Cordeaux (1802-1899)was the first President (1893) of the Lincolnshire Naturalists' Union, a role that F.L. was to occupy some twenty-five years later. His driving interest was bird migration, and his main study area the Lincolnshire and Yorkshire area of the Humber District. Smith, A. and Cornwallis, R. (1955) *The Birds of Lincolnshire* Lincoln: Lincolnshire Naturalists' Union, describe his work thus: 'It must be said, however, that Cordeaux did not always appear to demand of himself or others the highest standards of care and accuracy in identification and recording' (p 38). In this, he would have parted company with F.L.!

5.   According to Lorand and Atkin (p 110), the last breeding record of the stone curlew was in 1886.

6.   Lorand and Atkin, op.cit., page 170: 'Cordeaux and others' confirm the whinchat as 'one of the most abundant summer visitors in the county, breeding along many country lanes, railway embankments and in uncultivated areas...By 1950 it was reduced to a few pairs in the north west.' Now its occurrence is most likely on migration at coastal locations, in autumn rather more often than in spring.

7.   A farmer friend on the Leadenham Heath, south of Lincoln, used to claim that in the 1970s he had seen wheatears on the farm in every month of the year. They were certainly

obvious on the fens during migration, and some stayed presumably to breed. Though I have seen wheatears on passage in the area of Scotton, they seem much less frequent now in Lincolnshire overall.

8.   I occupied my present Lincoln property in 1978, a modest bungalow with an equally modest garden (10m x 20m) on a small estate with a playing field adjacent, on the southern edge of the city. At that time there was no major building on the former Skellingthorpe Airfield (2.5 miles away), and this birch-fringed area was not only extensive but was contiguous with the 88 acres of Hartsholme Park. Redpolls were regular in a small fir-tree in the garden throughout the year. In winter there were sizeable build-ups of redpolls, often with a few siskins. The same was true at this period in the Burton Pits reserve just north of the city. It was a daily occurrence, when mowing the lawn or walking to the corner shop to see the distinctive deep undulations of redpolls in flight and to hear their buzzing calls. I have not recorded this species in the area now for some three years (then only a single bird), and they have been scarce for more than a decade. Lorand and Atkin note a rise in the population of redpolls in Lincolnshire from the 1960s but by 1989 were detailing a decline; in 1955, Smith and Cornwallis thought them scarce compared to Blathwayt's time. Clearly this is a bird subject to fluctuations in population, probably due to details of habitat availability that may not be fully understood.

9.   The *Pinguicula* is a species of butterwort, either the common butterwort (*vulgaris*) or the pale butterwort (*lusitanica*), both of which are bog plants according to Ary, S. and Gregory, M. (1960) *The Oxford Book of Wild Flowers* Oxford: OUP, p 138. Presumably these plants were growing in the wet areas where the reed warblers and similar species nested, rather than on the heath. However it is a nice piece of observation, and the flowering time fits the nightjar's nesting season (May-July).

10.   Lincoln city bird-watchers used, at one time, to hop across the border to Stapleford Woods, Nottinghamshire, to hear and see nightjars. In my own experience, individual birds have turned up at Whisby and Southrey but there has been no indication of breeding. On the other hand, being a nocturnal species, if they occupy sites sufficiently away from roads and paths there is a good chance that pairs escape notice.

11.   Pochard were recorded as breeding in the north west by Smith and Cornwallis (op.cit. p 63); and they record the first breeding in the Lincoln area as 1952 and 1953. Lorand and Atkin (op.cit. page 90) date the Lincoln area breeding as around 1960, with some other birds nesting in the Humber district. Fellow wardens and I became very excited when we established that breeding was taking place on the Burton Pits reserve in the 1970s, though the event is more common-place in the Lincoln area now. J.T.R. Sharrock (*The Atlas of Breeding Birds in Britain and Ireland* 1976 Tring: British Trust for Ornithology) documents the slow adaptation of this species to gravel pits. The story is one of expansion: though nesting regularly in only ten English counties in 1938, and sixteen in 1964, there was confirmed breeding in 192 of the 10Km squares across Britain and Ireland by the time of this first *Atlas* project, with a range from the northernmost tip of Scotland to the Isle of Wight.

12.   Gilbert White's *Natural History of Selborne*, reprinted innumerable times over two centuries is, of course, the diary of the classic parson-naturalist. He is the role model of all naturalists, and the tiny touches in his writing (such as weighing dormice in scales using a halfpenny as a weight) are what breathes life into the man. This passage from Blathwayt echoes that same curiosity. Julian Huxley's passage describing the courtship of the great crested grebe is a classic of descriptive writing which combines acute observation, excellent science, and mastery of the English language (1930, *Bird Watching and Bird Behaviour* London: Chatto and Windus, pp 69-73). Blathwayt does not rival this, but this incident, obviously extracted from his notebooks, is as they say, in the same ball-park.

13.   Op. cit. pages 164-5. Lorand and Atkin, reporting the county situation, paint a slightly bleaker picture of breeding success. The species is wide-spread from about July, when adults and birds of the year appear on the Lincolnshire fields where there were none before. It is common in winter in such locations as the Witham valley and on the coast, often in association with golden plovers. Flocks can sometimes number thousands, and are often into the hundreds. Impressionistically, the number of breeding birds seems to be rising in the farmlands around Lincoln city (compared with the 1970s), and some 'old' haunts have been re-occupied; but it hard to say what level of success these pairs have, given the intensive farming. I have just a slight concern here for F.L.'s accuracy. He seems to imply that the July birds he saw were all local breeders; this may not be the case.

14.   The drumming of snipe remained a mystery for many decades. Almost fifty years later – the year in which Francis died - in a New Naturalist volume (Vesey-Fitzgerald, B. 1953 *British Game* London: Collins) the issue is summarised thus: 'There are three theories: that the sound caused by the air passing through the funnel-shaped wings strikes the two stiff outer tail feathers, causing the drumming: that the sound is vocal: that the quivering wings cause the sound.' The writer concludes: 'how it [the sound] is produced has been the cause of much argument; still is the cause of much argument' (p 140). Not for F.L. Blathwayt!

15.   Almost all of my personal sightings in the county have been in the autumn/winter period, and Lorand and Atkin (p 128) speak of a 'scarce spring passage.' Individual birds turn up at the more obvious locations near Lincoln (Hartsholme, Whisby Nature Park, Woodhall Gravel Pits). I have also seen occasional birds on field puddles after torrential rain. This last scenario apart, the species may show a tendency to site loyalty.

16.   The *New Atlas* records that some half-dozen 10km squares nationally held green sandpipers during the breeding seasons of the census period, but that breeding was not established in any of them. Waders as a group do tend to wander far and wide, and throughout large portions of the year, so this outcome is not very surprising. David Bannerman, in a typically quirky entry in his 12 volume tome (Bannerman, D. 1961 *The Birds of Britain* Edinburgh: Oliver and Boyd, volume 10, page 58f.) declares (of a report on breeding in Inverness) that 'even so experienced a couple in bird lore as Nethersole-Thompson and his wife have yet to find a nest in the county with eggs or chicks and the parents in attendance.' Bannerman examines the evidence extant in 1961. He concludes that only two reports stand scrutiny: from Westmorland and Inverness. In the Westmorland case, the claim that two adults were seen at the same time as young birds was not made until twenty years after the event, and the first version of the account suggested adults and young were seen separately (thus leaving doubt as to whether the young were of green or common sandpiper). The Inverness record involved the photographing of a chick, which was thought to be a green sandpiper, though once again adult and young were not seen together. Bannerman rejects both records. Sharrock's *Atlas,* by contrast, accepts both records; and it is followed (presumably) by Prater, A.J. (1981) *Estuary Birds of Britain and Ireland* London: Poyser, since this concludes (p 389) 'Few green sandpipers breed in Britain and none in Ireland so that almost all those seen are of Scandinavian origin.' This first phrase suggests some green sandpipers do breed in Britain, and is a sweeping statement on the basis of such flimsy evidence. Yet it is followed by Cramp's work (Cramp, S. 1993 edn *Handbook of the Birds of Europe the Middle East and North Africa*, volume 3, Waders to Gulls, Oxford: OUP) which states baldly 'Bred Westmorland 1917 and Inverness 1959' (p 571). There is no discussion of the security of these records; and maybe this is a salutary reminder to us all not to accept at face value everything we see in print – even from the most prestigious sources! F.L. would have been somewhat bemused.

17.   Witherby's *Handbook* gives a list (volume IV page 311) of the species in whose nests green sandpipers have built. They are: fieldfare, mistle thrush, song thrush, blackbird, hooded

crow, jay, red-backed shrike, and wood pigeon. The *Handbook* also notes the use of a mat of pine needles, or of squirrel drays.

18.   This book returns to the black-headed gull in more detail in a subsequent chapter, where F.L. commentates more widely on the gulleries of Lincolnshire.

19.   Perhaps I should have said: it leaves *this* reader longing for more. While reading the log at the former Burton Pits reserve near Lincoln I came across an entry which neatly described the dawning of a beautiful summer morning, and the growth of bird-song as the light strengthened. Underneath, the next contributor had written: 'What a load of ****. Can't we just have lists?'

20.   Moss, S. (2004)   *A Bird in the Bush*   London: Aurum, (pp 90-94) gives a brief but interesting history of the rise of the binocular.

21.   This story is quoted by Armstrong, P. (2000) *The English Parson-Naturalist* Leominster: Gracewing, p 71. The parson in question was the Revd Andrew John Young of Sussex (1885-1971), 'poet and more-or-less full-time eccentric.'

CHAPTER 7
LINCOLNSHIRE BIRDS
Pits, gulls and herons

This chapter surveys the work of F.L. that relates, in the main, to studies of birding locations other than Scotton Common (dealt with in the previous chapter) and with published papers that relate to specific species in Lincolnshire. These papers, along with his study of Scotton Common birds, form the prelude to his County List, which is explored in chapter 8.

In 1908 winters were more severe than they are now, and F.L. was used to seeing one of his regular birding locations, what we have called a 'local patch', covered with ice and ice-skating Lincolnians- he even joined them!

The location was obscure enough: a narrow triangular spit of water nestling between the (then quite new) railway embankment and the Fossdyke. He describes it as 'an obtuse angled triangle, with the base perhaps half a mile long, and the corners...choked up with reeds, bullrushes and other aquatic vegetation'. This water was deep in some parts, and very shallow – subject to drying out in drought – in others.

The area attracted him not merely because of a variety of bird-life but because it was 'within a mile of the Lincoln Stonebow' – this meant that it was in easy walking distance of his parishes. His article on 'The birds of a Lincoln ballast pit' was, he says, based on notes taken mainly in the years 1901-1905. This covered the time when he was curate at the parish of St Swithin, a few yards only from the Stonebow and the early days at All Saints. He could have walked to the pit and back in a lunch-break! Certainly it gives us a clue about how his leisure time was occupied.

So the ballast pit – for that is what the area was – became one of his haunts, and it appealed to him for other reasons, too. It was 'not far from the site of the Skellingthorpe Duck Decoy'. We know he had interests in these now disused decoys: he laments that this one had been out of action for sixty years. It appealed, too, because he believed, correctly, that the fens had once encroached on the city right up to this point (1). He hoped that birds would be encouraged by this:

As birds are well known to be very conservative in their habits and return to ancestral haunts as opportunity or encouragement are offered them.

This was, perhaps, a touch optimistic. F.L. had not taken into account the vast expansion of the city that had impinged on the fen. Now, while the ballast holes, as the maps sometimes label them, are still visible they back onto a series of busy roads and trading estates, and any remaining birds are but a remnant.

As with his other location accounts, F.L. sets out to compile an inventory of species. His purpose, he declares, being to interest other members of the Lincolnshire Naturalists' Union to visit, and to realise that they 'need not go far afield to find material for the study of wild birds' (2).

He spends a little time in the article setting out some basic hints for the beginning ornithologist: especially a warning that 'the novice…must be very careful before he records the occurrence of a rare bird seen at long range across the water.' The main motivation for this warning, he explains, is that the plumage of wildfowl varies, of course, across age, sex and season.

F.L. himself gets round the problems by dint of knowledge, and of 'a strong pair of glasses.' He even insists – and there is a touch of his philosophy coming through here:

I have however identified all the birds mentioned, through strong field glasses, and so am sure of my facts.

Absolute certainty and accuracy of observation and identification is a Blathwayt trade-mark! In this paper - unusually - because it deals with his own 'patch' and is not generally watched by others, there are no other observers and no written records to consult; the notes are 'entirely from my own observations.' So what have these observations revealed?

First, his favoured ducks, all non-breeders: mallard, wigeon, teal, shoveler, pochard, tufted duck and goldeneye. The last three species, being diving ducks, he thinks spend more time on the water; the others disperse into local fields to feed. He notes that the numbers of mallard fluctuate: in November 1900, three hundred; in September 1902, four hundred; and in October 1905, more than two hundred drakes in full plumage. By contrast, teal occur in modest numbers, the most being fifty in both October 1905 and December 1907. Wigeon, too, are scarcer, usually winter visitors in ones or twos, and the most occurring on 21st March 1901 when there were twenty pairs.

Pochards are commoner than teals and wigeons, arriving after breeding. F.L. knows of some local breeding pairs at Twigmoor, but numbers on the ballast pit can build to sixty or seventy. They may appear in August but leave in March. They outnumber the tufted ducks, which never add up to more than ten birds. The only record of goldeneyes was of three on 6th December 1907, which were immature birds (3). Coots and moorhens were evident to F.L., the latter in small numbers and retiring in habit, the former a common species for the pit and in February 1904 rising to a maximum total of one hundred and thirty (4).

But F.L.'s eye is taken most by the great-crested grebes. This species is an interesting link with the old fen fauna. It was a striking figure on the stagnant pools of bygone Lincolnshire, in company with such marsh-loving birds as black terns, avocets, godwits, ruffs and bitterns (5). These have been lost as a breeding species, but the grebe, though at one time approaching extinction, has escaped that fate and is now extending its range in the British Isles (6).

F.L. goes on to record that he has been aware of the grebes breeding in Lincoln in four of the previous eight years:

I first noticed a pair with three young in the curious striped downy plumage on July 12th 1900. In the following year, on August 21st, the three young brought off that season were nearly as large as the parent birds. In 1902 and 1904 I think only two young were brought off each year.

Francis regrets that no proof of breeding had been established for four seasons, but puts the explanation down, perhaps, to his making too few visits to be sure. He is clearly entranced by watching these rare birds (7) in dynamic close-up. Nearly a quarter of the article is taken up with an extensive quote from his notebook, and it is worth repeating some of this. After explaining that two pairs were present on the pit at 4.45p.m. on March 10th, 1902, (a damp, warm, hazy day with no wind) and that they were relatively idle – preening and scratching – when he arrived, he then records the courtship behaviour of one pair:

After he had called for some little time, a few minutes, the female began to swim towards him. When she got fairly near to him he crouched down on the water, raised his wings and ruffled his feathers just as an angry swan will do, and also seemed to lay back his head as a swan does. When the female was only a few yards distant she dived and came up almost underneath her mate. The two then faced each other and went through most curious antics…

Francis reveals how he was too far away to catch any vocalisations during these actions, but that the birds appeared to be 'dancing.' The performance continued until:

Both had fished up a large piece of ribbon-like weed, and holding these (sic) in their beaks they faced each other and stood upright in the water showing nearly all of their silvery breasts and looking almost like two snakes. When facing each other holding the weed, their bills almost touched, and they began to move their heads and consequently the weed also, from side to side in a most curious manner…

There then followed a chase, which was vigorous enough that Francis could hear 'much splashing.'

Wonderful though this grebe courtship ceremony is, it seems common-place to a modern birder. We see grebes frequently, and in March and April have probably witnessed this ritual many times. But in 1902, few bird enthusiasts even would have had this opportunity; and the description provided by F.L. transports the reader in his or her mind's eye into the world of the grebe. There is more detail: about the kinds of calls made, about the birds' washing, about the time the birds spent submerged. But the point is made: this is a magic moment and one which Francis is inviting the less fortunate to experience initially through his eyes, and then by getting out on the ground in relatively accessible places. In this passage he has encapsulated all the 'popular' birding of

Birds magazine (8) and at the same time all the rigorous observation of a scientific journal. He has done it all without the 'sermonising' of a W.H. Hudson, or the anthropomorphism that dogged so many natural history books in the early part of the 20th century.

Among the other treasures of the ballast pit were dabchicks or little grebes, though F.L. is less moved by this species since it was, at that time, commoner and more widespread than the great-crested grebe. As now, lapwings and golden plovers turn up in winter, the latter in smallish numbers (9). He conjectures that various other waders turn up at the pit, but does not claim to have seen any other than dunlins, fifteen in all, which he watched 'through my glasses' on 27th October 1905, and snipe and redshanks. What he does claim is to have heard the cries of waders passing over Lincoln city on 'dark foggy nights', including curlews and sandpipers. Ringed as it is by gravel pits, this is still true of the city and the suburbs, with the most frequent cries now being those of oystercatchers, followed by the calls of curlews and redshanks (10).

A red-letter day was 30th August 1902. Francis, lamenting the passing of the true fenland with its typical bird species, is delighted to see a single example of a fen bird on that day: a black tern – 'an interesting visitor to ancestral haunts.' He records that it was an immature bird; and this fits with the modern pattern of black terns in the county (11).

Among the brooding herons, the 'little parties of goldfinches', the linnets and greenfinches, and the singing reed warblers, two other species deserve mention in this ballast pit location. The first is F.L.'s favoured black-headed gull. He records a high total of forty birds on 23rd November 1903, and jogs his readers' memories that the county is favoured with gull colonies. As some mention of these forms a later part of the chapter, discussion of black-headed gulls can be put aside until then.

Intriguing among F.L.'s observations at the ballast pit is this last one:

From the end of October to the beginning of April, a characteristic bird is the Hooded or Grey Crow. He is only a winter visitor to Lincoln, but is much in evidence during his stay along the banks of the River Witham.

That hoodies are 'much in evidence' is no longer true. Hooded crows, with their smart grey bibs, are a northern species as far as we are concerned, coming from Scotland or Scandinavia to pass the winter. But their numbers in Lincolnshire have diminished greatly over the years (12). The accuracy of the historical record on matters like this is of great importance to identifying trends in bird populations, distribution and behaviour over time. Such insights are a knack that F.L. enjoyed because of the perceptiveness of his observation; and his next concern is no different.

•

The vision of one or two herons standing, in clerk-like grey, over the waters of the Lincoln city ballast pit is one with which all birders can empathise. Fewer have, perhaps, seen a heron's nesting colony. Lord William Percy (13) describes a moment in the life of a heron:

It comes in fair weather or in foul, on a calm sunlit day or in driving snow, punctually almost to the day on February 5, in the form of a series of wild yelps as the first scout of the heron colony returns to the trees of the little wood that fringes the reedbed.

Blathwayt's interest in heronries is triggered by a note in the *Zoologist* (14). In his own time, he suggests that only three of the quoted Lincolnshire heronries are still occupied: Skellingthorpe Wood, Swanpool, and Haverholme near Sleaford (15). He deals, as so often, with documentary evidence additional to the *Zoologist* article, quoting Yarrell (16) and Cordeaux (17).

Not content with mere reports, F.L. makes it his business in 1908 to visit the 'four existing heronries'. He has some difficulty with one visit, for he is not sure of the location of Swanpool. He believes that it is 'the piece of water overhung with trees, known by that name, close to Lincoln'; and he is probably correct (18). His arithmetic appears a touch flawed at times, and his writing uncharacteristically vague, but we can re-construct the situation thus:

First, no heronry exists at Swanpool (19). Second, the Skellingthorpe Wood colony was tenanted; F.L. counted twelve nests but only seven nests with sitting birds (20). At Haverholme, in the Evedon Wood F.L.

discovered up to twenty pairs nesting, and local intelligence suggested this number was stable. The fourth site was Manby, where the birds had abandoned the previous colony and moved to Rowland Plantation near Appleby station: twelve nests placed high in 'Scots firs.'

F.L.'s diligence threw up a further colony at Newball Woods, north east of Lincoln:

This colony is not mentioned in the above lists, so perhaps it is of somewhat recent origin. It has been known to me for about seven years, six or seven pairs of birds nesting there annually during that time. I have no knowledge of the date when the colony was established but the number of nests seems to have lessened of late.

The Muckton colony at Louth, F.L. discovered, had moved to Tothill Wood, three miles east. Caton Haigh (21) provides F.L. with intelligence of twenty to thirty nests but 'he has heard that an order has gone out that the birds are to be destroyed in the interests of trout-fishing' (22).

Thus F.L. reviews the state of heronries in Lincolnshire. The work has an almost prophetic quality about it, for herons were to become the major research project of the BTO for many years. In their own words, this is how the BTO sums up the rationale for this regular species survey:

As a predator at the top of the freshwater food chain, Grey Herons are excellent indicators of environmental health in the countryside. The aim of this census is to collect annual nest counts of Grey Herons *Ardea cinerea* from as many sites as possible in the United Kingdom. The Heronries Census began in 1928 and is the longest-running breeding season monitoring scheme in the world. Volunteer observers make counts of apparently occupied nests at heron colonies each year. Changes in the numbers of nests, especially over periods of several years, are a clear measure of the population's trend. In recent seasons, observers have counted also the nests of Little Egrets *Egretta garzetta*, which are now appearing in a number of southern English heronries.

Coverage is coordinated through a network of regional organisers. A core of birdwatchers and ringers monitor their local colonies annually, providing a backbone of regular counts. Around two-thirds of the heronries in England and Wales are currently counted each year, with major censuses carried out in 1929, 1954, 1964 and 1985. Rather few counts are made of heronries in Scotland and Northern Ireland. Counts are submitted to the BTO on cards and the data are entered onto computer at BTO headquarters. The number of heronries cards submitted each year is around 450. (23)

An early report of this survey appears in the *Bird Study* volume published in 1956 and related to the census year 1954 (24). This established that nationally 6,225 occupied nests from 520 heronries could be accounted for, and in England and Wales there were 4,708 nests from 301 heronries – an increase of 19% over the first year of the Census, 1928. Smith (of Smith and Cornwallis) was the Lincolnshire representative for this activity. The fate of F.L.'s heronries was as follows:

- Muckton remained stable
- Appleby had become extinct in the 1930s
- Skellingthorpe (now called Doddington) has diminished from 18 to ten nests
- Haverholme and Newball seem to have been lost to the record
- F.L. had demonstrated that Swanpool had no nests even in 1908.

Twenty-two Lincolnshire sites were listed, however, of which thirteen appear to have been active in 1954, suggesting a rise in the population of these birds or, as Francis had astutely pointed out elsewhere, that having a larger team of observers tended to find more birds. For F.L. to have drawn attention to the species gives a clue, perhaps, to the sensitivity and insight of the man, for he had realised that it was possible to use an individual species as a barometer of change. The same insight holds true for his next subject – almost, his next passion: the black-headed gull.

●

F.L.'s paper on the black-headed gull is probably the most loosely written and least exciting of all the papers among either his early writings or those that deal with the county of Lincolnshire. This assertion is made on several grounds. First, the introduction to the paper is rather rambling and deals first with a range of other species found in the vicinity of the gulleries. Second, the style falls neither to the 'scientific' approach that he adopts when 'listing', nor to the anecdotal and literary style that he demonstrates when reviewing some problem of bird behaviour based on his personal note-taking. Third, there are several rather rambling acknowledgements to the landowners on whose sites the gulleries are situated. All this makes the paper somewhat unfocused.

So what is there to learn from this item? First and foremost, the location of the extant Lincolnshire gulleries of the time: at Twigmoor, Crosby and Scotton Common. Second, important information about the status of these locations for the species in question.

Twigmoor seems to have a history that dates, F.L. thinks, from about 1843, when birds previously nesting at Manton Common migrated to this site. The circumstances of this move are described:

I have learned from reliable sources that when, about the middle of the last century, Twigmoor was planted with trees and the small ponds converted into a considerable lake by the forester of the late Sir John Nelthorpe, Bart., the Manton gulls, being much persecuted in the nesting season, migrated to Twigmoor, and have now, owing to careful protection, grown into a mighty host.

Francis notes that the vagaries of the weather determine the start of the breeding season, but that the first eggs are usually laid in the first half of April. The colony is significant:

I once tried to make a rough estimate of the number of gulls breeding in this famous colony, and set it down at five thousand pairs, but counting being a sheer impossibility, my figures may have been very wide of the mark…

F.L. thinks that the Crosby gullery, five miles to the north, is an off-shoot of Twigmoor, founded about 1865. The owner reports that it has been used ever since, but that about fifteen years ago there was a seven-year hiatus caused by 'some poaching gentlemen.' An unnamed visitor to the area in 1905 claims that the colony was 'enormous' but F.L. thinks its days are numbered because of 'steady encroachment of the workings for iron ore.'

The third colony, at Scotton, is six miles to the south west of Twigmoor not far from the Trent. Francis has it 'on good authority' there were no gulls here in 1860, and he concludes it is an over-spill site from Twigmoor. He believes that this site 'is safe from persecution' under its present ownership; and notes that it can be visited, though on private land, subject to the payment 'of a small fee, which is, I believe, devoted to some charitable object.'

Beyond the information about gulls, there is some small, tangential attempt to survey other birds that inhabit the gull ponds; but to a large extent these observations are replicated in other papers for other audiences. Though opposed to 'poaching gentlemen', F.L. is not opposed to the legitimate husbanding of the birds, for of Scotton he can write:

[I] have visited it on many occasions, having spent many pleasant hours watching the habits of the birds, or discussing them with the keeper over a substantial tea of fried gull's [sic] eggs and home-cured ham.

This paper is more trivial than his other work, it is suggested, not only for the reasons previously listed, but because it lacks the carefully reported insights into bird behaviour and distribution that one has come to expect of Francis. But it still has worth. It anchors our knowledge of breeding black-headed gulls at that period, which can allow later comparison. Sources (25) suggest that few black-headed colonies nationally diminished in the period 1958 to 1973, though numbers at Scotton had fallen from an earlier figure of 900 pairs to about 200-250 pairs. Black-headed gulls, over the last century, have proved to be in general both a national and a local success story.

There are no extant records to prove the matter, but it is possible that the *Zoologist* article was a factor in provoking an early, and very detailed study of the species. Another Oxford graduate, F.B. Kirkman, set about researching the black-headed gull, and came to the Twigmoor gullery to do so (26). Kirkman was also a photographer, and his resulting book of the study records not only that he watched the Twigmoor gullery from 1913-1935, but includes photographs of the location. Kirkman's book is a interesting blend, containing both insightful field notes, but also a now rather dated attempt to deal with the 'mentality' of birds based on the emerging theories of psychology.

•

Of all the species that make birders excited, the raptors are those most commonly cited. We may marvel at the citrus feathers of the yellow wagtail, at the jewelled glory of the kingfisher or at the agility of the swift. But the imagination is captured by the killers of the bird world: the owls and hawks.

F.L. was no different. Always seeking information about kites or buzzards from the old keepers and woodsmen, it was clear he had a keen interest in these birds. No doubt it was this interest in these elusive species that triggered a further paper (27) to which, if only for completeness, some reference should be made. For this was a paper not about living birds but, substantially, about dead ones.

To suggest that this paper has an unusually (for F.L.) polemical motive one need stray no further than the first paragraph. It is about the 'birds of prey', the 'Striges and Acciptre' (sic), and 'though commonly regarded as enemies of the game-preserver and poultry-farmer, and accordingly terribly persecuted, most…should be looked on far more as man's friends than as man's foes.'

The paper reviews a case of owls and hawks in the Lincoln County Museum, about which institution Francis shows a passing but repeated interest. Francis argues that these bird species keep down vermin; and uses as his proof the contents of their pellets, dissected by the Curator at the museum. So his intention is to encourage 'an intelligent interest' in birds of prey; and he summarises the contemporary laws on bird protection and decries the activities of the 'prowling gunner.'

Having set the scene, F.L. deals with the Lincoln specimens of barn, long-eared, short-eared and tawny owls. Of the first, he suggests they are not uncommon, and are known by their shriek, which terrifies the superstitious. The long-eared, he says, is also far more common than most credit; but the nocturnal habits cover its tracks unless one ventures into night-time woods and is familiar with the sounds made by adults and nestlings. By contrast, the short-eared is a bird of the open fields, mainly an autumn/winter visitor. He claims it was once a common bird, and a breeder, on Scotton and Manton Commons; and records twenty being flushed by gunners from one field at Scotton in January 1908. The tawny's calls are a 'still common country sound.'

The museum has an example of the little owl, shot at Coleby in 1899; and F.L. records the species being released into the county. He notes in passing only that the Tengmalm's owl was shot at Saltfleet Haven on 22 October 1880.

Though there are some few details given about these species to distinguish the one from the other, the notes about them are sparse. When he moves to the other birds of prey, F.L. is more expansive. He notes, correctly, that harriers form a kind of half-way-house between owls and other birds of prey. The specimens of the marsh harrier before him – just three – were all taken in the Scotton area half a century before; though the species was believed to have nested in the Isle of Axeholme in 1836. He regards Montagu's as an 'occasional straggler', which is roughly the position today. F.L. seeks out sources for the status of the hen harrier, and finds the Revd E. Elmhirst informative: this species was once common in the Market Rasen/Middle Rasen area as a breeder, with up to ten pairs in the gorse. Though this delight has long gone for F.L., one bird was shot at Nocton in December 1906; and this is precisely where one would look near Lincoln for this species today.

Buzzards, for F.L., are 'only wanderers' to Lincolnshire. He would have been delighted with the modern spread of this species in the county; the museum specimen comes (inevitably, one feels) from Scotton about 1850. The rough-legged buzzard is listed as an autumn visitor from northern Europe; and it still is. Honey buzzards are rare in F.L.'s England and in ours: the museum specimens being from Scotton about 1850 and Market Rasen in 1896. Two birds of the species were shot at Grantham in autumn 1908: and F.L. draws attention to the thickly feathered lores that protect the bird when it seeks its food (not, as Francis points out, the honey, but the bees).

F.L. does not feel that the golden eagle, the sea-eagle, the osprey and the goshawk can truly be called Lincolnshire birds, though each may be encountered very occasionally in suitable locations. Of the sparrowhawk he writes: '...the gamekeeper, not without some cause, keeps down its numbers...The two museum specimens are in the immature plumage, the adult birds having the upper parts of a slate blue colour.' This, of course, is not strictly accurate, as the female also has brown plumage.

The discussion of the (red) kite is interesting. The museum has no specimen but would 'gladly accept one' if it were offered! He has consulted Cordeaux's work and found that, in his youth, the latter had seen kites over the woodlands at Louth. Cordeaux had talked in turn to an old man who, as a boy, had been sent to mind geese and goslings at Louth, to keep kites away (about 1820). F.L. quotes the line of Shakespeare: 'When the kite builds look to lesser linen' (28). For the birds will, apparently, rob clothes-lines. Francis goes on to gather other records of kites around the river in Lincoln, and about the cathedral towers, with the last eggs obtained near Wragby in 1870.

So F.L. comes to the 'true falcons': peregrine, hobby, merlin and kestrel. The last, he says, is common and protected, though those that nested round the cathedral have moved away (more recently they have returned). The merlin is mainly a winter visitor, though eggs were taken in Manton; it is basically a moorland bird and thus not favoured by the Lincolnshire habitat (29). Hobbies had apparently decreased in numbers in F.L.'s time, and these birds are still not common though in some years more appear than in others, and they can often be seen following the hirundine flocks at migration time. Francis knows of no breeding records of peregrines but knows it as a winter harasser of coastal flocks of waders and small ducks. Again, it is by no means uncommon now in Lincolnshire, even inland, outside the immediate breeding season (30).

So F.L. draws his paper to a close (31). He concludes:

For a lover of wildlife there can be few sights more sickening than that which is presented by a row of carcases of owls and kestrels exhibited on 'the keeper's tree', and it is much to be hoped that in the future the law of the land in this respect will be both observed and enforced.

He would have been interested, if appalled, that a 'keeper's gibbet' was photographed by the author just a couple of miles from Doddington, in the 1970s, and that among the species exhibited was a female kestrel!

•

The published papers reported in this chapter and the previous one have confirmed Francis Blathwayt's approach to birding in Lincolnshire, setting out his methodology, his style and his particular interests. It comes as no surprise, then, to find that towards the end of his sojourn in the county, his thoughts turned to creating a County List, using the data he has collected from these studies and excursions. It is to this attempt that the next chapter is devoted.

NOTES TO CHAPTER 7

1.   The 'old' fens attracted great affection from those who knew them. J. Wentworth-Day owned a small acreage of fen over the border in Cambridgeshire and tells (1961 *The British Birds of Wild Places* London: Blandford, pages 25-7) of its loss: 'You might go, as I did, on countless enchanted dawns, in a punt, gliding like a ghost, through waterways and up reedy channels, the bows cleaving like a knife through the lilypad and watermint, until the punt broke with a rustling crackle through a thin wall of reeds and there, flat and ghostly in the dawn fog, lay the waters of Swan Mere, or the Cottage Pool, or the Bittern's Pulk. The duck, mallard and teal, tufted and shoveller, gadwall and garganey, rose in a frenzy of wings and swept back and forth through the pale bird's egg blue of a sky, empty of smoke and silent of man...But alas, that fen of mine is no more. It was drained in 1940, when the land was needed to grow food in time of war...They set fire to the reeds and for a day or more my secret fen roared and crackled...The duck rose up and fled on whimpering wings. The moorhens and rails, the bitterns and warblers, went no man knows whither...When the wind blew the dust and the ashes and the smoke away, my secret fen lay burnt and black and scorched.'

2.   Earlier, we referred to the work of EMBSC in the period 1975-1980 especially in relation to the Hartsholme area (which is only a mile or so beyond the ballast pit mentioned in this article). The EMBSC, motivated by precisely the concerns of Francis Blathwayt, also published trail 'guides' to other areas in and beyond Lincoln. These included 'A visitor's guide to the birds of Lincoln', which gave species present in locations such as the cathedral precinct, Brayford pool, the Arboretum (a stone's throw from F.L.'s lodging as a curate in 1900-9), South Common, and the nearer fens – all based on my own sightings and those of fellow member Mike Willey. They also included a walk on public footpaths from Hartsholme towards F.L.'s ballast pits. However, the text of this (which spoke about 'poppies bleeding into the barley' – a statement of pure fact) had to be withdrawn because the farmer over whose land the footpath ran saw this as some kind of slur on his competence and complained to the City Council!

3.   A similar trawl of ducks on a modest-sized pit near to the city today would produce similarities and differences. Mallard might still be the dominant species; indeed a few swim up and down among the shoppers only yards from the ballast pit today. Tufted ducks would also be in relatively high numbers (though the total numbers for all species might be depressed over F.L.'s time). A few teal would probably hide away in the reeds; though wigeon might seek more open ground for grazing. It would be surprising today if no gadwall were found – very unusual in F.L.'s time; and it would be no surprise if the occasional sheld-duck dropped by.

4.   Coot counts have been undertaken sporadically both nationally (by the British Trust for Ornithology) and locally (by the Lincolnshire Naturalists' Union). The mid-winter coot census by the LNU in 1974 (*Transactions* vol 18 no. 4 pp 175-178) indicated 110 birds were present on Lincoln LNER pit, which may equate with Blathwayt's ballast pit. The count was taken on 8th December 1974, and I recall carrying out the Hartsholme count. On the day of the count there were only five birds present; the day before numbers had been in three figures! Winter total for coot in Lincolnshire was 3,819 birds; while the summer peak was at that time about 500 pairs. Winter birds come through on migration from Scandinavia and elsewhere.

5.   In recent years, some of these species have made some recovery. Bitterns, though by no means regular, do turn up in Lincolnshire, mainly in the area of the Isle of Axholme and the Humber Bank (Lorand and Atkin, p 72). It might be worth recounting a short tale here about a local bittern, not least because it epitomises all that is worst about birding! Lorand and Atkin (p 72) record the finding in Birchwood, close to Hartsholme Park, of a little bittern on 26th August 1976. This bird was discovered in an almost dried-up drain at the foot of a garden by

the friends of one of EMBSC's young members, Richard Arden. He alerted me, and I took a camera and we went in search of it. It hadn't moved: it was standing, bittern-like (!), among the reeds and was clearly going nowhere. I was able to crawl on my belly to within three feet of it: I know it was within three feet because the camera (in my rush) had only been equipped with a standard 50mm lens and it was at its closest focusing point. I reeled off twenty shots, though the low light (it was about 8.30p.m.) and the location meant I was shooting on *f.* 2.8 at 1/30th of a second. Sadly, I had to leave home at 5a.m. next morning and the bird died overnight, the skin passing to a local 'expert', who identified it as that of a little bittern. It was little, certainly; but the skin showed no signs on the typical buff patches that distinguish the little bittern species. However, it was noised abroad as such. Not being satisfied with the identification, I sent a colour slide to the BTO for their opinion, and meanwhile set out the facts of the matter as they were known to me (letter, Lincolnshire Chronicle 10th February 1977, page 15). This challenge to the authority of the 'in-group' produced a violent verbal attack on me by a very eminent local worthy when our paths happened to cross on a local nature reserve: integrity and truth mattered less, it seemed, than acceptance of the word of 'people in the know'. On 1.8.77 a response to my letter came back from the BTO, from an eminent member of this august body (whom I won't name) saying this was 'almost certainly a bittern and probably a young one.' Meanwhile, because the BTO wanted to see the skin we managed to retrieve it briefly; and in due course the SAME eminent BTO ornithologist wrote: 'there is no doubt the skin is a little bittern, a juvenile, probably male...The transparency you sent some weeks ago was however a common bittern and there can be no doubt in my mind that you had both species present.' That might have been the end of the story except that we now had a mystery – unless someone had 'swapped' the skin while it was out of our control [and I don't believe they did], BOTH the skin and the slide were categorically of the SAME bird! Unhappy with the outcome, a picture was sent to *British Birds* journal, and one of the staff there wrote querying whether we were claiming an American bittern on the basis of it. So now there were three potential identifications! As luck would have it, my wife and I were to visit the greatest bird photographer of the day: Eric Hosking. With some trepidation I offered him my slide (I thought it was good, but alongside his...). He took it graciously and put it into a sequence that he showed to his friend Bert Axell. His subsequent letter runs: 'I...confirm that Mr Axell, who was for seventeen years warden of Minsmere and has probably seen more bitterns than anyone else, is quite positive over the identification, and I myself had already identified it as this bird' – the bird being common bittern. The most recent 'expert' to whom I have showed the slides also confirmed the bird as common bittern and, like us, felt it was a very young juvenile – hence the small size. IF, this is the case then one can conjecture a) that the bird could not have flown to its location from its nearest normal breeding ground and b) that therefore a common bittern had tried to nest in a drain close to Hartsholme Park in the summer of 1976. However, there is one more twist to the tale. In a chance meeting in a bird hide in Norfolk, in casual conversation, I mentioned this sighting. My listener turned out to be a most talented bird artist (again, I will not name him). He took huge trouble to view the slides, to write an assessment, and to demonstrate (at least to his own satisfaction), by minute examination of the feather detail, that the bird in question was – a little bittern. His four pages of hand-written notes and exquisite drawn details are still in my archive! But if there is a moral to this story it is that you can't believe everything you are told by experts or read in County Lists. I still would not give a verdict on the real identification of this unfortunate bird. But F.L.'s desire for absolute accuracy counts for something: mistakes are human, but integrity and truth are the birder's watch-words!

6.   The reader will recall that the great-crested grebe was, above all, the species that sparked the conservation movement that came to be headed up by the RSPB. Though common-place now, grebes were then in serious danger of extinction, so F.L.'s excitement is understandable.

7.   Some measure of the rarity of great-crested grebes in former years can be felt in this quotation from Lorand and Atkin (p 65): 'Large numbers bred in the fens before the final

drainage in the early nineteenth century...nesting apparently ceased in the county until 1900... At least eight waters were known to be occupied by 1914...In 1931 there were twenty-six pairs at twelve sites...In 1965 a hundred and six adults were located on twenty-four waters...by 1975...no fewer than a hundred pairs were present.' Now, it would surprise if any suitable lake or pit failed to hold at least one pair; and large numbers sometimes winter on the coast

8.   *Birds* is the members' magazine of the RSPB, which aims to make birding accessible to the Society's more than one million, often 'hobbyist', members.

9.   For a number of years I, like many others, undertook census work locally on behalf of the British Trust for Ornithology in relation to wintering golden plovers. This species seems to have 'traditional' wintering areas and to be very site-loyal. At this time I was able to conduct the counts from my upstairs window, the view covering fields leading down to the River Witham as it winds out of Lincoln city. Though counts varied, there were rarely less than a few hundred golden plovers; and sometimes thousands. They would fly in, in high, fast groups, about 7.30 a.m. throughout the winter; and would eventually pack and settle. Often, heavier, darker flocks of lapwings would oar across the sky below these little scimitar-shaped plovers. Some large counts for 'goldies' were as follows: 1100 on Christmas Eve 1999; 3000 on 27th December 1999; 2000 on 11th January 2000; 2000 still on 16th; and 1500 on 5th February 2000; plus 1500 again on 11th November 2001. Lapwings occasionally topped 500 birds in this area, though much bigger counts are known in the county. Over the last two or three years conditions seem to have changed, and the flocks are much smaller and less frequent, though may simply have moved further along the river valley.

10.   Both redshanks and oystercatchers turn up quite often at the local gravel pits in North Hykeham, off the western ring-road, for example. I have not seen curlews at the pits, but they certainly call in on the nearby fenland during autumn passage. Dunlins are probably more frequent over-flyers than one gives credit for, and occasionally a small group will drop into a wet field or along the margin of a lake or pit. Both common and green sandpipers are passage visitors to local waters.

11.   Lorand and Atkin, pp 143-4.

12.   It is interesting to compare the entries for this species even between Smith and Cornwallis' day and Lorand and Atkin's. The former calls it 'an autumn passage migrant and winter visitor', while the latter rates it 'scarce.' Smith and Cornwallis imply through their semantics that the birds turn up in some numbers, at least on the coast. They record an instance of nesting in 1900 on the basis of Blathwayt's own work, at Market Stainton. Lorand and Atkin note 'numbers have declined considerably since [the 1930s]... most records refer to single birds or small parties'. My personal observation of the species in the county is limited to the fen at Nocton, and even there not for many years now. Lack, P. (1986) *The Atlas of Wintering Birds in Britain and Ireland* Staffordshire: Poyser, pp 372-5, shows a winter distribution round the Lincolnshire coast of groups of 1-15 birds in about fifteen locations; and four inland sites of the same magnitude, all except one in the north west of the county.

13.   *Three Studies in Bird Character*, London: Country Life Limited, 1951, p 17. This is a delightful book with a collection (for its time) of superb close-up monochrome photographs of the three species concerned.

14.   He refers to 'the List of British Heronries' printed in that journal in 1872.

15.   Those that had passed out of use were: Leake near Boston; Spalding; Donington; and Cressy Hall: 'all in the south east of the county.' A colony at Manby was in decline since 1851

and extinct by 1872; Muckton Wood near Louth is regarded as doubtful.

16. Yarrell's *British Birds* volume iv (1884-5), in which Manby is claimed to be reduced but active.

17. Cordeaux, J. (1872) *Birds of the Humber District* adds that ' a single nest was built on a tree in Nocton Park, near Lincoln.'

18. The map of Lincoln for 1900 marks a Swan Pool close to the city, and this is the location that F.L. identifies.

19. Though the area was extensively watched from 1975-1980 by EMBSC there was never a suggestion that a heronry existed; nor has one since, as far as I can ascertain.

20. On his move to the Rectory at Doddington, F.L. was to become a close neighbour of this heronry, which remains a traditional site. It is certainly common enough to see herons passaging across the Doddington road.

21. Lorand and Atkin (p 59) summarise the work of G.H. Caton Haigh, a 'fine ornithologist' who 'began regular visits to the coast at Tetney and North Cotes' towards the end of the century and 'shot many rare birds including several new species for Britain, such as Radde's and greenish warbler, and showed that yellow-browed and barred warblers occurred with some regularity. However he was also an excellent field observer...' It emerges from *British Birds* he was, in later life, afflicted with arthritis, but still managed to shoot from crutches!

22. Maybe because F.L. regards this paper as rather brief, he adds a second section on the heronries of Somerset, which seems somewhat out-of-place. Perhaps it should have been a free-standing note, possibly in another journal. For the present purpose, which is to focus on Lincolnshire birds, I have ignored this element of the article.

23. These data are taken from the BTO web-site: www.bto.org.uk .

24. Burton, J.F. (1956) 'Report on the National Census of Heronries 1954' *Bird Study* (3) 1, pp 42-73. The heron surveys by the BTO have continued into recent years. By 1993 it was into its 64th year of operation, and its methods were being reviewed (BTO News, July/August 1993. No. 187, p 1). It is worth noting in passing that numbers of herons crashed after the severe winter of 1963, but then recovered. By 1974 survey techniques had taken a turn of which F.L may not have approved. Reynolds, C.M. (1974) 'The Census of Heronries 1969-1973' *Bird Study* (21) 2, pp 129-134 identifies methods for dealing with uncounted heronries, and those that become extinct or start up and thus distort the results of the count. He suggests: 'The uncounted heronries affect the population estimates in two ways. Firstly, changes in individual heronries may differ considerably from the general trend. By calculating the confidence limits for the changes by the method used for the Common Bird Census..., as if for a small sample, and applying these to the estimated uncounted total, the limits of the estimated population can be obtained...' Somewhere, in the great birdopolis for dead parson-naturalists I think I can hear F.L. saying something that sounds suspiciously like: 'What you need is a powerful pair of prism glasses and a bicycle to visit all the sites...' But I could be wrong!

25. Gribble, F.C. (1976) 'A census of black-headed gull colonies in England and Wales 1973' *Bird Study* (23) 2, pp 135-145.

26. F.B. Kirkman (1925) *Bird Behaviour: A contribution based chiefly on the study of the black-headed gull* London: Nelson. Kirkman later collaborated as author with Jourdain on other titles.

27. F.L. wrote this item 'Owls and Hawks of Lincolnshire: with special reference to the collection in the City and County Museum, Lincoln' in January 1909, to be sold at the museum, price one penny. The modest booklet has a superb 'electro' of a Barn Owl on the back cover, lent by the RSPB.

28. *Winter's Tale* Act 4, scene 2.

29. My own experience is that merlins have increased over the years, still mainly outside the breeding season but not exclusively so. I recently saw both sexes in the Waddington area, though not at the same time, and have had other sightings on the fens. Prior to this I saw individual birds as follows: North Hykeham (Dec 1978; July 1980; March 1985; September 1987; March 1988); Waddington (October 1990); Brant Broughton (March 1992); Bardney (September 1993).

30. The peregrine described by Jake Wildmann ('Wild Ways: February 2005' – in www.sourceuk.net) is a Lincolnshire bird.

31. Lorand and Atkin are heavily dependent on Blathwayt for early raptor occurrences. It is worth noting that, in modern times, Montagu's harriers have tried to breed. Red kites are at least wandering through the county from release schemes elsewhere, and there is suitable habitat for them to settle. Goshawks are recorded occasionally and may breed in secluded woods. Rough-legged buzzards are fairly regular wintering birds in small numbers, but very local.

CHAPTER 8
LINCOLNSHIRE BIRDS
County Lists and speculation

There is an inherent contradiction, it may seem, between field ornithology and the compilation of scientific data such as are found in County Lists. Yet F.L. carried out both functions and was effective in both arenas.

Think back to his wading, up to his knees in water, to capture and examine the sheld-duck ducklings, or being attacked by black-headed gulls for handling their chicks, or jumping off the boat onto the shingle in an easterly wind on Lundy. Then, see him in his study in the Doddington Rectory, surrounded by books and journals, pouring over ancient and obscure records to investigate the bird species that have turned up in Lincolnshire over time. These mind-pictures form the enigma that shapes the man. For, while there are birders who can perform one of these operations outstandingly but singly, there are others who can engage in both functions with enthusiasm, slipping from one to the other seamlessly. F.L. was one of these.

So, in this chapter it is the intention to look at two further substantial papers that Francis compiled about Lincolnshire. The first is, despite the modesty of his presentation, quite simply the most definitive review of the bird species of Lincolnshire ever undertaken up to that time. In the second paper, a more informal affair, he allows himself the indulgence of a little speculative thought.

•

In 1914 the *Transactions* published 'The Birds of Lincolnshire' – F.L.'s impressive attempt to draw together from historical sources a review of species recorded in the county. The item is written with considerable economy, and this is a characteristic we have noted before. F.L. does not flaunt his deep and wide-ranging knowledge. He does, however, in this instance give us an insight into how he went about the task.

115

Of Roseates *and* Rectories

The paper begins with a statement of its aims: to produce a County List, but not just a list of occurrences. F.L.'s list will make some judgements about the status of the birds in question. It lists the major sources, which include books and journal articles, many by 'greats' of earlier and contemporary birding (1). But F.L. has also used notes and papers 'too numerous to mention' which have appeared in periodicals and books not otherwise included in his bibliography (2).

As in his survey of Somerset Birds (3) F.L. begins his account with a 'short sketch of the physical features of the county', but this is curtailed because the paper is written specifically for a Lincolnshire audience, and a naturalist audience at that, which will be familiar with this context. He does allow himself the regret that the only 'wild' area of the county now remaining is that of the north west, while much of the remainder is under cultivation. However, he applauds the coastal marshes as a potential location for birds, and feels it has been under-watched. He pays tribute to the great names of Lincolnshire ornithology, Cordeaux and Haigh, for he is always generous in his appreciation of the labours and knowledge of others.

Drawing up a County List requires judgement: which records to accept, which not. We know he is a stickler for accuracy. He bows to Cordeaux's huge experience, but can't disguise a tinge of scepticism, though it is delivered in a guarded form:

All Cordeaux's records have been allowed to stand, in consideration of his great knowledge of the subject...

So far, so good. But then:

One or two of his records, as for example those of the ortolan, lesser kestrel and little crake appear to rest on somewhat slender evidence.

This leaves 286 species on the County List, plus nine listed but not included nor given a number on account of the doubt attaching to them.

To transcribe the list, or replicate it in detail, would merely bore the reader, who can refer to it at source (4). Instead, the choice has been made to commentate on only a small number of the species included within it, often chosen for very personal reasons or because there is some specific information about the bird in question that is of particular interest.

The final version of the County List compiled by Francis follows an order no longer used in ornithological texts (5) and this chapter deviates even from F.L.'s order to suit its themes. The names of birds are also sometimes not those we would expect to read today: for example, the greenish warbler becomes the greenish willow-warbler; the willow warbler is called the willow-wren; the tits are labelled titmice, and the pomarine skua is named the pomatorhine skua. In all other respects, the list is easy to follow.

Among the species worthy of note are two warblers. The wood warbler is reported to be a 'summer visitor, preferring large beech woods', which is logical. However, this habitat is lacking over much of the county, and Smith and Cornwallis suggest that, since Blathwayt's time, the only breeding records have been from Broughton Woods and the Normanby Park estate in the north west of the county; otherwise it is a scarce passage migrant in spring and autumn. By contrast, Lorand and Atkin leave open the possibility that the very occasional breeder may be missed by birders (6). The great reed warbler, a large version of the reed warbler in looks, with a call like a spinning football rattle, F.L. regards as 'perhaps an autumn straggler' and 'never obtained but twice reported as seen near the NE coast' (7). Lorand and Atkin accept five records – one emanating from Cordeaux (i.e. on F.L.'s list); and then one trapped at Huttoft on 3rd May 1967, one in the Chapel Pit area of the county during the summer of 1976, one present at Burton gravel pit from 6-22 July 1979, and one at North Cotes in May 1980. The Burton bird was heard by dozens of birders and glimpsed by a few (8); the song is very distinctive and not easily overlooked or mistaken.

Shrikes – great grey and red-backed – feature on F.L.'s list. Of the former he suggests they occur in most years in coastal areas, but are rare winter visitors. With respect to the latter, he records breeding in the county on a number of occasions between 1907 and 1914. Smith and Cornwallis confirm that the great grey is scarce but regular, adding some inland records, twice near Brigg and once near Grantham; though these and other records are all, except one, for single birds (9). More recently, Lorand and Atkin record the great grey as 'a winter visitor chiefly inland' and mostly associated with conifers. This may seem an odd contradiction but the clue could lie in the latter authors' belief that more intensive observations have extended our sightings of this species (10). My own first experience of the great grey in Lincolnshire mirrored Wildmann's (11):

Fighting the fatigue of over-indulgence we sought...the freshness of a country park...The whistle of bullfinches on snow-berries drew us to their leaden backs, washing-powder-white rumps and salmon breasts. Rounding a corner...a harsh 'shack' call and an undulation of flight swept up the caller to the pinnacle of an old, bare silver birch...A great grey shrike, starling-sized in dapper grey and black-and-white, like a gentleman in morning dress, sat hook-billed watching us watching him.

Nevertheless, despite many more birders watching for it, the great grey shrike remains a very unusual sighting, its coming a red-letter day (12). It seems likely that F.L. had not seen one – not in Lincolnshire anyway. The red-backed shrike seems to have been reasonably well known in the first two decades of the 20th century. Smith and Cornwallis note its demise by the 1940s; and Lorand and Atkin suggest a steady increase since 1963 while in 1977 'more than fifty were seen.' Autumn records outnumber spring occurrences. Impaled beetles - the shrike's macabre larder - found by Hartsholme wardens at Birchwood in the autumn of 1976 may have been the result of a visit by a red-backed or a great grey shrike; the bird itself was not seen.

Another quite 'exotic' species noted by F.L. is the waxwing; and he records irruptions in 1850, 1867, 1883, 1893 and 1914. The phenomenon of groups or flocks of these wonderfully plumaged, dapper and dumpy, crested birds arriving suddenly and departing with as little warning is well documented now, of course. One such flock appeared locally a few years ago. The birds arrived, about twenty in number, in the garden of a suburban bungalow on the A607 in Bracebridge Heath, Lincoln, just on the city side of Waddington RAF camp. A herring-bone *Cotoneaster* against the property wall, under the window of the sitting room, was - for about a week - raided for berries. When disturbed or sated the birds flew across to the remnant of village green opposite, where they rested on a small deciduous tree about twenty feet high and to the unwary would have passed for a group of chattering starlings. Then, of a sudden, a few days later they disappeared. Smith and Cornwallis add the winters of 1932-3, 1936-7 and 1946-7 (a fearsomely severe one) to the irruption dates given by F.L.; and Lorand and Atkin can expand the list further: 1956-7, 1957-8, 1958-9, 1959-60, 1961-2, 1963-4 (another harsh winter), 1965-6, 1970-1 and 1988 (13).

F.L. is assiduous in noting population trends, and even for quite common birds these can provide interesting data. For example, among the finches he recounts that the goldfinch, which was becoming scarce, is now gaining ground. It 'deserves every encouragement', he declares, doubtless entranced, as most birders are, by its tinkling calls and by its good looks and acrobatic behaviour. Goldfinches, in earlier centuries the victims of bird-catchers, are now relatively common even in the heart of Lincoln city (14). A similar acrobatic finch, the siskin, is a winter visitor to the county; and F.L. was pleased to record a single male at Hartsholme on the comparatively late date of 11th April 1910 (15). By contrast, we have documented in a previous chapter, for our own time, the demise of the redpoll since F.L.'s day. Likewise, the hawfinch has diminished. F.L. rejoices that its numbers 'have greatly increased in recent years' but notes its destructiveness in gardens. That very characteristic has spelled its persecution. Lorand and Atkin call it 'scarce...and local' though its secretive habits may mean it is marginally commoner than the records suggest (16).

Another small bird of F.L.'s time that was scarce, indeed, 'very scarce', was the woodlark; a fact corroborated by his contemporary M. Peacock for the north west. Today, the woodlark is still, regrettably, scarce; for it has one of the most delightful songs of all songbirds and would probably come in most birders' top three songsters. Over the last century, the places most likely to hold woodlarks are the north western area, Haverholme near Sleaford, and Woodhall (17). Today the county stronghold may be on the Lincolnshire Trust reserve at Woodhall; but perhaps the bird is sometimes overlooked (18).

Francis allows himself one moment of poetic indulgence in the list, speculating that the 'sea-blue bird of march' in Tennyson (19) is the kingfisher, which he says is an uncommon resident with a spring and autumn passage especially on the coast. Smith and Cornwallis add nothing to this picture, and Lorand and Atkin refer to the severe winter of 1963 which almost wiped out the species county and country-wide (20). There is no question that kingfishers do turn up on most suitable waters, and can be very site-loyal if somewhat elusive. It is perhaps surprising that F.L. recorded the kingfisher neither at Hartsholme, where it was regular but hard to find in the late 1970s, nor on the Brayford where – on very rare occasions in winter – one might be traced to the little drain that runs under the Old Central Warehouse (21).

A group of birds that always attracts the notice and comment of birders, past and present, are the raptors. F.L. notes the release of little owls by Lord Lilford in Northamptonshire in about 1888, and that this species has spread into Lincolnshire. He has made personal observations in Doddington around 1914, and there are other local records as well as some from the north of the county. The little owl is, of course, now a relatively common species; fears about it having a detrimental effect on the balance of native birds have been largely unfounded. It is now a welcome sighting for most birders, and many keep a sharp eye on the tops of telegraph poles or fence posts for its diminutive form, especially at dusk and dawn.

The harrier group is a partial success story. F.L. rates the marsh harrier as a 'very rare visitor', though individual sightings are widespread across the county. By the time of Lorand and Atkin's County List it had begun breeding again, though it was still regarded as unusual (22). However the last two decades have seen a substantial turn-around in the birds' fortunes. Leaving Lincoln city for the fens it is now possible to discover many successful breeding pairs within a radius of only about ten miles; as well as at least one winter roost. I have put up five birds from a single field – a male, a female, and three birds of the year – on a single occasion, and on another noted as many as three males in the sky (each with a subtle plumage variation, making it individually recognisable) within the space of twenty minutes. On one occasion I met a birder making detailed records of harrier sightings who claimed he could pin-point seventy territories in the Lincoln area.

The same optimism cannot be said to attend the hen harrier in Lincolnshire, again 'very rare' as an autumn and winter visitor to Francis. Lorand and Atkin re-tell the story of the extermination of twenty-six birds in one day at Market Rasen moor in the 1820s. The largest gathering at a roost in recent times has been eighteen birds (23). Males, with their smart grey plumage, are quite unusual; but in the winter 'ring-tails' are sometimes seen both on the coast and inland. The Montagu's harrier, named after the famous Colonel Montagu, has always, in modern times, been rare; F.L. regards it as 'probably a former inhabitant of the fens' but by 1908 any records were 'many years ago'.

Among the other raptors, rough-legged buzzards winter in variable numbers now as in F.L.'s time. Numbers of observers, and improved optical aids, have stepped up sightings. Francis would have been pleased that there is now a fairly strong chance of finding this species on the fen, within a short distance of Lincoln city, in most winters. Meanwhile, the common buzzard, which he records as a common resident of woodlands, went through a huge crash because of the use of pesticides and the myxomatosis disease in the staple food, rabbits, but is now expanding its range and numbers at a very good rate in the county (24).

F.L. devotes quite a lot of space to the red kite, 'at one time a common resident in Lincolnshire; now quite extinct.' For once - and one assumes it is because the collection has some pretension to a scientific study - Francis notes a visit to R.N. Sutton-Nelthorpe at Scawby who, in his 'fine' egg collection, has kite eggs taken as follows: from Branston Wood, Newball Wood (1846), Barlings Park (1857), Stainfield Wood (1858), Wragby Wood (1859), and Bullington Wood (1870). Ian Carter tracks the decline of the red kite in Britain from a high in medieval times to serious persecution through the 18th and 19th centuries (25). He includes a record of kite slaughter at the Burley Estate in Rutland between 1807 and 1816 in which 183 birds were dispatched. Since then, there have been several re-introduction schemes, and these have resulted in great success. Kites are now relatively common in parts of Wales, and also in the English Midlands. They have yet to spread significantly into Lincolnshire (26), though the habitat for them certainly exists and there is no intrinsic reason why they should not do so in due course.

Leaving aside the exceedingly rare raptors, F.L. notes that occasional goshawks are shot or trapped (27); and that sparrowhawks are common 'wherever allowed to exist by gamekeepers' (28). Among F.L.'s osprey records is one shot near Hartsholme Lake in 1881. Recent occurrences tend to be on spring and autumn migration, often along the coast, with a tendency for numbers of sightings to increase, and for some birds to be associated with areas that Francis would have known (29).

Among F.L.'s beloved ducks, the one most worthy of note is the gadwall. Francis records this as a 'very rare winter visitor', and states that 'recent records are wanting.' This species is a great story of success. Lorand and Atkin note that an attempt was made to introduce gadwalls into Lincolnshire in 1915, though no details are given; the attempt apparently ended in failure. Breeding probably began in the 1960s, and by the 1980s the species was not uncommon on freshwater (30). In the two decades since, the trend has continued and there would hardly be a lake or pond in the county without a pair of these subtly marked birds.

The gradual diminution in corn-crake numbers seems to be heralded by F.L.'s entry on that bird which though 'not uncommon in some districts' is 'more numerous in some years than others' and 'in some parts of the county it has of late years become unaccountably rare or absent altogether.' This species still occurs as a passage bird, and may sometimes spend the summer, though breeding is not proven (31). In fact, corn-crakes have been adversely affected across the UK by mechanised farming and by the earlier cutting of crops, and only special protection and management now affords the species a breeding slot (32). The same demise has affected the great bustard, which may not have occurred since 1902 (33). F.L. notes that even in his day 'there are not sufficient records to enable one to trace the extermination of the species with any degree of accuracy', and identifies as the last reliable birds females shot at Weelsby and Tetney respectively in 1902 and written about by Caton Haigh (34).

While the bustard was a wold-land species, the crane was a bird of the fens; and this habitat, too, has been eroded. F.L. records a bird shot at North Hykeham, only a short distance from Lincoln and Doddington, but before his time (35). Lorand and Atkin, however, do tell a more encouraging story, with sightings at Humberstone (nine birds, 25th October 1953); Skegness (4th November 1966); Gibraltar Point (4th September 1967, 23rd August 1972); Scotter (December –March 1978-9); and there were other sightings in 1984, 1985, 1987 and 1988. There was a record at Gibraltar Point in 1993. It is not impossible that the crane could become like the little egret, and make a gradual come-back into suitable habitats eventually.

Of the species list offered by Francis Blathwayt, the remaining group of interest is that of the waders, and two species are worthy of particular mention. F.L. listed a little ringed plover on Holbeach Marsh in 1894 but thought that the record was suspect. The story of the spread of this once-rare little wader is known to most birders through the wonderful account in Kenneth Allsop's book (36). Little ringed plovers first bred in Lincolnshire, apparently, in 1950 at Woodhall. Through the seventies one was aware of increasing sightings at gravel pits. By the mid-90s pairs were even present on F.L.'s home territory: Whisby. Even as these words were being written two adults and a juvenile were present on the main pit there.

Finally, Francis regretted the passing of the avocet, a once-common bird of the 'old' fens. Yarrell and John Cordeaux had suggested that the last eggs of avocets taken in the county dated from about 1840; and F.L. thought that the species might turn up on the coast on migration, but 'very rarely'. By the time of Lorand and Atkin, the story had changed little. Yet now the avocet has re-colonised a great deal of the eastern side of England (37) in suitable habitats; and F.L.'s heart would be gladdened that for several years pairs have been breeding at the scrapes created at Gibraltar Point nature reserve. Though it has to be said that not every birder welcomes the avocet: they are noisy and very aggressive not only to other pairs of avocets but to other species of waders, so that they tend to bully other birds away.

As predicted at the beginning of the chapter, this has been a very personal review of F.L.'s list, the emphasis being on birds of particular interest or on places of special importance to Francis. His list, a monumental piece of research, has been the backbone for County Lists of modern times: by Smith and Cornwallis, and by Lorand and Atkin. This is, of itself, not merely an achievement but a mark of excellence. Francis ends his review with some suggestions for how birding in Lincolnshire should be developed; but as he expands on these ideas in his next published work it is best to put these matters on hold for the moment and to consider them in detail later in the chapter.

•

Francis Blathwayt left Lincolnshire in 1916. He was married and had started a family. He had been offered the living of Melbury in Dorset, a small rural parish much on a par with Doddington but closer to his family home at Dyrham, and to Colonel Linley Blathwayt and his family in Batheaston. It was a move he felt impelled to make. Yet he had not quite finished with the birds of his adopted county for the last seventeen years. He was elected the President, for the year 1918, of the Lincolnshire Naturalists' Union. He had accepted the nomination; perhaps he felt he had deserved the honour, for he had started his modest amateur birding career while a curate in the city in 1900 but was now the Revd F.L. Blathwayt MA MBOU (38), and a person of some standing in the Lincoln community and the birding community in general. However – given his personality – it is more likely, not that his thoughts were of self-aggrandisement, but that he had unfinished business. It was a pattern to be repeated later: and for now, he had a message to convey. One of the duties of President was to give an Address. His was close to his heart and he was anxious to deliver it.

The Address appears in the *Transactions* for 1918. It draws together his favourite themes. Its very first words are 'Gilbert White', the first unambiguous indication we have that this, the greatest parson-naturalist, though of the 18th century, may have been a hero of our own parson-naturalist. The similarities are clear. He draws on this mentor to justify a view that watching 'one district' is more valuable, scientifically, than chasing shadows: twitchers take note! It was just this view, so implicit in his published Lincolnshire work, that drew me to his activity in what I now think of as my 'Hartsholme years', described briefly in a previous note.

The Address chooses to review the birds of Lincolnshire, past, present and future. This is apt: so much of F.L.'s writing begins by looking at what is known (the past), relies on his observation (the present), and is prepared to draw lessons from these two strands (the future). His attitude to the past is summed up in this powerful paragraph:

In the days when the vast stretches of fen, the primeval forests between the unenclosed Chalk Wolds and the Oolite Ridge, the expanses of heath, and the sandy warrens of the north west of the county, were all in their pristine glory, very many species of birds inhabited Lincolnshire which have long vanished, or which, if they do occur today, are little more than isolated stragglers, drawn by some conservative impulse to visit the haunts of their remote ancestors.

Among the 'stragglers' are crane, bustard, bittern, black tern, bearded tit, avocet, ruff, black-tailed godwit, buzzard and kite; he is drawing on his County List. F.L. would be less than excited to know, one suspects, that another 'straggler' – the grey-lag goose – has returned as a travesty of its former self; but he would be delighted with the little successes (avocet, ruff), and with the real achievements (buzzard) of modern times. This paragraph is as close to passion as F.L. allows his scientific persona to get; yet there is, within it, a depth of feeling for the losses of the old world – for the missing black terns and the varieties of grebes that once inhabited the fen (39), for the avocets of the Fossdyke, the short-eared owls of Washingborough. He longs for the sight from the old decoys, of duck 'streaming in for eight hours continuously!' and mourns the demise of his nearest decoy at Skellingthorpe.

Francis has a real feel for what we would now call local or 'living' history; it is a very modern concept. He wants to gather the 'old men' and their wisdom before it is all lost: T.H. Roberts of Stainton wood and his keeper; Old Perrin, the wildfowler of Gibraltar Point, now deceased, who once killed sixty terns with one shot from a punt gun (40) that were sold for sixpence a piece to be made into fans; former Presidents of the LNU such as John Cordeaux; and the late F.M. Burton who can recall red kites 'soaring round the Towers of Lincoln Minster!'

Then he wants to learn from the present, by which he means his own seventeen-year sojourn in the Lincoln area. He claims to have watched most assiduously in Lincoln city itself, around Scotton common, and to some extent along the coast. He mourns the cutting of woods at Langworth, Bardney, Nocton, Doddington and Skellingthorpe. He follows his interests by noting the effect on herons in particular. He expresses doubts about the introduced little owl, though – uncharacteristically – does not explain why. He suggests that the three woodpeckers, along with nightingale, garden warbler, lesser whitethroat, grasshopper warbler and wood wren (warbler) are common enough for 'those who know where to search' (41). F.L. notes the presence of corn buntings and yellow wagtails, the latter around the Witham (42). He notes also that whinchats, once common, have now disappeared for no known cause (43). He identifies large winter flocks of bramblings and tree sparrows, with which he would have been familiar from his wanderings in the Hartsholme area and elsewhere (44). He rehearses his observations of crossbills at Hartsholme and the birds of the ballast pit, grebes and his beloved duck species. He also notes flocks of geese – probably pink-feet – migrating across the city, a phenomenon that has continued to this day, though less frequent than formerly.

So he moves territory to the Scotton area. This survey is the result of 'many a happy day' that he has spent there. Here are the black-headed gulls discussed earlier, and the many duck species he is so fond of. Here is 'truly a delight for the naturalist' as he watches wheatear and whinchat, short-eared owl and curlew, nightjar and rough-legged buzzard. Here the green sandpiper passes through and black grouse are occasionally seen. A 'friend' has found the nest of the garganey, and another 'friend' had also discovered its eggs. There is just a hint here of the social side of birding; and though the 'warping' of this area drains the land, the result is not all bad as the resultant mud attracts ducks and gulls and waders.

So he moves his attention to the coast, where there are no cliffs to attract breeding sea-birds; but he knows of colonies or nests of ringed plovers, redshanks and lesser (little) terns – and even a secret place with a common tern pair or two. He has seen 'the knots rising like a cloud of smoke' and 'other waders in dense flights', while 'the hedges near the coast are perhaps full of travelling birds such as blackbirds, robins [and] goldcrests.' He has seen the snow buntings, shore-larks and twites on the 'fitties', that still draw annual swathes of birders (45). Scoters and wigeons colonise the winter seas, and in-coming migrants may include lapwings and skylarks and hooded crows.

This review captures the essence of the places F.L. describes; this is his nostalgic review of Lincolnshire birding before he finally quits the local stage. It has the ring of authenticity and the hall-mark of experience about it. People and places are missed now he has gone. There are rich sights and sounds stored in the memory. Yet he is not a man for public emotion. Rather, he must push forward with all his scientific detachment to consider the future, even if he himself is not directly a part of it.

•

The final part of F.L.'s Address is the most 'modernist' of the three sections, for the backward look was more characteristic of the era from which he emanated. For F.L., however, it is the future that holds out the prospects of improved scholarship. Not that this future-gazing is devoid of its past roots. So his first recommendation for the future is to gather up the old records, from men who had watched and worked in the habitats of Lincolnshire, and who knew the changes and chances of bird distribution. He urges the LNU membership:

First, to gather up before it is too late, by word of mouth, from very old fowlers, gamekeepers, punt-gunners or decoymen, reminiscences of the past, and to publish the results...

This is an entirely modern aspiration, and one that now fires organisations such as the BBC history section. And for once – and it is the only time in the collection of Lincolnshire articles that we have reviewed – he refers obliquely to his clergy status:

And while gathering up the past, it should not be forgotten that old Churchwardens' Accounts often contain records of the payment of money for 'vermin' such as kites and buzzards. These records, when hunted out, should be printed and published, as they throw much light on the abundance and distribution of the large birds of prey...

Then there is the need to preserve more effectively what now exists but is under pressure – a conservation theme that has, again, a thoroughly modern ring, and which we still action erratically and sometimes ineffectually:

...It is a duty to guard and preserve carefully the few remaining examples of locally vanishing species. For instance, the colonies of lesser terns on the coast should never be molested; keepers should have strict orders to refrain from shooting the few hobbies which still breed in the larger woodlands.

And he is not convinced by legal protection measures:

The Wild Birds' Protection Acts are often nearly a dead letter, so those who have it in their power should do all they can to protect and encourage any species which shows signs of re-colonising the haunts of its ancestors – for instance the hen harrier...

This is powerful rhetoric, aimed at local landowners (and likely to offend), and also at politicians. From his usual scientific, almost academic, self as a writer, F.L. now has a platform and one that may receive through publication a wider audience than those sitting before him as he speaks. His intention is to use it.

So he moves to his final cluster of issues, that deal with 'fresh fields of observation' – again, not without a hint of controversy aimed this time perhaps at the local birding establishment (46):

The knowledge of the distribution of birds in the county is still far from perfect. Observers, or at any rate recorders, are lamentably few for so large an area of nearly a million and three-quarter acres, so that it is quite likely that many surprises are in store for the ardent ornithologist of the future. We want to know more of the comings and goings of birds in the Wash area...

Having set the scene, he provides an agenda. Scientist that he is, he lays out the research questions for the next generation who take up the mantle. Here are his priority fields for research:

- What are the respective ranges of marsh and willow tits? (47)

- Does the marsh warbler occur? (F.L. thinks he has discovered one at Washingborough) (48)

- Why have the quail and corn-crake become much rarer as nesting species? (49)

- What are the movements of the continental races of well-known birds (robin, song thrush, goldcrest, titmice, rock pipit, woodpigeon and others) and how do they relate to the status of native birds of their species? (50)

So he concludes:

There is ample work for the future. The distribution, wanderings, increasings, and decreasings of the birds of Lincolnshire are still very imperfectly known and recorded, and if future workers in this fascinating study get as much pleasure as the writer has received from his seventeen years' observation of the birds of the county, those future workers will be abundantly rewarded for their labour of love.

So ends F.L.'s public connection with Lincolnshire. It is realistic yet still optimistic, for it is based on a spirit of scientific enquiry. His views are clear and powerful, and they don't toady to those with influence at the expense of the birds (51). Ordinary people, even those who do not wholly support his or the LNU's aims, can be useful and are to be respected for their knowledge. He betrays his own philosophy: there is a kind of 'protestant work ethic' about his conception of birding. There is 'work' to be done, and it is a 'labour of love'; some of that labour is illustrated in the next chapter, through extracts from his bird diaries of the period.

To the end he has resisted any suspicion of sermonising: instead he has set an agenda which is both ornithological and political. In all of this he has anticipated the voice of modern conservationists.

NOTES TO CHAPTER 8

1.   These 'greats' include Pennant, Cordeaux, G.H. Caton Haigh, and an active contemporary, M. Peacock.

2.   Today's convention would, of course, require him to quote every source; but we are dealing with the custom of the time. The fact that he is so assiduous in drawing up a bibliography is a tribute to his 'scientific method.'

3.   See chapter 5.

4.   F.L.'s works are listed in Appendix 1. Copies of this article (and others) from the *Transactions* are available from the British Library via local library services.

5.   Saunders, H. (1907) *List of British Birds.*

6.   Smith and Cornwallis, page 120; Lorand and Atkin, p 184.

7.   Smith and Cornwallis (p 117) indicate that Cordeaux heard this species at Tetney on 28th July 1897, and that there had been a previous sighting some years before.

8.   I was a volunteer warden at Burton when this bird put in its appearance. At the time my son made a recording of the song put out by this bird, using a portable tape-recorder and a parabolic reflector.

9.   Smith and Cornwallis, p 125. The exception was ' a small party seen near Tetney Lock on October 30th 1942.'

10.   Lorand and Atkin, page 194. My own observation of my first great grey shrike in Lincolnshire (8th December 1974) was seminal in my interest in Hartsholme Park and in the formation of EMBSC. Another sighting there was reported in March 1977 but not confirmed. A more recent local bird was at Dunston, on the Lincoln cliff, on 3rd January 2003.

11.   Jake Wildmann's 'Wild Ways: December 2003' www.sourceuk.net .

12.   The paucity of numbers in the country annually is confirmed by the *Wintering Atlas.* This survey (covering the winters 1981-4) recorded great greys in 6% of all 10km squares, giving a total of 229 birds present in mainland Britain and the Channel Islands, well distributed

throughout coastal and, more commonly, inland sites, and all except ten sites with only a single bird (the remainder having two birds present). So this is very much a 'loner' species. Oddly, the *Wintering Atlas* (pp 361-2) also records that deciduous trees, as opposed to conifers, are favoured.

13.   Lorand and Atkin (p 164) note: one remarkable record was of a bird that appeared during a freak snow-storm at Kirton in Lindsey on 3rd June 1975.

14.   For example, while the new Lincoln University site, adjacent to the Brayford pool and railway line into Lincoln Central station, was being developed there were many rough corners that sprouted weeds which the birds visited. Regrettably, this is a species that may be affected adversely by our obsession with tidiness. In town parks and along verges, for example, the maintenance staff eliminate anything that might be considered to destroy the neatness of formal planting. Thus they remove (albeit without malice) the very items that birds like goldfinches need. Remonstrations with the local authorities, even in today's enlightened times, produce a sense of wonder at the complainer's eccentricity!

15.   During EMBSC's wardening and census activities at Hartsholme 1975-1980 siskins were regular winter visitors. Small groups could be relied on during December-January in the alders adjacent to the boathouse and at the entrance to the narrow stream bank on the east side. Lorand and Atkin (p 202) claim the largest county flock to have been in 1971, with 300 birds at Twigmoor – the largest Hartsholme flock was about seventy birds. The species has become more common in many places, and the county even has some breeding records: Hartsholme 1973, and Snipe Dales in 1985 and 1986. Siskins have adapted to taking food from garden bird feeders, too. My most confiding Lincoln sighting was of a flock of birds feeding on a sapling silver birch, barely above head high, in a two-metre square plot, in the middle of the car park at Homebase on the trading estate at the University roundabout, while shoppers loaded their car boots with pots of Dulux and half-price workbenches (02.01.97).

16.   The playingfield adjacent to my property in North Hykeham is bordered in part by flowering cherries. Hawfinches eat the kernels of cherries by cracking the stones with their powerful bills. Allegedly, the hawfinch is the only bird that is capable of doing this (most others tear off the flesh and discard the stone, and it is common to see blackbirds do this, and I suspect greenfinches do also). Scattered throughout my garden are neatly halved cherry stones, and the question remains: Are they evidence of local hawfinches? After ten years of watching, I have still to see a hawfinch in the locality! Yet this would seem to be the implication of the picture in Bang, P. and Dahlstrom, P. (1974) *Collins Guide to Animal Tracks and Signs* London: Collins, page 127; and of the statement by the guru of modern birding Ian Newton that 'the presence of split stones…of cherry beneath the trees is a sure sign of these birds…' (Newton, I. 1972 *Finches* London: Collins, New Naturalist, p 62). My only alternative explanation is that the locally abundant greenfinches have learned the art, and there is no evidence whatsoever for this.

17.   According to Lorand and Atkin (p 158), there were nests at Woodhall in 1898 and Haverholme in 1902, this last being recorded in Blathwayt's list. There have been other attempts by the species to breed in Lincolnshire, most notably at Skellingthorpe, just a mile or two from Doddington Rectory, but not until 1956. Birds do passage through the county, and one ringing recovery originated in Thetford.

18.   Every good birder knows the value of being *au fait* with bird song; and Blathwayt records, we have seen, how he found a number of species such as reed warblers by listening rather than observing. However, less experienced birders, if only because of lack of familiarity with the species, may not notice a specific song among others in the maelstrom of spring

sound. The following experience is worth recounting: Some years ago (c. 1994) I was doing some work on the education of minorities, and the local Travellers' Unit of the education authority provided some data and offered me a video of inter iews with Romany people about their customs and culture. As I sat and played through the video, on which an elderly Romany gentleman was speaking outside his caravan, I became aware of the fluting notes of a woodlark in the background. I re-viewed the tape to check; and I was certain. So I rang the Travellers' Unit and asked who had made the tape and where it was shot. The end of this investigation identified a traveller site about a mile from the centre of Gainsborough. So in the previous summer, anyway, there was at least one woodlark apparently holding a territory there!

19.   Tennyson's sensitivity to nature in general and birds in particular probably appealed to Francis. Elsewhere, Tennyson calls the kingfisher the 'secret splendour of the brooks'; and nowhere is Tennyson's eye and ear for wildlife better captured than in a published talk by Sir Charles Tennyson (1965, 'Bird and Beast in Tennyson' *The Veterinary Record* (77), 49 pp 1466-1473).

20.   BTO News no. 126 May 1983 (page 1) reports the 1981-2 kingfisher crash, also following hard weather – a 64% drop nationally, based on figures from the 1982 Waterways Bird Survey.

21.   This building has been renovated recently and is now the University of Lincoln's Learning Resources facility. My most recent sighting of a kingfisher on the drain here was on 5th March 2005.

22.   Lorand and Atkin p 97.

23.   Op.cit. p 98, quoting the Revd E. Elmhirst in *The Field*. The eighteen birds were in the Wash area.

24.   Smith and Cornwallis, writing in the mid-fifties called the common buzzard 'a scarce and somewhat irregular passage migrant on the coast and inland...occasional winter visitor' (page 69). In the 1980s Lorand and Atkin (p 100) retreat to 'very scarce' but note a few summer records. Now it is possible to see common buzzards on both wold and fen, and quartering farmland where there are suitable stands of woods nearby.

25.   Carter, I. (2001) *The Red Kite* Chelmsford: Arlequin Press.

26.   Smith and Cornwallis give 'no records during the present century'; Lorand and Atkin call it a 'very rare vagrant' of continental origin. The situation is likely to change. The Lincolnshire Bird Club's *Lincolnshire Bird Report 1993* listed (p 30) only one sighting for that year but asserted that red kite sightings had numbered at least twenty-seven birds between 1969-92. A single bird was picked up in binoculars making its way from north of Lincoln, on a ESE course, over Branston Booths, crossing the Bardney Road, and moving on out of sight over the Nocton fen towards Dunston on 21st September 1997.

27.   Lorand and Atkin suggest seventeen records from 1955 to their own publication date, 1989. The picture may be slightly more rosy now, though the *Lincolnshire Bird Report 1993* can cite only two examples.

28.   The definitive study of the sparrowhawk is: Newton, I. (1986) *The Sparrowhawk* Calton: T & A D Poyser. He charts the demise of the species during the 1960s from organo-chlorine pesticides, as well as studying other factors (such as weather) in its success rates. What can be stated categorically is that the species has now recovered and even exceeded its former

numbers, and in the Lincoln area is sufficiently common that individual birds can be seen thermalling over the city and surrounding areas on a regular basis, and many garden owners are treated to the sight of adults capturing small birds and tearing them apart on a suitable post within a few yards of house windows.

29.   For example, according to *Lincolnshire Bird Report 1993*, a bird was discovered at Whisby on 26th April of that year, and one at Boultham Mere on 11th May. Like kites, ospreys are subject to re-introduction schemes, the closest to Lincoln being at Rutland Water (Everett, M. and Cocker, M. 2002 'Ospreys in the UK' *Birds* Winter 2002, pp 32-38). Local reports list a sighting for 1st May 2005 again at Whisby: 'Lincoln Area News', in the Lincolnshire Wildlife Trust mailing for that date).

30.   Op. cit. pp 85-6 gives a fuller account, and the *Lincolnshire Bird Report 1993* records a high of 66 birds at Swanholme.

31.   Lorand and Atkin (pp 105-6) seem rather more optimistic about this species than may seem justified.

32.   Corncrakes are being actively assisted by the RSPB in Fermanagh, Tiree and the Uists.

33.   Lorand and Atkin (p 108) follow Blathwayt on this. There is currently a plan to re-introduce this species into the fens of Cambridgeshire. However, elsewhere in Europe, reservoir schemes are threatening this species: 'Spain's damaging water plan' *Birds* Spring 2004 page 74.

34.   On July 20th 1869 according to *The Zoologist* 1869, p 1842; but a later victim of the gun was at Spalding 25th October 1882, again noted in *The Zoologist* of that year, p 463.

35.   *Lincolnshire Bird Report 1993*, page 35; records one bird at Gibraltar Point.

36.   Allsop, K. (1962 edn) *Adventure Lit their Star* London: Macdonald. This tells the story of the first successful breeding by little ringed plovers in modern times (1938), and the 1962 edition of the book has up-dated material on the growth of success rates for this bird.

37.   Piotrowski, S. (2003) *The Birds of Suffolk* London: Christopher Helm, page 139, rightly asserts that the avocet 'has a special claim in the county's [i.e. Suffolk's] natural history.' It was here that the bird returned – to Minsmere and Havergate – after more than a hundred years of absence, during WWII. Build-up of numbers at Minsmere took place from about 1963; by 1976 there were 50 pairs there and 90 at Havergate. Since 1976 birds have also over-wintered; there can be several hundred birds on the Rivers Alde and Ore; highest counts reach four figures. Birds have been noted at inland sites as numbers have built; and there has been a spread into the rest of East Anglia. In fact, avocets have been nesting in the Suffolk area since the 1940s, anyway: there is even a report of this by Philip Brown in *Bird Notes* 'Avocets in East Anglia' vol xxiii no. 5, pp 155-7.

38.   It is claimed in his obituary that F.L. 'was proud' to have been a Member of the British Ornithologists' Union for fifty years, which would mean that he was admitted by 1903. I have tried to verify this information and to establish more about the BOU in F.L.'s day by contacting the BOU, now based in an Oxford University department. Sadly, the BOU was unable to supply any information, the only organisation I contacted unable even to manage the courtesy of a response.

39.   He quotes Camden's *Britannia*, 1806, enlarged by Gough, on this issue.

40. The point of the story is not to glorify the killing but to illustrate the sheer volume of birds, the bio-mass as we would now say.

41. Grasshopper warblers are cryptic birds and may be more frequent than the casual birder might suppose; though it is some years since I have found them in the vicinity of the city. There was a report of several at Whisby in 2005. Whisby still hosts lesser whitethroats and nightingales, as well as garden warblers, and the occasional grasshopper warbler. Nightingales also turned up at Hartsholme on a number of occasions and held territories between 1975 and 1980. But wood warblers are now a very scarce commodity in Lincolnshire.

42. My property faces down a long slope to the Witham valley over a playing field where, in the 1980s, yellow wagtails were common. Their numbers in the immediate area have definitely reduced, though they can still be found along the Trent valley and on the fens. Local reduction is almost certainly the result of the over-tidying of the grassland and verges by enthusiastic but ecologically insensitive employees of the local council and other official bodies. The loss of water meadows is crucial as farming methods change.

43. The causes attributed by Marchant *et al* are several, and may have been creeping in when F.L. was writing (Marchant, J., Hudson, R., Carter, S. and Whittington, P. 1990 *Population Trends in British Breeding Birds* Tring: BTO). These include the loss of good habitat (neglected pastures with small hawthorns), opening up of more land to intensive arable agriculture, the spread of too dense scrub following the myxomatosis outbreaks, the use of chemicals, and the increasing disturbance of roadside verges (p 155).

44. The last big flocks of these species in the areas around Lincoln that F.L. would have known probably date to around 1976 when both the fields around Burton and the old Skellingthorpe Airfield held good numbers from time to time.

45. The 'fitties' are the areas of mud flat, often far out, where the low sea plants provide a living for these ground-feeders. The Gibraltar Point and Horseshoe Point areas still hold important areas for twites in winter.

46. F.L. generated the very first County List for Lincolnshire, as we have seen. The LNU took on up-dating this task through the medium of Annual Bird Reports until the mid-1980s. I cannot comment on the politics that then assailed Lincolnshire birding, but the task of compiling the annual lists moved from LNU to the Lincolnshire Bird Club. For a number of years (until 1996) the effort was sustained. Since then, written data have not been produced annually. In a personal communication (e-mail 06.05.05) the present County Recorder up-dates the situation thus: '...through sheer volume of records and lack of volunteers no reports have been published since 1996. We are currently beavering away to try to remedy this and are working on 1997-2000. All subsequent years are now computerised, approx. 30,000 [sightings] a year. We regularly supply data-base information...We also have in preparation a Lincolnshire Atlas.' This mirrors F.L.'s fears about county recording; and doubtless he would note with regret that counties adjacent, such as Norfolk and Suffolk, can produce a glossy, book-style Annual Report each year that is highly acclaimed. Each has produced a book, *Birds of Norfolk* and *Birds of Suffolk*, in substantial published form (even these have sometimes been up-dated several times). Lincolnshire remains a poor relation despite the toil of the few. Without wishing to carp, neither the Smith and Cornwallis volume nor that of Lorand and Atkin compare to the East Anglian outputs. Even the restrained *British Birds* (vol xli) claims: 'ornithologists in Lincolnshire are either relatively fewer or less well-organised than in many parts of England. The present publication (i.e. *LNU Transactions)* includes a section on ornithology, but it hardly achieves the status of a proper County Bird Report'. It was a situation F.L. would have recognised when he wrote in *Transactions:* '...it is *much* to be regretted that so few bird observers seem to exist

in the county. Our President is a tower of strength but I know scarcely any other observers who keep and publish records and very few members of the LNU send me bird reports' (volume 2, 1912). This may be because of the apparent characteristic retentiveness of natives of the county, noted also elsewhere. F.L. would, I am certain, also deplore another trend in modern birding: that of élitism (and this is NOT a comment on Lincolnshire's situation specifically) – where only the in-group have county records accepted, however questionable, and good records from 'outsiders' are rejected, which in turn leads to fewer records being submitted. The cause of science is best served by completeness as well as accuracy. My own view is that the whole system of county recording nation-wide probably needs a degree of overhaul at a time when more birders and more sightings exist than ever before, and communication is better, but the wheels of acceptance grind, it seems, ever more slowly. Nor does one have to look further than the many web-sites for twitchers and others, for example, to see one result of the problem; where sightings are simply added daily and not always on the basis of any substantial evidence.

47.   In his chapters on the marsh and willow tits, Christopher Perrins (1979 *British Tits* London: Collins New Naturalist) outlines some of the problems, which include the difficulty that less experienced birders have in distinguishing these two birds by sight, and even by sound though this is more reliable. On balance, marsh tits prefer deciduous woodland, and willow tits are at home in conifers, but there is much overlap between the species.

48.   Marsh warblers have always been occasional visitors in very tiny numbers, and not in every year by any means. The F.L. dream of these birds establishing themselves has not been realised. A few turn up on the coast, and inland records include individuals at Bardney (1964) and Ancaster (1966) (Lorand and Atkin pp 177-8).

49.   The issues regarding corn-crake numbers have been discussed earlier, and it is probable that similar factors relate also to quails.

50.   This question is really too advanced for those of F.L.'s generation to tackle with any substance. Though Gilbert White wrote to Pennant to compare migration in one location and another, it was not until the invention of radar that studies of bird movements entered a truly modern phase and these questions could be addressed with certainty. This story is told compellingly in Garth Christian's (1961) *Down the Long Wind* (London: Newnes), chapter 5 in particular. Ringing helped, of course, and Annual Reports from the counties now include ringing recoveries, though often these are very sparse and the pictures they paint somewhat ambiguous. This is an area where there are still huge gaps in ornithological knowledge.

51.   Though not alone, Lincolnshire has its ups and downs in terms of attitudes to conservation. Sir Dudley Stamp (1969 *Nature Conservation in Britain* London: Collins New Naturalist, p 150) rejoiced that Lincolnshire had 'Gibraltar Point...the first local nature reserve to be declared in England (1952).' But attitudes are by no means universally positive to the conservation movement. John Sheail (1976 *Nature in Trust: The history of nature conservation in Britain* Glasgow: Blackie, pp 222-3) tells the salutary tale of Waddingham Common in 1963. 'The site was first proposed as a nature reserve in the early 1940s as the only surviving example of a peat bog overlying limestone in Lincolnshire. It contained Grass of Parnassus...and other wetland species. The Nature Conservancy scheduled the site in 1951, and the Lincolnshire Naturalists' Trust began to negotiate a nature reserve agreement with the parish council when a local farmer to everyone's surprise, proved he owned the common. He decided to plough up the site, and the Nature Conservancy first learned of the threat to the wildlife when the Ministry of Agriculture informed it of an application from the farmer for a grant of £12 an acre towards the cost of reclamation...[So here was] the anomalous situation where one government body scheduled the site for protection and another used public funds to destroy it.' If ever there was a sorry tale, this has to be it.

CHAPTER 9
THE BIRD DIARIES
The Lincolnshire Years

To sustain keeping a diary for well over half a century is a major achievement and a measure of tenacity, yet this is what F.L. did. His bird notebooks were written up with hardly a hiatus from youth (1893) into old age. Now bound, courtesy of a benefactor, and housed in the Dorchester museum, they run to 22 volumes of unequal size and thickness.

To handle these volumes is to be tied by touch to the man: there can be no doubt that they were his treasured possessions. Yet they are workbooks: always systematic, sometimes neat, never showy. For our present purposes those that deal with the Lincolnshire years are of most interest, though a preliminary word or two generally about the diaries and some observations on the earliest volumes are in order.

Each diary has a title page indicating that the volume contains the bird records of F.L. Blathwayt, though the wording varies from one volume to another. For example, in volume 2 the front page is annotated: 1899 Natural History Annals, Saltaire, Weston-super-Mare.

The dated entries fall to the right-hand pages; and the left-hand sheet is left for notes, corrections, addenda, and later reflection. Indeed, in one diary F.L. actually explains this system, which evolved early in the recording process; and also that the left-hand pages contain natural history notes that are not bird-related. Often there are several days between entries; but at times recording occurs on a daily basis (e.g. during some of the Doddington years when he is noting sightings in the garden) though entries may be minimal – a few bird species listed, and a location, against a date – the things he might have seen through his study window. Entries are sustained when he goes on vacation to other locations. At the back of some notebooks he begins to draw up notes that later form systematic lists for specific areas. In one volume over seventy of the entries that made up part of the 'Birds of Somerset' chapter in the *Victoria County History* are drafted.

Here and there, the diaries contain sustained prose accounts of particular sightings. These are often recognisable as elements that have been worked up later into published articles: for example, the passage describing the behaviour of the great crested grebes on the Lincoln ballast pits, previously quoted, appears in similar form in the appropriate diary, as does his record of snipe drumming.

Some entries have crosses against them, usually in blue crayon; and though it is hard to be certain, these crosses seem to be the work of F.L. himself, indicating passages of relevance to articles in hand or lists that are extant in print (one initialled annotation is also in blue crayon).

Loose between the pages are various cuttings taken from local newspapers; a couple record an unidentified bird (heron or cormorant) that perched on the towers of Lincoln cathedral and led to much local speculation, one describes the auction of land in the Skellingthorpe area. There are some pieces of scrap paper with pencilled notes on them in F.L.'s hand. One includes notes about the occurrence of geese. Another is the corner of a piece of notepaper with an embossed address on it: 1 Stonefield Avenue, Lincoln, today a semi detached house in a private road near the Stonebow arch (1).

When Francis uses the left-hand pages to correct or add to an entry, he makes the note and then initials it, as if the diary were already a public document and he was certifying the authenticity of his addendum, which may be in pencil. The scientist is looking over the shoulder of the diarist, extracting every last molecule of accuracy from the records.

In a previous chapter it was noted that, when Francis made entries in the School Log at Doddington, during the period around 1914-6 his writing deteriorated. The same phenomenon is visible in the bird diaries, too. Indeed, sometimes the words are too obscure to read (here this is indicated with >> in the text). The reason for this deterioration is a matter for speculation. Since he did not lose his acuity of vision, perhaps we must assume a condition such as arthritis in the hands. The later diaries are not as badly affected as those about this date, but when he is afflicted in this way the letters are either very small or very large, and they are only partly formed so that they give the impression almost of short-hand.

The notes are made in plain, ruled, notebooks not in pre-formatted logs. Maybe the idea to keep such a record was his own invention, or maybe he was given the first notebook as a youngster and it seemed an opportune way to use it. Either way, the first volume is dated 1st January 1893 (he is eighteen) and it begins with a flyleaf indicating his address as Walney House, Herefordshire. The first entry consists of a map of the Bromyard area, in intense detail and annotated in singularly minute writing. The entry for this first date is modest: including carrion crow, blue titmouse (sic) and redwing. He also surveys other forms of wildlife than birds: voles, moths, butterflies and wasps do not escape attention and record, including Latin names. An undated entry in April 1893 lists two 'sea-gulls' flying over the garden – his first interest in gulls. He records a pair of lesser spotted woodpeckers, and even at this early stage there is then a footnote about suspected breeding signed 'FLB'.

These early diaries show a wide-ranging interest in natural history: long lists of moths found, complete with Latin names and gender; and also items like fossils. The early diaries have been worked over later, and there are corrections made in the light of increasing knowledge and experience. His interest in 'listing' birds in relation to events such as migration starts early. By 1896 he is recording his earliest dates for migrants as follows:

Chiffchaff	March 23	Frome Bank
Willow wren	April 10	Edwin woods
Swallow	April 13	Downs
Grasshopper warbler	April 15	Avenbury
Tree pipit	April 16	Bromyard
Cuckoo	April 19	Edwin woods
Blackcap	April 19	Hardwick
Redstart	April 22	Frome Bank
Greater whitethroat	April 22	Frome Bank
Sand martin	April 23	Knightford Bridge
Nightingale	April 23	Oakerdine (?)
Lesser whitethroat	May 1	Frome Bank
House Martin	May 1	Frome Bank
Swift	May 2	Hereford House
Whinchat	May 5	near Edwin woods

These 'earliest date' migrant records are sustained over time, Francis using the fly-leaves and end-papers of the diary to make the list up for various locations including Doddington until 1910 (2). In volume 2, on November 28th 1899, there is the first evidence of his use of the trade-mark field glasses as he watches Scaup through them at Sand Bay, Somerset. Two days later he returns to the spot and writes his first extended descriptive note, on the identification and behaviour of these birds.

From volume 3 to volume 9 the diaries record F.L.'s observations while curate in Lincoln city and then during his occupancy of the Rectory at Doddington, 1900-1909 and 1909-1916 respectively. The main intention of this chapter is to trawl the diaries of these periods for entries that augment the picture we have built up of F.L. as a Lincoln-based birder, and about the birds that he watched in the city and county. This intention is pursued thematically rather than chronologically.

●

Paramount, perhaps, throughout the diaries of the period is his interest in heronries, and his study of the heron mirrors that of other long-term interests and thus serves as an example of this element of his work. Typical of the heronry entries is the following:

10th March 1908…Biked over to Skellingthorpe Wood to see the heronry. Nests built at the Saxilby end of the wood near a rookery. I counted about twelve nests and saw about seven or eight birds. I should think there are about six pairs nesting; possibly I did not see all the nests as they are rather scattered. Birds certainly sitting. I watched two back to the nests and they settled down evidently on eggs. On another nest two birds were standing upright. These birds moved within the last two years or so from the far end of the wood near the keeper's cottage. They have also diminished in numbers.

This entry has most of the Blathwayt trade-marks in relation to herons and those other species he watched consistently over time. It shows persistence in tracking the fortunes of the colony; it compares and contrasts other seasons; it involves careful observation of behaviour and counting; it is guarded in making judgements with the use of phrases like 'evidently', but notes what is 'certainly' the case. The style is clipped and economical, almost but not quite in note-form. Yet through all the thoroughness and detail oozes a genuine 'feel' for the event: every birder can picture the scene precisely, can empathise with the experience, in his or her mind's eye stands under F.L.'s trees.

This same note on the heronry has, too, a typical Blathwayt postscript. The Revd Cole (a former Rector of Doddington who had moved to a nearby parish) informs him that herons had dwelt 'from time immemorial' in Old Hagg wood which joins the Skellingthorpe wood to the south. F.L. concludes that 'the colony has doubtless shifted quarters in these old woodlands'; and he speculates 'From Old Hagg perhaps about 1896 when a new railway was cut through the wood.' Francis always seeks out local sources of information from those whose opinions he respects.

His persistence in tracking species is also a physical persistence:

17th March 1908…4 degrees of frost. By bike to heronry in Haverholme wood [Sleaford].

He goes on to note:

Counted 21 nests and saw numbers of old birds. Sitting had evidently commenced. The gale of 22nd February had blown down the old nests, so the nests I saw must have been new. If so, there are 21 pairs in the heronry. The usual number is about eighteen pairs…

In 1908 tracking heronries is well under way, and on 2nd April he checks out an alleged site of a heronry at Swanpool, near Lincoln and finds 'no sign' of it. 8th April sees him back in Skellingthorpe wood, this time with Sylvia (see below) where they hear the cries of the young in the nest. The next year continues the quest on 2nd February at Top Hill wood near Louth where workers tell him that:

Last season herons were much shot at and disturbed with the object of driving them away as they took trout from the >> stream. This heronry apparently originally came from Muckton wood…

There is a nice touch in an entry dated 21st March 1911, where F.L. sketches a map of the Skellingthorpe Big Wood, 'called on the map West Wood'. He locates each heronry with a cross. There are ten nests marked, and there is an adjacent rookery shown.

Three years later, on 26th March 1914, he is still patrolling the Big Wood and counting herons' nests, though the article on Lincolnshire heronries (described earlier) which triggered this research has been published for some years: his interest is intrinsic and scientific, not merely public. On this occasion there were 'noisy young and egg shells below the trees'. He comments: 'Herons do not build where the undergrowth is cut down.'

The entry for the following spring is more detailed, with nice touches that bring it alive:

21st April 1915 …about 20 pairs were breeding in the western plantation…most of the nests appeared to have young birds in them and these were very noisy and kept 'chattering'. The parent birds were sitting close (on eggs or newly hatched young) and did not leave when I struck the tree with a stick. Most of the nests were in trees (oak) not far from each other but a few were some distance off the main colony. Several trees had two nests in them but none more, I think. The rooks whose nesting trees a little to the north have been felled during the last winter had now invaded the heronry and I saw a heron sitting on his (sic) nest with two rooks in the same tree. The birds chase each other about a bit but on the whole seem to agree.

His last annual survey in the Doddington woodlands took place in 1916 and he found (on 13th March) a few nests in the district but the trees formerly occupied by herons in the Skellingthorpe Big Wood had been felled. The issue is recorded as a fact, without emotion. But then on 13th April is a final little triumph, recorded equally factually:

Went to Skellingthorpe Big Wood in the morning. The herons are still nesting in the western plantation in a long rather narrow strip of trees left by the woodcutters about a quarter of a mile long running east/west to the south of the main ride…I counted about twelve or thirteen nests which appeared to be tenanted…there were two herons' nests in one tree and about 200 rooks' nests.

One can't help wondering if he had had a word in somebody's ear, but that is merely speculation!

Another long-term interest is the black-headed gull, hardly a favourite of today's birders, but one F.L. was intrigued by from an early stage in his birding. Earlier the first (1893) reference to this species ('two sea-gulls' flying over the garden) was quoted; and he watches flocks of fifty to a hundred come in off the sea in January 1900 at Berrow. By May of that year he is in Lincoln and on May 21st there is the first mention in the diaries of the gull colony at Scotton. A note on a left-hand page indicates that he had investigated the black-heads' nests. One had six eggs in it, which he concludes was the result of two females laying in one nest. His interest is sustained throughout, though without the lengthy descriptions one might have imagined, given the fascinating paper on this species which he published in 1909.

Likewise, his interest in ducks and decoys is maintained throughout the diaries; in any suitable location, such as the ballast pits or by the coast, he records the species seen and the numbers. He has less good fortune with decoys than with the ducks themselves as the following entry (24.1.16) shows:

Went to look for South Carlton duck decoy. Not very clearly defined. A swampy pool between the main and catchwater drain. Close to the east bank of the Cormer(?) a little to the west of the decoy cottage, still inhabited. Saw there two or three mallard flying over...

Then there is a later marginal note:

This NOT the decoy but a swampy marsh.

Again, he records (2.12.14):

Revd Canon R.E.G. Cole, late [he means 'former'] Rector of Doddington...told me that he cannot remember the Skellingthorpe duck decoy ever being worked but his father (1837-61) who was Rector before him told him that thousands of duck used to be taken. He thinks that the rent was raised and the man who rented it gave it up in consequence.

F.L.'s willingness to be critical of his own sightings or activities is compounded only by equal willingness to test the soundness of the reports of others. After a detailed set of his own observations of putative marsh warblers (see below) he returns to the entry and notes:

I do not consider it proved that these birds were examples of *A. palustris.* I visited the withy bed again today and saw nothing of the bird...some undoubted reed warblers were nesting.

He is equally severe on poor Spencer (whoever he was!) on 11th July 1900:

Spencer saw two birds on the ballast pits which he thought were black terns. (I expect they were the young of *L. ridibundus*).

But when F.L. does decide to investigate a species or an aspect of bird behaviour in some depth, he is able to add to his scientific scepticism and his commitment to 'integrity and truth' another dimension – that of detailed and captivating descriptive prose. Several of these passages have been quoted already from his published works; but it worth looking at others from the diaries that, as far as I am aware, have no public dimension. The first is the incident of the marsh warblers:

27th July 1901...I found a pair of birds with nest and 4 young in a thick withy bed opposite Washingborough. Vegetation was very thick including meadow sweet, rose-bay willow-herb and wild raspberry. I am inclined to think the birds were marsh warblers. I did not hear the song but the alarm note was a short, harsh rattle, lower in pitch than that of a sedge warbler. The birds appeared paler than the reed warblers and the legs were flesh or flesh/brown coloured. Their throats were white and their flanks were tinged with sulphur colour, darker in one of the birds, presumably the male. The female bird was remarkably tame coming sometimes within a few feet of me as I stood near the nest. This latter was built on a raspberry cane of which one young shoot was woven into the nest and the cane pierced the >>. Another (nest) was similarly placed, which had apparently been robbed.

F.L. would have been keen to substantiate this observation because the marsh warbler had not been recorded in Lincolnshire, though it had bred spasmodically in other counties (3). It is hard to separate from the reed warbler unless one can count primary feathers in the hand (4), or one is sure of the differences of call; and F.L.'s description is by no means impossible for the species. But we have noted earlier in the chapter he is his own harshest critic. Though he goes back to try to confirm his suspicion he concludes that he does 'not consider it proved' that these birds are the coveted marsh warblers: it is just one of those tantalising open verdicts that birders have to settle for.

Some consolation for this disappointment may have come early in the next year, after a mammoth cycle ride, when the records 'the first shorelarks I had seen' and describes their habits in some detail and with perception:

9th January 1902…Rode from Lincoln to Saltfleet via Louth. The wind SW and strong. Saw a number of hooded crows on the way. I saw three Shorelark together sheltering under the sand dunes at Saltfleet. One seemed to be an adult male, the other 2 females or immatures. They were remarkably tame and came within a few yards of me as I sat on the sand dunes and when alarmed flew only a short distance and worked back to the place where I first noticed them. Their flight was swift and darting; and more like that of a pipit or a wagtail than like that of a lark. On the ground they kept very low and proceeded by short and very rapid runs after the manner of sanderlings. Occasionally but seldom they hopped. They looked almost like mice as they ran about in the [?]dune. Their call-note was a low and sweet 'peep' but when disturbed they uttered, when rising, an alarm note somewhat resembling that of a skylark but quieter and different pitch. The black crescent below the throat was very conspicuous and in one the ear tufts were noticeable.

A shorter but equally apt observation involved a black tern, which he valued as an 'old' fenland species, and his favoured location, the ballast pits:

30th August 1901…Black tern – one immature bird hawking over the water at the ballast pit. Very restless and twisting about like a swallow. Occasionally dipping down and picking something off the surface of the water. Upper surface of the back, wings and tail a smoky grey, under-parts white, head appeared black with a conspicuous black mark on the side. Did not get a really close view. Flight reminded me >> of ringed plover except that it was not straight but very erratic, with many twists. [The note is hastily or excitedly written, and falls off the bottom of the page].

F.L.'s encouters with warblers extended to the grasshopper warbler; another cryptic bird, difficult to see and sometimes hard even to identify certainly by song:

3rd May 1915...I got a very good view of the grasshopper warbler. It was in the Skellingthorpe Big Wood near the north boundary hedge of the part called Mag Tree Hill, a little to the west of the white gate leading out of the main ride of the wood. I got my glasses on the bird for a good long time but it then took alarm and dropped into the herbeage and dead branches and skulked away. The warm brown colour struck me and it was conspicuous in the sunshine; the marks down the back and <u>very</u> long under-tail coverts were also conspicuous. While watching this bird, perhaps a female, I thought I heard a male 'singing' near at hand. I also thought I heard one singing not far from this place on May 30 1911.

The sting is in the tail of this sighting: a good, unusual bird which has probably escaped certain identification before, yet which was probably there in that spot every year!

But F.L. is no rarity chaser, and it is appropriate to end this brief selection of prose descriptions of encounters with birds by detailing his concern for even the commonest species: starlings. The note in the diary is three pages long, and what follows is only part of it. He heads the item 'evolution of roosting starlings'.

10th November 1908... East wind, bright sun. I have lately noted large flocks of starlings hurrying over Lincoln to go to the south east. So I started off this afternoon to find their roosting place. Just beyond Bracebridge asylum (5) I found a large flock of starlings on a newly harrowed field about 3.40 p.m.... With a mighty rush of wings the entire flock swept over their roosting wood about half way between there and Branston Hall. Seen from a little distance it had the appearance of a vast cloud of smoke drifting over the wood; this cloud contracted and expanded; now it was a long bar, now a huge shapeless mass. One half would suddenly wheel around and cross the other; and then the entire flight was a confined whirling mass of black specks coursing in every direction like snow driven by a whirlwind. All this time the noise of a hundred thousand wings sounded like the noise of the clouds of escaping steam. Suddenly...the whole with a mighty roar swept down into the trees. The sound of hard chirruping voices now almost eclipsed by the noise of the wind. It was some time before the birds could settle down, many large parties kept winging above the trees for a long time after the majority had settled but at last by 4.37, twenty minutes after sunset, the...roar of wings gave place to a confused chorus of chattering like...the rush of a passing train.

These descriptive passages show F.L.'s empathy with his subjects, the birds themselves. But he exhibits another kind of empathy – with people. The people of the diaries fall into two groups. On the one hand there are friends and family members; on the other there is a mixed group of informants, keepers, plover-catchers, bird-stuffers, woodsmen and their relatives who provide contemporary and historical data about Lincolnshire birds. It is with the latter group that we begin.

Despite the huge social divide that must have separated this aristocratic, educated clergyman from the woodsmen and others whose knowledge he coveted, F.L. clearly mingled with them happily, enjoying their company, eating with them on occasion, and seeking their specialist information. The 1908 entry for 2nd March epitomises one aspect of these contacts:

I bought a hobby, female adult, from Fieldsend, shot 21st September 1899 at Stainton wood, Wragby Road, for ten shillings and gave it to the Lincoln County Museum. This, I believe, was shot by the woodman, T.H.Roberts, and sold to Henry Nash for two shillings and six pence by him in the flesh.

Another appears in the entry from 23rd August 1909:

Had a talk with Perrin, the old fowler, who has lived at Gibraltar Point about forty years.

Among the things he was told was that lesser (little) terns had always nested about the Point, and that there were a few larger terns (Perrin called them swallows) which also nested (probably common terns, thinks F.L.). Perrin illustrates their numbers by indicating how many could be shot with single blast of the punt gun. F.L. was sufficiently interested in the old man to record that he died the following winter though, as we shall see shortly, he recorded few events that were not actual bird appearances or behaviour. Naturally, he talked (16th February 1901) to the woodsman at Doddington, George Dodsworth:

He had worked for many years for Lord Scarborough at Stainton wood by Langworth. He told me that last year a pair of wrynecks nested in an old tree...at Doddington. Also caught a white owl that is often about the Dees.

A couple of days later he is chatting again to the current woodsman of Stainton, Mr T. H. Roberts (mentioned above). F.L. records (19th February) that this gentleman had worked in Newball woods for about seven years, and was aged about sixty-five. He ran through with him a list of birds, to which the old man responded that he had no knowledge of kites there; common buzzards were regular nesters from about 1855-60, and nested again about 1875 but were practically never seen by 1910:

He described to me in his younger days how he had often watched buzzards soaring in spiral circles over the woods and had admired their flight. He had seen four at the same time during this time. (6)

Later in 1910 F.L. records a conversation with Henry Nash, bird-stuffer of Lincoln (14th October):

[He] had spent many days shooting in his earlier years on the coast about Gibraltar Point.

Again, Francis plies him with a list of species and discovers that Nash has recorded white-winged black tern, two spoonbills about 1905, a Temminck's stint and two pectoral sandpipers there. Closer to home 'old Barnes', woodman for the past thirty years in Skellingthorpe wood, tells him, in a 'talk…mostly about herons' that he had counted as many as twenty-nine nests five or six years ago. As well as talking to woodsmen, F.L. frequents the bird-stuffer's shop and Nash allows him to inventory the stock! Thus, on 22nd December 1902, he records:

Adult male flamingo, shot off river Welland, Boston, 22nd November 1902
Greater shearwater, shot by John Hall about 27th November 1902, Welland
Bittern, shot 1st December 1902, near Washingborough
Male redwing, shot 11th November 1902, near Branston – a curious variety of a pale buff colour with freckled breast and tail >>white
Black-throated diver, immature, shot near Boston 14th December 1902

A similar entry appears for the taxidermist S.A. Nobbs on 22nd February 1907, which is notable for some species brought in from the local area. These include a great grey shrike from Canwick, a water rail from the ballast pits, a puffin from (land-locked) Folkingham, and male and female rough-legged buzzards from Coleby. In all this one can feel F.L. building up his data bank for what, eventually, will become the County List for Lincolnshire.

His friends are equally 'grilled' about their birds or accompany him on his forays. He visits Mr Sutton-Nelthorpe's collection of stuffed birds and of eggs, including a kite from Branston wood (22nd May 1906). We have noted that he converses from time to time with Canon Cole, a former Rector of Doddington (7). A Mr Coward sends him 'some bird notes' on 17th March 1908, including a record of a red-backed shrike in the previous year. On April 8th of that year he visited the local heronry with Sylvia, who is otherwise unknown. Occasionally he takes a dog with him on his walks, for example 'Jack'; but the names of dogs seem to appear in inverted commas. Once (9th February 1909) he 'biked with HWB and GFB' to Louth looking for herons. It seems certain that HWB was Henry Wynter Blathwayt, his brother, who was to be killed in the Great War in 1917; the identity of GFB is unknown. On 23rd February that year he lunched in Gainsborough with Mr F.N. Burton, 'aged about seventy-nine' who:

...told me that when he was a boy living at his father's house, Lindum Holme(?) near Pottergate, Lincoln, he had counted as many as eight (red) kites soaring around Lincoln Minster tower - that would be about sixty-five years ago. Once he saw a kite rise out of his father's garden. In the 1860s they began to get rare around Lincoln. Buzzards were also common [then].

In 1912 (October) he receives a letter from Caton-Haigh and goes on a birding expedition with him at North Coates on 5th November. During their walk they spend time talking to Henry Stubbs, aged about seventy, 'whose family for generations have been plover-catchers about North Coates. I saw his plover decoys and nets. The most he caught in a day was somewhere around one hundred.' Caton Haigh wrote again in September 1914, and they once more patrolled the coast on 8th October of that year. There are other friends and correspondents, too: Mr Allison (there were probably two brothers), the Revd Peacock, and Mr Jarvis. Another heron-watcher was Mary, on 21st April 1915; but one can merely speculate that this was his cousin, the suffragette daughter of Lt Col Linley Blathwayt, or possibly Mary Gibbons from the 'Bird Dinner' (see chapter 3).

A unique personal encounter is dated 22nd May 1906. F.L. is researching black-headed gulls at Twigmoor, whither he normally goes by cycle. But on this date:

Mr Melville took me to Scawby and back by motor – went to see the gull ponds at Twigmoor...thousands of black-headed gulls on the ponds, groups of young in various stages but none out of the down...a nightingale not far from the lake, Scawby Hill.

One has the impression that the birds were much more interesting than the new-fangled mode of transport! Almost nothing personal intrudes into the bird record; not changes of parish or home, which merit only a new heading. Not people in general, who are often merely initials. Only one event captures a glimmer of awe outside his beloved birds:

31st May 1907...Saw the Cunard liner Lusitania out at sea off St Ives in her steam trials. When off Land's End she turned and seemed to steer WNW. (8)

But even she is like a migrating bird whose course has to be logged!

There are, of course, individual records of rare or unusual birds, some F.L.'s own sightings, some reported to him. A catalogue would become boring, but a few mentions are worthwhile. F.L.'s first curlew sandpiper occurs on 9th October 1902 at Saltfleet, in company with Mr Allison. Corncrakes turn up, for example on the Nettleham Road (now the main A46) on 18th May 1907 and 3rd May 1909. A hawfinch is stunned against the Rectory window on 16th February 1911, and subsequent entries suggest they increased in numbers and stole the peas from the vegetable plot ('got a lot lately'). A little auk was reported from Boston on 12th February 1912. F.L. recorded a nuthatch near the church on 3rd August 1913 – a rare bird indeed in this part of Lincolnshire. In 1914 he heard nightjars from the garden, too. Mrs Sipthorpe reported a roller seen near Louth at the beginning of October 1901.

But as well as the unusual, F.L. was the birder of the usual, of distribution and of the local 'patch'. This must not blind us to the vast area that he covered, on foot and by bicycle, to sustain his recording; Appendix 3 sets out the bare facts of the case and they are impressive. But, among all the travels, there were nevertheless favoured spots. So this chapter draws to a close with a place that began to loom larger in his consciousness from about 1910: Hartsholme. In the early days in Lincoln he had made the ballast pits his 'patch', and they appear in the published works. In Doddington, the local woods were his 'patch'. But from 1910, when the crossbills turned up and alerted him to the area, Hartsholme began to feature quite frequently in his notes.

The first mention of this location is incidental: on 15th November 1900 three shoveler he was watching on the Lincoln ballast pits flew off 'towards Hartsholme'. A long silence is broken in 1908 when, on 7th April, he heard three chiffchaffs calling, and saw a large party of redpolls near Stones Places (at the western end of the Hartsholme Park - the house still exists). On this date there were noisy green woodpeckers and a pair of stock doves. These 'would turn up into the wind and continually pass under and over one another; they repeat this for some time.'

Then, in 1910, his awareness of the area is raised by the crossbill incursion recorded earlier in the book. The first entry in the diary reads:

7th April 1910...Crossbill, a party of about twelve or perhaps a few more, in the Scots firs... Some of the birds very tame; one fine red cock sitting on the hedge near the road, quite close to me, and then flew up to a fir tree and sang various chattery and wheezy songs for some minutes. Call-note a sharp 'gip-gip'. Sung in a different key by different birds. Did not have any glasses so could not make out all the shades of plumage.

Going without glasses must have been an unusual occurrence for F.L. to note it; and one imagines that he had not set out to go birding. However, caught on the hop once, he returned next day:

8th April 1910...Went to Hartsholme fir wood to look for crossbills. Saw one flight of about twenty over the firs. Also others in small parties; several were red birds. Sometimes they would leave the woods and fly down to a stubble field with other birds such as buntings and sparrows; noisy when in flight, uttering a 'gip-gip' call all the time when on the wing.

9th April 1910...a few calling...

11th April 1910...I saw parties in twos and threes, and one party of about nine; there must have been twenty or thirty birds. Keeper, Mr Radley, said he had seen droves about since January or February chiefly in the evenings. Sometimes he thought he had seen sixty birds >>> He thought he had seen them in March 1909.

12th April 1910... 1 singing in the Lodge

16th April 1910... about 6

18th April 1910... about 10 in the usual place about 6.30 AM

5th May 1910... single crossbill singing, Hartsholme Lodge

12th May 1910... crossbills, party of perhaps 6 still in firs

30th July 1910... Saw Mr Radley, keeper, Hartsholme Lodge. He had seen large groups of crossbills still about the fir wood, about the middle May and well into June but not he thought into July. About May he had noticed one plucking dry grass from the roadside and flying with it into one of the fir trees. This is, I think, almost conclusive proof that the species has nested in Hartsholme woods.

These sightings led to further visits to the area, so that in 1911 F.L. records a pair of great crested grebes probably breeding on the Hartsholme Lake (26th April). Twenty or so redpolls were recorded in the woods on 28th December that year. In 1912, on 1st June, the grebes had downy young.

In his last Lincolnshire summer, F.L. is still visiting and recording in the Hartsholme area:

20th July 1916...I saw a pair of great crested grebe and three young at Hartsholme ballast pit. Did not get a close look but about three young about half-grown. Little grebe, a pair with young...

Earlier in the year, Francis had been following up the birds of the Hartsholme district in familiar fashion:

31st January 1916...[Note on LH page] went to see Mrs Charles Watson, North Hykeham. She is the daughter of the late Mr Potts who died some 8 years ago, formerly keeper at Hartsholme to Mr Shuttleworth, then publican at Reading Hotel, Thorpe-on-the-Hill. His daughter, aged about 35, had in his house, a cormorant, immature white-breasted, shot there 30 years ago by her father on Hartsholme lake. A great crested grebe from the same locality and probably about the same date. No dates on the cases but both set up by Barber of Lincoln. She remembers her father told her he had shot an 'eagle' at Hartsholme, more than 30 years ago; this was probably the osprey recorded in the Zoologist by J F Muskham, Barber's assistant, 1887, page 70, shot early in 1883.

The diaries of the Lincolnshire era are a wealth of information about the birds of the period 1900-1916. They have collected together personal observations, the tangible evidence available from sources such as the taxidermist's shop, and the sightings and reminiscences of others. What emerges is a unique record of the period and one that built ultimately to the first attempt to establish a County List for Lincolnshire.

We have found F.L. a harsh task-master, not easily satisfied by identification until proven beyond doubt, whether the view is his or another's. His search for integrity and truth has served later generations of Lincolnshire birders in good stead – though it has to be said, one wonders if he was easy to live with! To illustrate this last remark, the chapter closes with a final quotation from late in the Lincolnshire period and leaves you to make your own judgement:

11th April 1916... Went to Kirton at Lindsey, [to see stuffed birds at the] ??Unicorn Inn exhibited for the Red Cross which were said to be golden eagle and kite and found them to be 1) an immature sea eagle trapped by W. Dennett of ...Kirton Lindsey, keeper of Marton(?), on the Twigmoor side of Marton Warren on Feb 9 1916. The bird was caught by one toe in a fox trap, and he had been seen about for a week or so previously. The other bird was a rough-legged buzzard and was shot by the beater of W. Dennett on Marton Warren on November 12th 1915. I biked back through Scotter and over the Common...

In the middle of November 1916 F.L. moved parish from Doddington to Melbury. The school log for Doddington records his final farewell on 17th November. The bird diary presents this event merely as a change of location, with the very first entry on – 17th November! There is no mention of the change of job; no record mention of his family (9). Just an entry on the left-hand page: a small and very perceptive drawing of a Slavonian grebe, measuring about an inch square but shaded and detailed - one of the first Dorset species to come under his scrutiny.

NOTES TO CHAPTER 9

1.   The address belonged in 1907 to Frances Sophia Mitchinson, who may have lived there for some time; by 1909 it was taken over on her death by Helen Frances Mitchinson, daughter. Neither name appears, so far as I can trace, in the diaries.

2.   There is massive debate in the birding and environmental worlds currently about whether or not 'global warming' is a reality, about its causes, and even more importantly what its effects might be. Some birders maintain that the dates of migrant birds are becoming earlier year by year; but I at least am extremely sceptical of this view. Others maintain that individual species are affected differently: this approach at least has some scientific credibility. F.L.'s 'earliest dates' recorded in the chapter can be usefully compared with others recorded mainly in the Lincoln area by Jake Wildmann in his April 2005 column for www.sourceuk.net which are as follows:

1st chiffchaff	1st willow warbler	1st house martin	1st swallow
1966 - 6.3	1976 - 11.4	1981 - 12.4	1977 - 13.4
1973 - 28.3	1982 - 6.4	1982 - 2.4	1980 - 10.4
1977 - 6.3	1988 - 15.4	1984 - 12.4	1982 - 10.4
1978 - 2.4	1989 - 29.3	1989 - 28.3	1986 - 7.4
1979 - 10.4	1994 - 5.4	1992 - 21.3	1987 - 12.4
1980 - 7.4	1996 - 5.4	1994 - 4.4	1991 - 9.4
1981 - 31.3	1998 - 6.4	1995 - 12.4	1995 - 12.4
1982 - 22.3	2000 - 7.4	1996 - 15.4	1996 - 15.4
1984 - 7.4	2004 - 6.4	1997 - 13.4	1997 - 10.4
1988 - 2.4		2000 - 23.3	2002 - 7.4
1992 - 8.4			
1994 - 20.4			
1996 - 3.4			
1997 - 23.3			
1999 - 27.3			
2000 - 8.3			
2003 - 21.3			

There are two interesting things to note here. First, that there is no short-term trend between 1966 and 2003 for birds of the four species listed to arrive earlier. Second that the 'average' dates for willow warbler, house martin and swallow are not excessively different from F.L.'s 1896 dates: (respectively 6-7th April, and 10-11th April for JW; and 10th April and 13th April for FL) – no more different than might be due to chance alone. F.L.'s swallows came on 1st May, a bit later than the average dates for Wildmann, 10-12th April; but this was unusual as in 1916 he comments that 23rd April was late for swallow arrivals. Sighting of 'first migrants' by individual observers is a very hit-and-miss affair! The fact is borne out in so far as, from time to time in his Vertebrate Section reports for the LNU *Transactions* he gives arrival dates for Lincolnshire. These vary widely from year to year so that he is constrained to comment on individual years as either 'early' or 'late' e.g. in 1914 willow warblers arrived early on 4th April.

3.   According to Holloway's *Historical Atlas*, in which the nearest breeding birds between 1875 and 1900 were in Nottinghamshire, but most were more westerly.

4.   According to Lars Johnson's (1992) *Birds of Europe* London: Christopher Helm

5.   This is presumably the former St John's (mental) hospital, which was converted into a new housing development some years ago.

6.   As this chapter was being written, I drove past the wood just west of the Doddington Rectory. There, over the wood, was a common buzzard, wings held in the characteristic V, circling low over the canopy. It was my first sighting in that immediate area, though the species has been increasing locally for some years. F.L.'s heart would have leapt.

7.   The Revd Cole in fact wrote , during his incumbency, a tome on the Doddington parish: Cole, R.E.G. (1897) *The History of the Manor and Township of Doddington – otherwise Doddington-Pigot – in the County of Lincoln* Lincoln: James Williamson. This is a fascinating account of the parish prior to F.L. One learns many things from it: for example the original church had a timber spire about 1700, which was replaced by a new version in the 1771-5 re-building, but no longer exists. The Jarvis family kept 'negroes', some of whom were bequeathed from one member of the family to another in their wills. There is a detailed account of rainfall figures measured in a guage at the Rectory (they varied from about sixteen inches to twenty-nine inches annually). Cole records that Old Hagg Wood and Skellingthorpe Big Wood had been 'the immemorial breeding place of herons.' His account of the road system suggests three main routes: to Drinsey Nook and Dunham, to Hartsholme and Lincoln; and to the main Lincoln-Newark road.

8.   The official Lusitania web-site gives a great deal of historical detail about this ship. It was eventually sunk by the Germans in WWI with huge loss of civilian life. But when F.L. saw her she had been named by Lady Inverclyde on 7th June 1906 and then moved to a fitting-out berth. F.L. saw her on 31st May 1907, and she furthered her sea trials in July off Ireland, though failed her acceptance trial. Her maiden voyage came on 7th September.

9.   Francis and Marjorie produced their first son in July 1916; they also had daughters: the eldest was Barbara, who was ninety in 2004; a younger daughter, Jean, was to be Captain of the Dyrham Girl Guide Company according to Mrs C. Poole (personal communication) – see chapter 12. Two boy children failed to survive infancy.

CHAPTER 10
FROM DODDINGTON TO
DORSET AND DYRHAM

Late in November 1916, Francis and Marjorie made a move from the parish of Doddington, Lincolnshire, to the parishes of Melbury Osmund and Melbury Sampford in Dorset. F.L.'s bird diaries do not even remark on the event: he ceases recording in one place and, with no more than a change of heading on the page, is recording in another.

In the years preceding this, F.L.'s family/parental home seems to have changed from Sussex to Saltaire, Weston-super-Mare (1). The date of this move has not been discovered precisely though the location is mentioned in the early diaries; nor do we know for certain whether at the time his father was in England having left the Indian Civil Service. What we do know, from the diaries described in the previous chapter, is that F.L. vacationed in Somerset while he was a curate in Lincolnshire; the diaries contain periodic surveys of Somerset birds collected during these vacations. It will be recalled that F.L. had researched and published the 'Birds of Somerset' for the *Victoria County History,* to which his uncle Linley had contributed sections on insect natural history. Maybe the decision to move was conditioned by the fact that at some time in 1916 his father died.

Melbury was only a few miles from Colonel Linley Blathwayt's home at Batheaston; and not much further from the family seat at Dyrham. If Doddington appeared rural, then the countryside around Melbury was more so! If the Rectory and church at Doddington seemed small and quiet, then the livings at Melbury were positively isolated.

The two parishes were grouped quite early in their history (2), in fact from 1750. They were in the gift of the Earl of Ilchester, and the tiny church at Sampford probably acted almost as a family chapel for the manor house adjacent. The village of Melbury Osmund was also small and somewhat isolated. It is still accessed down a lane only wide enough for a horse and trap.

A visitor to Melbury Osmund (the church is named St Osmund) today would find it hedged around on one side by picturesque cottages, and on the other flanked by the old Rectory. The church is a yellow stone building with a short nave and a low tower set in a tidy churchyard. Two smart wooden boards commemorate the former clergy. One lists F.L. as also holding the living of Stockwood in plurality. There are rows of dark pews now adorned with embroidered kneelers. A banner commemorates the patron saint, and another the Mothers' Union, established during F.L.'s time there. The clergy stall is a modest affair and the pulpit does not tower over the plain interior; though there is some pleasant stained glass in the style of the time, dating from the late 1800s. The body of the church is light, a result of the mainly clear glass windows. There is a welcoming feel, and even a little book of historical information that mentions Francis.

Francis remained here until 1929, and it is certainly a rural idyll. Maybe he was persuaded to the area by the Earl of Ilchester. The Earl was a Trustee of the Dorset Natural History Society; and later President. F.L. became Vice President. The Earl wrote a paper (3) on 'The Abbotsbury Swannery' nearby. Maybe he had marked out this serious clergyman as a safe pastor and a talented birder, and could see a way to advancing two causes at once! The Earl's paper shows clearly his antiquarian interests, as well as a concern for the swans that had passed down the family line.

His life in Melbury provided F.L. with an opportunity to continue his birding alongside the duties of parson, though his output of more lengthy published papers at this time is apparently modest, being just two papers in *Proceedings* (4). These closely mirror the work he began in Lincolnshire in recording the gulleries and heronries. However, the private recording of birds and bird behaviour in his diaries continues; and maybe these quieter years were a time when he was simply researching his new surroundings carefully. It is also a time when he is compiling annual bird reports for two counties (Somerset and Dorset), and writing Notes for *British Birds*.

In 1929 the opportunity arose for F.L. to leave Melbury and take on the Rectorship in the parish church adjacent to the family home in Dyrham. He was fifty-four, and he seems to have jumped at the chance. It was yet another rural living; and one in fine countryside. Though just outside the county of Dorset, it was close enough for him to keep up his watching and his writing about that county. He could also continue his membership and offices in the Natural History Society, which he did almost until his death.

His writing was now at its most prolific (5). He was producing material from his own observations, but also acting as editor and 'clearing house' for the sightings of others. It was a role to which he was eminently suited because of his talent for accuracy and 'complete lists.'

As today's visitor approaches Dyrham, across the Dyrham Park estate, he or she is presented with typical 'parkland' ecology. The house itself, described in chapter one, nestles in a deep fold of the surrounding hills. Cattle still graze around it. The little square tower of the church pokes out from above the right-hand corner of the house. To descend the hill to the house is to lose sight of the church almost totally, except for a momentary glimpse of its tower. But a narrow lane leads down to the opposite side of the church, and there is enough space – just – to park a car and walk along the handsome, stone-walled path to the church building.

On close approach the church is surprising. Built into the hillside as a kind of after-thought to the house, it is almost as if it has been half-buried so as not to steal the glory of the secular building. To the south there is a narrow, sunken path to the house itself, still accessible to National Trust ticket-holders. To the north, the hill rises sharply, so that half the height of the church on this side is below ground level. Despite clear windows the church is thus very dark, a situation exacerbated by the heavy over-hanging trees (6).

But it is the churchyard that is most depressing. Nettles rise higher than many of the grave-stones. Few of the plots are cleared and tended. Some kind of heave operates on the slope, and grave-stones are tossed about and displaced, even over-turned and broken. The atmosphere is dank and few birds sing. One might expect a robin to warble or a spotted flycatcher to burst from a grave-top. Nothing! (7).

F.L. produced his most prolific bird writing while Rector here, and served the causes of both birding and the church until his death in 1953, when he was aged seventy-eight (8). The next chapter tells in brief the story of his birding during the 'Dorset years', that is during his Rectorships of Melbury and Dyrham. It is only then that one can re-visit his life to make some assessment of it, and to recount the events regarding his death.

NOTES TO CHAPTER 10

1.   The diaries show this move was made by 1899.

2.   The list of Rectors goes back to a surprising 1324 when Peter de Blictor was the first Rector. The board then lists the other Rectors until March 1750 when the parish was combined with Melbury Sampford. In 1885 Stockwood was added to the responsibilities of the Rector, and F.L. belongs to this period. At the bottom of the board, the gold lettering is crammed together to include as many entries as possible; but the attempt was in vain. Plurality took over, and the parish became the two original Melburys, Stockwood, Evershot, Frome St Quintin and Melbury Bubb. The role of the clergyman was changed to Team Rector; the first holder of the new role was the Revd Linley D. Blathwayt, F.L.'s son (whose tenure was from 1975-1981).

3.   The paper was read to the Society on 20th February 1934 and was included in the *Proceedings of the Dorset Natural History and Archaeological Society* [hereafter *Proceedings*] in that year, pp 153-164.

4.   'Dorset gulleries' (1920) *Proceedings* vol 42 pp 81-86; 'Dorset heronries' (1923) *Proceedings* vol 45 pp 75-80. Conversation with Mrs Gillian Blathwayt (July 2005) confirmed my impression that 'Uncle Frank' took this living substantially because of the birding opportunities that it offered.

5.   The list of writings contains the following: (1932) 'The Etiology of the Occurrence and Dispersal of Birds in Dorset' *Proceedings* (54), pp 181-194; (1932) 'A revised list of the Birds of Dorset' *Proceedings* (55), pp 165-209; (1934-1943) 'Reports on Dorset Natural History' *Proceedings* (56-65); (1944-1948) 'Reports on Dorset Birds' *Proceedings* (66-70); (1939) 'A revised list of the Birds of Dorset' *Proceedings* (61), 136-167); (1945) 'A revised list of the Birds of Dorset' *Proceedings* (67), pp 95-126. It will be noted that many of these items are compilations of sightings that form, in many cases, the basis of the County List. Birds do not exhaust the subject-matter of these works, however; it is again opportune to note that F.L. was an all-round naturalist even if his specialism was birds.

6.   Not everyone agrees with this perception: 'The exterior appears a simple Perpendicular structure. The interior glows with Tudor warmth, as light floods in from the garden, enhancing the pink limewash on the walls. On a summer's day, with flowers on the pulpit and bees humming about the rafters, the interior might still be a set for *The Remains of the Day*, which was filmed at Dyrham... Dyrham has six fine bells, one of which is apparently from the reign of Edward I, making it over six centuries old. There is a battered but decorative tryptich on the altar.' (Taken from Simon Jenkins' *England's Thousand Best Churches*).

7.   During my visit I cleared the nettles from the corner of an oval head-stone and discovered, hidden below the weeds, the Blathwayt eagle surmounted by a cross. The legend read: 'Christopher George Wynter Blathwayt, MC, Croix de Guerre' – the final resting place of F.L.'s nephew (see chapter 1, note 18). Christopher's father, Henry Wynter had married the Hon. Elizabeth Helen de Grey; but his life was claimed in 1917 at Cambrai (one of the earliest tank battles where, ironically, Lincoln-made tanks caused consternation among the enemy). Christopher (1912-1990) was married to Gillian Butcher, who is credited in the Acknowledgements for information supplied to me.

8.   See further, in Chapter 12, for his death and funeral.

CHAPTER 11
DORSET WRITINGS

Sometimes in an antique shop one comes across a superbly-made piece of furniture which is exquisite in every detail except that it is smaller than one would expect for the object concerned. Such items are often described as apprentice pieces. There is a very real sense in which F.L.'s work on Lincolnshire birds was a beautifully constructed apprentice piece for the even more significant role he was to play in Dorset birding of his period.

This chapter attempts to do no more than survey this role in relation to the published works. This present text concentrates on the Lincolnshire years; to have added diary material, for example, about Dorset from 1916 until 1953 would have required a work of considerable more substance and wider scope. But the Lincolnshire picture needs a context not merely in its antecedents, but also in the events that it sparked in the birding life of F.L.

If Francis made the transition to his new county with a mere change of heading in his diary, then he just as rapidly began forging a name for himself there as a birder of consequence. On 11th December 1917, just twelve months after his move from Doddington, he read to the Dorset Naturalists a paper which was to set a new pattern for his work. F.L. had been remarkably canny in his choice of title:

'New Species of Birds Observed in Dorset since the publication of Mansel-Pleydell's *Birds of Dorset* 1888'

The selection was a master-stroke, playing to his own birding strengths and picking up the work of a local hero of the bird world. Thus his first Dorset paper was published in the *Proceedings*. He is able to note that he has personally added two new species to the Dorset County List in the year of his sojourn there: marsh warbler in June 1917, and possible breeding roseate tern, that source of wonder with which he had been entranced many long years before in Somerset. As well as definite records he is able to raise the hope of merlins from Chesil beach, garganey from Abbotsbury, and black tern from this last location. He is following the old ploy of collecting records from a circle of birding acquaintances: Mr Parkinson Curtis contributes records of greenshanks and red-breasted merganser. Nor does he retreat from his 'old' themes:

...though the swelling of a county list by the record of an occasional visitant is of interest, the most useful form of work is the study of the distribution of birds, even the commonest, in the county with special notice of their migrations, breeding range, and increase or decrease of recent years.

New audience, new location, to some extent new birds; but the same old message. He notes changes to ranges in the county of dipper and nightingale. He poses questions: the situation for herons, whether the Montagu's harrier, the chough and the stone curlew still breed. He asks about the status of the Dartford warbler. He seeks to know more of the breeding status of the great-crested grebe; and he enumerates the richness of the county for his favoured duck species. He trawls the records for missing birds: mealy redpoll, rarer pipits and waders. He asks questions about the continental forms of common birds such as song thrush, robin, goldfinch and tits. He exercises some tact in eliminating certain species from Mansel-Pleydell's list and revising others: three rare woodpeckers go on the grounds of insecure records; the Polish swan is not considered a separate species from the mute; and the Egyptian goose can be considered an escape. Finally, the remains of a golden eagle in Dorchester Museum are, he avers, those of a white-tailed eagle.

What follows is a list of addenda to Mansel-Pleydell's list that satisfy F.L.'s criteria of integrity and truth. Many of the records are authenticated from the key sources: specimens, records in publications such as *The Field, British Birds,* and *The Zoologist.* Twenty-two species are thus added to the County List for Dorset between 1888 and 1917, some of them emanating from the Dorchester Field Club.

As an example of how to win recognition and influence people whose acceptance counts, this paper is a classic. F.L. immediately took over the editing of the annual bird report of the county (1918) and continued in that role until 1948 (1). Green described his contribution to Dorset ornithology thus:

Blathwayt pioneered a new attitude to ornithology in Dorset, away from the collection of rare birds and towards detailed field studies, recording the local distributions and numbers of birds, the changes in these and their causes. (2)

But if F.L. was the driving force of the Dorset County List for three decades, he lost little of his enthusiasm for the birds themselves and the places where they were to be found. If a contemporary birder made his or her home in Dorset, where would be the location of greatest priority to visit? Many would respond: the Chesil Beach. F.L. was no exception, and after just two years in the county, he was ready in 1919 to publish his first thoughts on the area (3).

Chesil Beach is a natural phenomenon that runs for some fifteen miles from Portland in the east to beyond Abbotsbury in the west. It consists of a bank of shingle several dozen metres wide and about ten high that traps the brackish waters of the Fleet on the landward side, and is washed by the English Channel on the other. From an aircraft this narrow stone spit is an unmistakable landmark on the approach to the southern coast; from eye-level the bank is quite simply awesome in its scope: on a good day, a wide, flat, yellow cobble road, straight as a die, under an egg-blue vault of sky. It is inexplicable: even the geologists who study it cannot explain its origins nor why precisely the sea washes larger pebbles onto it at one end and smaller ones at the other. While it is possible to walk its length, this is best done along the strand rather than on the summit, for the pebbles heave under foot and yield at each step, sapping the energy and dragging with a pull like positive 'g'.

For sheer impressiveness (and convenience!), the bank is best viewed from the bar of a hotel near the summit of Portland Bill, where picture windows give onto the model-village houses laid out far below, and a view along the whole length of the beach to the setting sun in the west. Cobalt and ultramarine, and heliotrope, and gold and orange and purple light reflects in turn off the waves of the rolling sea and alters the hue of the pebbles. The white tops of the waves cream the strand-line or, in a stiffer breeze, are wafted in fine droplets up and over the crest of pebbles to drop their rainbowed moisture inland. In the resulting haze, the distant line of the beach and the even more distant headland appear and disappear like the cat in *Alice*.

To the west there is a large car park from which it is possible to walk through idyllic fields, accompanied in late spring by bounding lambs and the chomp of sheep in the grass, to the Swannery at Abbotsbury. Skylarks hang on invisible spiders' threads in the vault, singing over their territories, and a green woodpecker yaffles into a distant tree below the cawing rookery. The gothic ruin of a derelict abbey looks down from the north, and sedge warblers scold the intrusion from exotic tamarisks. On the bank itself there are wardened areas where the little terns breed; waders scour the muddy embers of the Fleet; and a peregrine hugs the stony contours foraging after a meal. Alone on the shingle bank, dwarfed by the sea and sky, one could be treading with F.L. himself in this awesome landscape.

F.L. called it 'one of the wonders of the world', and 'last June...tramped these miles on the pebbles, no light undertaking.' He discovered the 'beautiful lesser terns nesting', and some colonies of common terns. There were wheatears, and he pointed to the high ground of Portland as a key area for watching migrants. Francis found ringed plovers and, like all birders, harboured a secret wish: that he would find a Kentish plover too. It was not to be. Redshanks were about, but there was no evidence of breeding oystercatchers.

Black-headed gulls, of course, did not long escape attention; but F.L. could find only one breeding record – for 1910; the main breeding colony was in Poole. He could not resist listing all the duck species he encountered, but these required winter visits, which yielded: 300 mallard, 1,000 wigeon, 500 tufted ducks and 500 pochards, 100 shovelers, a few teal, 10 goldeneye, 4 scaup and 3 smew. The small birds of the Fleet edge and adjacent fields were the same then as now: larks, linnets, meadow pipits, reed buntings, and sedge warblers. He also recorded marsh warblers (4); and speculated that the habitat would support bearded tits (5). Other interesting sightings included gannets and pomatorhine (sic) skuas.

The most lyrical passage in F.L.'s report is reserved for the common terns. He first speculates about how long the ternery has existed, and finds that it has pre-dated even the oldest of those birders he has consulted on the matter. Then he tries to elicit support from those in other disciplines: he argues that since the nests are mainly in growths of *Lathyrus maritimus* and *Silene maritima* a botanist could perhaps establish how long the plants had grown there and thus indicate an 'earliest' date for tern colonisation, and he issues the implicit challenge. Then he describes the 'charming experience' of visiting the colony:

As one approaches the colony all is animation and excitement. The angry cries of the birds are incessant, and the vast fluttering, drifting, wheeling cloud of the long-winged graceful birds is almost bewildering…From an observation I made last year, it seems probable that the female bird does not always recognise her own nest, as the mixture of two extreme types [of egg colouration] pointed to promiscuous laying, though it does not actually prove the fact. When the young are hatched they soon creep or run from their nests and hide among the vegetation, and, when a little more grown, many scramble down the steep bank of the shingle towards the sea, in which their parents are procuring food.

The prose has the immediacy of personal observation, but is tempered with the usual Blathwayt guardedness about drawing conclusions without specific proof. In a way, the passage, fine in its own right, has its punch-line in the tail:

The colony consists almost entirely of the common terns, but on July 12th 1917, I saw also a roseate tern there, but unfortunately could find no proof that it was breeding.

This bird – and every birder has one or two such species – still haunts his dreams! (6). But F.L.'s interest is also captured, as always, by more mundane birds, too. So his next two papers (1919, 1923) consider those other favourite species, black-headed gulls and herons. The first paper begins with some rather tortuous debates about the interpretation of the word 'pewitt' in 17th century writings. Let us leave this aside, and note that black-headed gulls seem, as far as can be discerned, to have begun (or re-commenced) breeding in Dorset from about 1877 at Littlesea (7). Francis is keen to point out that black-headed are marsh (not cliff) gulls; and that their eggs have a market value as food (often as 'lapwings' eggs'), which has caused them to be pressured by humans. However, he is able to give an account of four colonies by dint of personal visits and information received:

- Littlesea: which has been affected by climate but which now hosted sixty pairs to F.L.'s own knowledge
- Rempstone Heath: which had been variously estimated at up to 2,000 pairs, but which had recently declined; F.L. could find only thirty pairs in June 1919
- Arne: in spartina grass and consisting of about 800 pairs, though there were also off-shoot colonies from the main group that had had varying fortunes
- Morden Heath: not visited personally by F.L., but may have started about 1908, and possibly modest but flourishing.

The paper surveys a number of smaller nesting groups, and ends with a description of the breeding cycle of the gulls. It is a workmanlike paper on a favoured species; and maybe he was wistful for the clamour of the large and dynamic gullery at Twigmoor. If so, it is as nostalgic as he ever gets. The second paper – on heronries written in 1923 – is likewise limited in scope and is a plea for more information from other observers. It is based on sources, as far as these existed, and also on personal visits to the colonies known or thought to exist. Of the four locations, Sherborne Park (in private ownership) could boast about seven pairs; More Crichel (which had existed from 1835) hosted about fifteen pairs; Knighton Heath Wood which held about a dozen pairs and was of recent (1912) origin; and Arne, which had the most at fifty pairs (reports of more proved to be unfounded). Each of these locations had probably been colonised at some stage by birds moved from other areas, not least because wood-cutting for the Great War had caused some disruption. There is one very interesting note about the Knighton Heath group:

It seems quite likely…[the herons] migrated originally from the Duddle Heath heronry which has now apparently ceased to exist, but which formerly flourished in a picturesque position in some firs on rising ground by the roadside just north of Norris Mill. This was once a well-known colony of perhaps twenty or more pairs of birds, and has historic interest, as Mr Thomas Hardy, in a letter to me dated March 15th 1917, wrote that this is the heronry he mentioned in *The Return of the Native,* published in 1878. (8).

The two papers pick up old interests and apply them to a new situation. But they are, in the end, a prelude to a different kind of publication. The list of Blathwayt publications (Appendix 1) demonstrates that, from now on, he was responsible as an editor for specific sections of the *Proceedings*. He became the 'correspondent' for the:

'Phenological Report on the first appearances of birds, insects &c., and the first flowering of plants in Dorset...with other notes on natural history'.

It is important to note in passing that F.L. sustained and actively pursued an interest in, and commitment to, natural history in general. In birding terms, he took on a role we would now call County Recorder, processing the data about species year by year, and punctuating the annual reports with revisions and up-dates to the County List. In this fine-grained work of counting, collecting and classifying he found his métier. He continued in it until 1948 although he had moved out of the county, to the parish of Dyrham, in 1929.

One of the *Proceedings* articles deserves mention, perhaps, above the rest; it was one that was probably to seal his reputation in the county: 'The etiology of the occurrence and dispersal of birds in Dorset.' It was submitted for the Mansel-Pleydell essay prize in 1931, and won.

In this paper F.L. sets out to explore the intriguing, and sometimes, vexing question for birders: why do species apparently quite prolific a few miles away fail to spread into equally usable habitat in my area (9)? He cites tawny pipit, crested lark and Kentish plover (10) as examples of 'common breeding species of birds on the French side of the Channel', but rare visitors and non-breeders on the English side. His analysis of the Dorset situation points up the advantages of the county:

Only two counties in England extend further to the south, it has a varied coastline of some 75 miles in length, and no spot in the county is more than forty miles from the sea. Portland Isle reaches out towards the Channel Islands and strives to form, with them and a projecting promontory in France, a bridge or line of migration-flight from the Continent into Dorset and *vice versa*...the writer cannot help feeling that here we have the remains of a flight line into Dorset, which has gradually been formed during the slow change of conditions in past ages...

Having examined the physical geography and found the answers tantalising, he goes on:

Place a geological map by the side of the physical map and study both together, and it becomes more and more obvious that here we have a county which certainly ought to abound in bird life. A backbone of chalk sweeps the whole length of the county from Cranborne Chase to the Devon boundary; two splendid-looking vales, those of Blackmore in the north on the Oxford Clay, and Marshwood in the West on the Lias give promise of rich pasture lands and sturdy timber; a huge area of sandy heath extends from Dorchester to the eastern boundary...while sands, rocks and the finest pebble-ridge imaginable add attractions which birds surely could not resist. (11)

Then comes a passage – a purple passage – that is fine writing regardless of the subject-matter:

Leave the maps, and come to actual experience of the county, and what is found? The vales are full of 'blue goodness', the downs of breezy solitude, the Heath of unspoiled primitiveness; the cliffs display a perfectly magnificent series of formation, size and colour; Poole Harbour and its islets and tides, an enchanting lake district; and the Chesil with its ten or twelve miles of raised pebble-beach, a golden bank without equal.

Here is a man captivated by his subject, enthusing with personal joy and trying to convey that enthusiasm and joy to the reader. Furthermore, the ornithological expectations of habitat, shelter, food and nesting space are all met in the county; and these factors and this variety mean that Dorset holds almost every species found elsewhere in southern England. Yet he wants more!

So F.L. begins to build the picture of why one place is occupied, and another neglected. He quotes the example of that 'little gem' the Dartford warbler (12): it survives heath fires, and predators (including human ones); but what it cannot withstand is the erosion – he does not use the word – of its habitat. Montagu's harriers attract a 'melancholy interest', but what they really need is protection. Cormorants and shags 'formerly nested in several spots' but 'the price set upon their heads in the interests of fishing' has driven them away (13). Collectors of skins and eggs have done away with the chough population (14). Bustards and grouse have disappeared because of 'the improvement in firearms, increased persecution by man and a certain amount of restriction of suitable habitats'. Land rails have been affected by the earlier cutting of hay (no new problem in our times!). Though conservation work has been admirably done at Radipole, Lodmore has a 'perfectly astonishing amount of rare and interesting species' visiting the area, but will lose its charm to 'drainage and exploitation.' Guillemots are threatened by oil from ships. The review covers scores of species, but its approach is entirely modern, combining an erudition about the sheer magnitude of bird-life in the county with a perception about conservation that today's birder would grasp instantly.

Warp and weft of the text are challenges: not only conservation challenges, but research challenges to the birding community:

- Why is the whinchat only a passing visitor? (15)
- Why is the tree sparrow seldom if ever found nesting in the county? (16)
- Why is the lesser black-backed gull only a spring and autumn migrant? (17)

This paper sets the seal on all those lists and statistics and up-dates and revisions of the County List that follow from F.L.'s editorship of the bird sections of the *Proceedings*. It shows how this work will proceed over the years, and culminates in his 'Revised List of the Birds of Dorset' (1945). It would be inappropriate to give a blow-by-blow account of these records; suffice it to say that they laid a seriously important and modernistic foundation for today's Dorset County List, a legacy contemporary birders still acknowledge.

•

In so far as Francis turned his hand to other kinds of bird writing at this time, he did so using those other sets of skills: acute observation, and recording of his own sightings and those of others. Alongside the records in the *Proceedings* must be set a collection of short notes in *British Birds* that advance the cause of recognition and solve some of the little mysteries of bird behaviour and distribution. Forty of these are listed in Appendix 1 (18). Three examples will suffice here.

First, an item from 1932 which summarises the calls of waders – an attempt at vocalising wader calls into something that passes as a means for the birder to recognise an unknown bird by sound as well as, or instead of, sight (19). F.L. presents the item with diffidence, since it is treading in difficult waters. Then a piece on the drumming of lesser spotted woodpeckers, written in 1938, uses the now famous prismatic glasses to assure the reader that the sound is made by impact of the bill not – as had been suggested in earlier pages of the journal – by vocalisation. The latter note was also selected by Jim Flegg in his review of seventy-three years of *British Birds* articles (20). The description of the drumming process is 'pure Blathwayt', and Flegg's judgement on the piece is apposite: it is 'a cut-and-dried account'.

Finally there is the item from volume 15, 1921 in which F.L. finally proves the breeding of the roseate tern in Dorset: he and two companions armed with prism glasses and telescopes 'mark' the birds 'onto two eggs' on a nest that was 'very scanty and not concealed'. The note has description, detail and brevity; but F.L. cannot mask his excitement nonetheless!

NOTES TO CHAPTER 11

1.   This in spite of the fact that there were other notable birders in the county: for example, the Revd F.C.R. Jourdain of *Handbook* fame, W.J.Ashford (1879-1970) – both egg-collectors – and W.R.G. Bond (1880-1952) who campaigned for the establishment of what is now Radipole RSPB reserve.

2.   Green, G. (2004) *The Birds of Dorset* London: Christopher Helm, p 22; [hereafter *Birds of Dorset*]

3.   'The birds of Chesil Beach', 1919, *Proceedings.*

4.   *Birds of Dorset* accepts breeding records up to 1945; and birds have turned up most years until 1985. The *Atlas of Breeding Birds* located breeding in one 10km square. Tiny numbers have been recorded most years until 2000.

5.   These birds did surface in Dorset in 1964, and for a time numbers grew in areas like Radipole, with tiny numbers breeding into modern times, but larger counts occurring in winter. The habitat in the Chesil area is suitable but not extensive.

6.   Roseate terns are such a rarity in my own watching that I scarcely ever considered them until I began reading F.L.'s work. Then as this chapter unfolded I visited Dungeness, where a huge group of terns had just flown in from the sea on their spring migration. Some were feeding in the warm water of the out-fall from the nuclear power station; others were lazing on the pebble beach. About thirty Sandwich terns, ragged crested and lemon bill-tipped, sat aloof from the rest – a party of about a hundred commons. Remembering F.L., I lay in the shingle and set up the 'scope, denying my usual idle habit of a rapid scan of the flock. As I searched each bird (I thought I might come up with an arctic among them) I realised just one individual had a marginally different head pattern and a black bill. There, among the commons, lurked the coveted roseate! In his monograph, Hume (Hume, R. 1993 *The Common Tern* London: Hamlyn) has some interesting comparisons between common and roseate tern behaviour: in studies, both species fed in an area up to 5.5 kilometres from their colonies; roseates tended

to form smaller feeding flocks than commons; commons fed more successfully in dense groups than roseates; roseates were quite aggressive to their own kind; but in the 'feeding cones' formed by mixed terns (a few low over the water, many higher up) roseates fared less well than commons at the point of feeding.

7. Pike, T.M. (1877) in a paper (untitled) in *The Zoologist* is the source. There is an extended note on black-headed gull numbers in *Birds of Dorset* (pp 237-9). Individual locations in the county may yield counts of 20,000 in winter; and breeding numbers in Poole Harbour reached 6000 in 1996.

8. Sherborne Park heronry ceased to exist in 1990 according to *Birds of Dorset* (p 129); More Crichel was destroyed in 1931, and Knighton Heath Wood in 1962. Arne had disappeared, it is said, by 1948. Current heronries are detailed in *Birds of Dorset* (p 129), along with numbers of wintering birds.

9. Some years ago my wife and I were invited to work for some days on Guernsey, and our hosts provided a small hire-car to get around the island. In our free moments we followed the beautiful coastline, and became excited by our first views of little egrets on British soil. We were aware, even as we watched them, that these sightings must herald the northern march of this species, which now sees them as common-place on the south coast of mainland England and round to the north coast of Norfolk and into Lincolnshire.

10. *Birds of Dorset* would have disappointed F.L. into modern times in relation to the tawny pipit, for the only record is of the one shot at Christchurch harbour in August 1879. The crested lark doesn't even merit a mention in the index of this publication; so it is left to the Kentish plover to come good. *Birds of Dorset* (pp 172-3) lists many sightings in modern times, though not the elusive proof of breeding despite mid-summer records.

11. The same sentiment is echoed by Green's *Birds of Dorset* (p 11), where the author notes that the Dorset List includes 124 species regarded as 'official rarities', and 405 species in total (72% of the entire British List) recorded in the county.

12. The 'little gem' is subject to habitat destruction and interrupted success by virtue of bad winters. However, there has been an up-turn in its fortunes, especially since 1990 (*Birds of Dorset* p 389-390). Peak breeding numbers seem to have been reached in 1994, with 650 birds.

13. Cormorants and shags both occur in numbers in the county, though actual breeding populations are quite modest.

14. Basically extinct from Dorset – and from many former haunts – four birds did turn up in the county in April/May 2001 (*Birds of Dorset* p 445) – 'the ornithological highlight of the year!'

15. Whinchats can be found in the county from March to November (*Birds of Dorset* pp 357-8); and a few have been recorded as breeding.

16. The *Atlas of Breeding Birds* did find some evidence of small numbers of tree sparrows breeding, but in general the bird is elusive in the county. The crashes of tree sparrow numbers are well known to ornithologists. In F.L.'s previous county of Lincolnshire, this author had tree sparrows breeding in garden nest boxes in the early 1970s. Today even single birds are hard to find, though there are a few at Whisby currently.

17. F.L. answers his own questions with a hypothesis, notably that the lesser black-backs are not cliff birds, and thus are only on passage 'to and from the flat isles and moorlands near the sea further north.'

18. For anyone trying to track down these writings, the issue is complicated by the fact that *British Birds* maintains an index driven only by the names of birds, not the names of authors. They suggest that finding articles is best when one already knows the subject matter – a kind of ornithological psychic insight! So to be successful in finding material it is useful to discover a library with a run of copies that can be consulted manually.

19. It is believed that the original handwritten text of this article now resides in the Zoology Department of the Oxford University Library.

20. Flegg, J (1981) *A Notebook of Birds 1907-1980* London: MacMillan, pp 66-68.

CHAPTER 12
F.L. AND HIS LEGACY

Too much biographical writing sets out to turn its subject into either saint or sinner. Such an approach would have drawn opprobrium from Francis Linley Blathwayt, for he is concerned above all with 'integrity and truth'.

It has to be acknowledged that the evaluation of the man and his work in this chapter is essentially mine, even though the views of others will be quoted. Therefore, it is my intention to depart from the mainly third person approach of the text at this point, and to write a personal assessment using my own criteria (1). This book has tried to establish the truth, or at the least some truths, about F.L. In assessing the outcome it is my integrity which is on the line, not his.

For months I have been following F.L. on his birding journeys and on the journey of his life. It was President Clinton (2) who said that life makes more sense when played backwards than lived forwards. It is a luxury, of course, which none of us has for ourselves. I have been following F.L.'s life backwards: I have been the spectre at his meals with bishops and woodmen, the silent watcher of his birds, the invisible coachman on his translations from parish to parish, the stalker on the footpaths of his birding. I have visited his locations, touched his possessions and, quite literally, read his thoughts. Despite all of this, in some ways he is still a mystery to me; I have seen only what he allowed me to see. To that extent my judgement may be flawed, and for that I can do no more than apologise to him and to my readers.

Yet assess his contribution I must: I owe him that in return for the intrusion. To do it I intend to survey six aspects of the man and his work and, using the evidence, to form a view of the nature of each. The reader will, of course, be free to do two important things: first, to judge whether I have manipulated the evidence unfairly in forming my own view and second, to return him or herself to find new evidence on which to base some other interpretation. The six aspects of F.L. that this chapter will pursue are these:

Pastor
President
Editor
Writer
Man
Birder

There is one other important preliminary remark. Historical individuals should, first and foremost, be viewed against the standards of their time and not against criteria invented by later generations to suit a different social circumstance. If a person's influence transcends their own time, well and good; but the modern trend of re-writing historical events from a current perspective is at best mischievous and at worst distortion.

F.L. Blathwayt – pastor

At the turn of the 20th century it was the custom in aristocratic families for second or third sons to enter Holy Orders. This required on the part of the man himself no over-blown commitment to religion, but a sense that Christianity was part of that established world order to which the aristocracy itself belonged. Like entering the army (one recalls Lt Col Linley Blathwayt) and the civil service at home or abroad (F.L.'s own father), it was a civic duty to hold such a profession.

Throughout my research I struggled to find evidence of F.L. the pastor. Then I discovered an archive at All Saints' Church, Lincoln, with warm letters from Bishop King, to F.L. on his engagement and agreeing a change of lodging. Francis gave the Bishop some binoculars. On leaving for Doddington the All Saints' parishioners gave F.L. a parchment extolling his 'good qualities and extreme kindness', and the simple directness of his preaching. My enquiries in the parish of Doddington drew a total blank; though I did find one tiny shred of evidence concerning this period: a 'flyer' tucked into his diary to mark a place. It outlined the church services for a period in the summer of an undisclosed year (3). Though both of F.L.'s Lincoln city parishes were 'high church' and he served under a bishop of that persuasion, there is nothing about this flyer that suggests other than main-stream, middle-of-the-road Anglicanism (there is, for example, no use of words like

'Mass'). If this suggests anything, it suggests an intention to be, as far as possible, 'all things to all people.'

Rogation Sunday May 21st
Holy Communion - 8am
Mattins, Litany and Sermon - 11am
Evensong and sermon - 3 pm

Rogationtide is an occasion of prayer to God for the fruits of the earth and the nation's welfare. It is right that in this country parish all who can should come to God's House on Rogation Sunday and ask his blessing on the growing crops

Ascension Day Thurs May 25th
Mattins & Holy Communion - 11 am
Evensong and sermon - 6.30 pm

Whitsunday June 4
Mattins and sermon - 11am
Holy Communion - 12 noon
Evensong and sermon - 3pm

The offerings on this day will be given for the church expenses. It is hoped that all, and especially those who are not called upon to pay the voluntary rate, will on Whitsunday contribute something towards the necessary expenses connected with the church

---

The flyer contains two extended paragraphs explaining the nature of particular religious observances. One might have guessed that Rogationtide would have a special meaning for F.L. because of his interest in all things rural and connected to natural history. The connection is made in the mildest manner possible. The second paragraph, on Whit Sunday, contains the Anglican pastor's constant (through the ages) concern with offerings to support the fabric of religion. What is interesting about this flyer is not what it says, but what it does not say. There is no word that could be given any theological meaning of any substance even about such a key festival as Whitsun.

Cast your mind back to F.L.'s period in the Doddington parish recounted earlier. Some of our knowledge of the period came from the school Log, where the mistress of the school recorded the assiduous attention of

F.L. to teaching the scriptures to the children; and the inspectors were generally impressed by the children's learning. But most of the material was rote learning (the Log implies as much). As Rector, it was clear that he was attentive to his duties to the school, but we can deduce little more.

On moving to Melbury, Dorset, the only glimmer of activity we can discern from the records in the church is that during F.L.'s time the Mothers' Union branch was established.

Finally, from 1929, he ministered in the tiny parish of Dyrham. In his (birding) obituary for F.L. Dr Rooke makes two brief references to his status as a clergyman: 'He was an inspiration…as a parish priest…' and 'devoted to the end to his parishioners and much loved by them', a view echoed by Christopher Salmon (4).

I have moved a lot of sources to try to find an article, a sermon, any written product by F.L. on a religious topic. The All Saints' archive has one: a sermon dated 3.11.07. In it F.L. makes clear that we don't 'learn morality from God's works in nature… Think of… the survival of the fittest.' Science reveals the 'orderliness' of the 'master mind', but not God's morality nor his love. A trawl of the Lincoln Diocesan Magazine for the years 1909-1916 found a single article by F.L. It was called 'Lincolnshire Gulleries'. It was his only contribution (5). The silence is yawning. Conversely, I have searched throughout his diaries, through all his published work, in every shred of birding material I can find to reveal even a single link between the wonder of nature and a story of Creation, the supremacy of the Deity over nature – in fact any theological mention at all. Nothing.

The most that can be said goes like this: for F.L. his world as a parson and his world as a birder were entirely compartmented, the one never impinging on the other. He never enters the debates that were contemporary with him about the relationship between science and religion. While there is much extant writing of his about birds, and on other aspects of natural history, there is no immediately accessible source through which to review his role as theologian or pastor. In each of his parishes he seems to have been effective in his job, satisfying his superiors; as far as we can tell he satisfied the parishioners and was liked. He does not seem to have had any clerical ambition beyond being a parish priest.

What can one conclude of F.L. the pastor? The Lincolnshire archives show he had excellent relationships with both his bishops. A vellum scroll from the parishioners of All Saints' records their esteem, his work with the Men's Groups being singled out for praise. Evidence from Doddington is sparse; he was attentive to teaching the school pupils. In Dyrham he was regarded with enduring affection: Mrs Hitchings recalls him walking or cycling daily to visit his parishioners, and his concern to place youngsters in employment. He kept theology and ornithology at arm's length from each other, yet served both causes with integrity and truth.

F.L. Blathwayt – President of the LNU

Though he had left the county at the end of 1916, F.L. accepted the presidency of the Lincolnshire Naturalists' Union for 1918 and kept up writing its Vertebrate Zoology report for some years after his departure. In its review of his presidency, 'R.W.G.' writing on behalf of the LNU surveyed F.L.'s biography and his achievements: the latter, a kind of interim evaluation of F.L. as naturalist. He noted that Francis had since been appointed President of the Somerset Archaeological and Natural History Society. His published work was also noted. Of his achievement as a naturalist and birder, this is what the short appreciation says:

From his youth Mr Blathwayt has been interested in birds, and the problems connected with their migration. Some ornithologists consider the gun a *sine qua non*, but Mr Blathwayt was not a naturalist of the sportsman type. It has been his practice to make observations of living birds by means of field glasses.

This statement is factually true, but there is no value judgement in it. He goes on:

Some of the Presidents of the Lincolnshire Naturalists' Union have been what may be termed all round naturalists. Others have been specialists in particular branches of natural history. Three of them have been Members of the British Ornithologists' Union. The first of these, the late Mr John Cordeaux, was one of the best ornithologists of his time, and had a great and widespread reputation. The second was that keen and competent observer, Mr G.H. Caton Haigh, who was President in 1913; and the third was Mr Blathwayt, whose abilities and personal qualities admirably fitted him for the office. Not only had he a thorough knowledge of the subject of his own special study, but he had a significant faculty for fellow-work.

This summary is the nearest the article gets to an analysis of F.L.'s work or praise of it. It concludes:

In whatever county he has resided, Mr Blathwayt has paid attention to local bird life, and from time to time he has made interesting discoveries as to the habitats of rare birds, one of his latest discoveries being the fact that the roseate tern breeds in Dorset.

Little else of substance is said. Earlier, I defended the stance taken in this chapter of putting forward a personal view. This is a moment to assert one.

R.W.G.'s assessment of Francis Linley seems to me at best to praise with feint damns, at worst to imply a second-rateness to his work. The key to understanding this passage lies, it seems, in its semantics. For, it might just be saying: here is a third good birder, an MBOU, who has been President of the LNU; he has been a rather 'different' character from what we have known by virtue of his beliefs about observing the living bird; his talent is now appreciated by other counties, who are fortunate to have his expertise for a time.

But that is not the way it reads to me. I construct the argument, based on semantic clues, to run covertly as follows: Francis Blathwayt was a birder President, but was a second-rater in comparison to fine birders of the past like John Cordeaux and Caton Haigh. He was not as good as Cordeaux (one of the 'best of his time'); nor was he a good observer like Caton Haigh. He was a fly-by-night who had too many interests out-of-county. His style contradicted the shooting/collection culture that many of us admire. His local studies are rather jéjeune; and his success with important rarities has itself been rare and not of significance to Lincolnshire. He is insufficiently committed to Lincolnshire since he has not, and will not, spend his whole life here.

You might think I am being harsh about R.W.G., but his is an evaluative synopsis which fails to mention or give enough credit to:

- The value of local/species studies to ornithology
- The significance of F.L.'s observational approach to science, and his part in replacing the preservation of rarities in death with their preservation in life
- The importance of F.L. as a birder of wider experiences which could bear on county issues in Lincolnshire
- The achievement of F.L. as a nationally published writer on birding, even at an early age
- F.L.'s insistence that a record, to be valuable, had first to be secure

The piece also underplays F.L.'s undoubted all-round ability as a naturalist, even though his prime interest is indeed in birding. It is, in my view, a grudging piece, redolent of prejudice (6). I suspect that the piece was written by someone, perhaps not the most appropriate person for the task, with an axe to grind. The R.W.G. in question turns out to be R.W.Goulding. Goulding was a long-term Honorary Assistant Secretary to the LNU, a joint editor of *Transactions,* but never Vice-President or President. He was the librarian of Welbeck College, Worksop, Nottinghamshire but at some stage lived in Louth. His own obituary in the *Transactions* describes him as lovable but somewhat pedantic; and his interests were not ornithological. Interestingly, Goulding's assessment was not the stuff of F.L.'s earlier death notice by the Honorary Secretary in the journal, which described him as a 'great ornithologist' and a 'keen entomologist' as well as a pioneer of modern conservation. The argument here is that Goulding's grudging tribute has coloured F.L.'s status in the county ever since it was penned, a status that stands in contrast with the appreciative assessment of him elsewhere.

The impression was confirmed to a degree when I consulted Lorand and Atkin's book on Lincolnshire Birds (7). Though their assessment is more balanced and even a touch more generous, there is still a hint of Blathwayt treachery:

Another ornithologist of note, the Revd F. L. Blathwayt, was secretary of the vertebrate zoology section of the Union [i.e. the LNU] for many years. His interest in the distribution of birds led him to study them in other parts of the county such as the Lincoln area which had previously been neglected. He published an interesting paper on the birds of Scotton Common (1906) but his major contribution was the first complete annotated list of the Birds of Lincolnshire (1915) which appeared in the *Transactions for* 1914 [sic]. Blathwayt highlighted the need for more observations to be made in the southern half of the county but unfortunately he left Lincolnshire in 1916.

So it's no good having ideas unless you see them through personally! To have pointed others in the right directions is not enough! I'm sure that this is a little unkind to Lorand and Atkin, but the atmosphere of half-hearted credit still prevails. Though Wentworth-Day's assessment of Lincolnians is probably too harsh, the fact remains that 'yellow-bellies' (as the true natives like to be known) are suspicious of anyone whose family, within recorded history, has not occupied the same house in the same village for the whole of living memory and beyond. F.L. could have stayed until he was a hundred, but he would never have received the recognition he merited. We have seen, from *Transactions,* how little active support he got in the way of records submitted.

In the event, Francis left Lincolnshire in 1916, of course; though the year 1918 in which he served the LNU in the capacity of President was not his last foray into an office for a County organisation. For an assessment of his later work we shall wait to review his contribution to birding in general. At this stage, however, it must be said that his embryonic contribution to ornithology was already being more readily recognised, and his talents sought more assiduously, elsewhere than they were in Lincolnshire. By contrast, his own commitment to the county, however, did not diminish; and in 1937 he wrote a letter in his hard-to-read hand which I discovered between the pages of the *Transactions* at the Lincoln Museum. It recorded his reading of the latest edition 'with much interest'; regretting that Caton Haigh seemed no longer to publish his bird notes; and correcting an entry that claimed a first for great crested grebes breeding at Hartsholme with a reference to his own note on this in the 1912 *British Birds* XXVI p 193!

F.L.Blathwayt – editor

In its 'Farewell Tribute' article to Francis, the Dorset *Proceedings* passed this judgement (8) on his editorship:

He was the editor of the annual Bird Reports from 1918 until he handed over to the present writer in 1949...Without this invaluable summary of more recent knowledge, present-day observers would find it practically impossible to bridge the gap of sixty-five years since the publication of 'The Birds of Dorsetshire' by J.C. Mansel-Pleydell (1888).

Of itself, this is a story of dedication, discipline, and persistence. But the writer goes on:

His ornithological activities were not confined to Dorset, but he continued to write the annual reports for twenty years after leaving the county in 1929. There was no-one adequately to fill his place, and it would be difficult to over-estimate our indebtedness to him for his long and devoted service to Dorset ornithology.

It didn't matter, then, that he raised a field-glass to look at birds that had the temerity to float beyond the county boundary, nor that his home was a few miles across that hallowed border, nor indeed that he had also edited the annual bird report for Somerset. What mattered was the enthusiasm, the consistency and the hard work of the man in the cause of the county's birds.

F.L. Blathwayt – writer

And so we come to a more complicated assessment: an evaluation of F.L.'s writing. For this it is necessary to set a little more scene.

We have observed that at the turn of the 20th century birding was a pastime engaged in substantially by landed gentry, the leisured middle classes (such as the clergy), and by those motivated mainly by considerations of collecting (of eggs or skins) or of estate management (game-keeping). Bird protection began only with the formation of the RSPB; even then it was slow to take hold of the psyche of the average person. Environmental protection and management is a comparatively modern and emergent phenomenon. Bird watching as a pastime might be argued to be essentially a hobby of the middle or upper classes at this early time, while birding for the poor or socially deprived was associated more with activities such as food-gathering or financial gain.

Nevertheless, we saw that writers such as W.H. Hudson had forged a tradition of writing narratives about bird-watching that had popular appeal, a tradition which was later to be expanded with the growth of interest in birds among people of all social strata. Bird writing suddenly became readable. These few paragraphs set out to trace the growth of bird-related writing within a social and scientific context during the period of F.L.'s life.

The first intention is to classify approaches to writing about birds or to create a typology of them; and the following criteria seem appropriate by which to judge bird writing of the time:

- Popular/informative
- Pre-scientific
- Scientific
- Post-scientific
- Post-modernist

These classifications can be defined thus:

Popular/informative: in these the main intention is to entertain the reader, but in this case to do so within a bird-watching context; birds are the 'pegs around which to hang the narrative' (9).

Pre-scientific: here the narrative itself forms the main thrust of the writing, the 'encounters with birds' forging the links which move the story along. There may appear to be little attempt to provide the reader with a conscious framework of ornithological knowledge or add to scientific understanding of the species mentioned; the genre is sometimes marked out by anthropomorphisms; it relies on, rather than questioning, existing knowledge and is to that extent pre-modernist (10).

Scientific: this genre is first and foremost modernist and is designed to bring the reader to a greater scientific knowledge and appreciation of the birds encountered - their appearance, habits, songs and behaviour - and to encourage in the reader a scientific 'way of seeing' birds that they themselves might encounter. The genre exhibits itself particularly in the essentially episodic books built around chapters illustrating encounters with specific species (11).

Post-scientific: here, the author's fundamental concern is with material which is chosen to be located in a setting involving both birds themselves, and also an assumption that the reader is aware of ornithological/ environmental issues; while the birding theme appears to be incidental, it in fact demands a quite high degree of specialist knowledge from the reader (12).

Post-modernist: reverses or upsets conventional views by, for example, beginning from the 'natural world' as the 'ideal' and our interference in it as the factor that disturbs natural balances; it assumes that humans have lessons to learn from nature/ornithology rather than about nature or birds (13).

These categories, then, form a typology for classifying bird-related writing, it is suggested. However, the categories are not mutually exclusive. Just as fashion blends elements from previous and present eras to create a currency, so the writers of bird-related texts move - sometimes consciously, sometimes uneasily - from category to category.

Other literary ploys are employed in these birding contexts: e.g.

*   Suspense (14)
*   Humour (15)
*   Ecological values & attitudes (16)
*   Political and value-driven stances (17)
*   Characterisation of human and bird participants in the narrative (18)

The narrative forms employed by writers to pursue ornithological themes are varied, most notably:

*   Novel (19)
*   Diary - which focuses on the writer (20)
*   Calendar - which focuses on the seasons (21)
*   Itinerary (22)
*   Autobiography (23)

It is suggested that, between them, the categories of the typology, the literary ploys, and the narrative forms combine to provide a three-dimensional model that helps us understand better the minds of bird writers during this period. But where does that leave Francis Blathwayt?

His writing is interesting because it serves different audiences and different purposes:

The Diaries: the genre describes itself. They are essentially private and completely unpublished, though we have seen that, even from an early stage, there is a sense of the self-conscious in them, a hint that they may be accessed (eventually) by third parties. They are essentially notebooks: logs of occurrences with a few longer passages that describe events or explore issues – passages that often form the basis and *aides memoires* of later public writing.

The Lists: are unashamedly scientific. That is their function and purpose.

The Articles: vary in type. Some are unequivocally scientific: these include the Notes in *British Birds* such as the one on the calls of British waders. Some are scientific but tending to the post-scientific: in this category one might place his Presidential Address to the LNU, and the item on 'The Etiology of the Occurrence and Dispersal of Birds in Dorset' – both of which have passages in them which go beyond the recording of scientific facts. 'A visit to Lundy' has elements of the post-scientific about it. Finally, there are what might be called 'notes about bird behaviour' – these may be the whole of an article or just a portion of it (one recalls, for example, passages about snipe drumming, and his piece for *British Birds* on the drumming of woodpeckers).

So we have to conclude that F.L.'s basic style – and intention – is scientific, though elements of the post-scientific intrude from time to time throughout his writing life. He does not lend himself to literary ploys: he is not a man for suspense or humour, not even for political stances. He would reject anthropomorphism. There are strong elements of ecological and conservation values, but they are firmly welded to scientific principles. He does not resort generally to forms such as the story or the calendar to make his points; but there is, in the Lundy article, an early example of the use of itinerary as a means to hold the material together. It makes for good reading, but is never repeated. Sometimes there is the trace of an intention to educate but the work is not 'educational'.

In F.L. we have a serious man, writing serious scientific material much of the time, mostly in article form. Just as in his pastoral work he does not appear to promote any particularly powerful views, so in his scientific work he shows political tolerance. (There are a couple of exceptions in passages – such as in the Presidential Address – when he becomes angry at the law's lack of teeth to protect birds). Yet, one is left with the feeling that he could have added an attractive dimension to his work by indulging a little more often in that more personable style which creeps in when he wades into Twigmoor ponds after black-headed gull chicks, or follows the starling flocks to Bracebridge to watch their aerial evolutions. There are moments there of poetry (24), which perhaps he thought of as weakness. We shall never know.

F.L. Blathwayt – the man

In what we have said so far there are a few clues to the nature of F.L. the man. Let us review them.

He is above all a scientist. He is persistent, and dedicated to his scientific tasks. He is a man given to the collection and the collation of data – perhaps a legacy from his Civil Servant father. He shows touches of sensitivity to his subject matter, but never allows emotion to come between his observations and good science. His attention to detail may have been pedantic: one recalls his visit to Kirton Lindsey where he viewed specimens designed to raise money for the Red Cross, only to find that they were incorrectly identified! Again, on his curate's licence, he alters the clerk's error regarding the county in which his home is located.

He is a clergyman but not a preacher in any negative sense: he never imposes religious views through his bird-writing. He does not take umbrage with fellow birders who shoot or collect eggs, even though he does not generally support these practices. As a clergyman he appears to have been rather tolerant and open-minded. He lived through interesting and turbulent times – social and ornithological – yet he never joins any cause or thumps any tub. When he moved to Doddington, his predecessor said of him:

He brings with him the highest commendation from his vicar and the parish in Lincoln in which he has worked for eight years past...He is *ready to continue* [my italics – author] our several parish institutions, such as Sunday and day school, clothing club, penny bank and parish magazine...(25)

Of all his family members, he seems to have had most affinity with Lt Col Linley Blathwayt. This gentleman was a supporter of the controversial suffragettes, yet F.L does not distance himself from his uncle. F.L. himself went birding with female friends. He appears to have had a wide circle of male birding friends, acquaintances and correspondents. He went birding with some of them (though none regularly), and in some cases with their dogs. He was unpretentious, mixing and dining as well with the woodman as with the noble Lord: a rare gift indeed. He actively sought out people in lowly positions whenever he could learn from them and was not hesitant to do so.

We must assume that he was a leader: he was President of two County organisations (Lincolnshire and Somerset), and Vice-President for many years of the Dorset Naturalists. His *Proceedings* obituary calls him modest. The record also repeats that he was always interested in the work of others in fields other than his own specialism. He is generous: he purchased items out of his own pocket for the Lincoln museum.

F.L. served as curate in poor urban areas between 1900 and 1909; he would have witnessed and ministered to the least privileged in society; he was sufficiently competent at this that his first vicar wanted him as curate again when he moved to the next appointment.

Yet he does not seem to have had clerical ambitions. He spent his entire life from 1909 as the vicar of just three rural parishes, each isolated, in areas of low population, and without any apparent pastoral challenge beyond the regular events of birth and marriage and death. He was perhaps a man, modern in birding ideas, but representing an 'old world' – the *Proceedings* obituary again: 'Changing economic and other conditions make it unlikely that there will ever be another great amateur Dorset ornithologist...His death marks...the passing of an era.'

His wife barely features in his narratives of birding (at least during the Lincolnshire period); it seems unlikely that she shared his interest, though clearly she supported his pastoral work in the school at Doddington. F.L. continued his interest in passing on birding and related skills to young people: he tested the Guide Company at Dyrham on their Naturalist, Birdwatcher and Stargazer proficiency badges, while Marjorie was District and Divisional Commissioner for the Girl Guides, according to Christiana Poole (26), who recalls (as a member of the Company in 1945) his daughters, Miss Barbara and Miss Jean (who died about 2002). She says:

I owe so much to this wonderful family who gave us so much pleasure as Guides at their lovely home and garden. They were the last of the gentry clergy.

We have noted that F.L. is a man who does not often share emotion. Once or twice he became impassioned about the failures of the law to protect birds; here and there he spoke with poetic appreciation of particular habitats; but his entry on the death of the mistress of the school at Doddington has a clipped 'stiff-upper-lip' Englishness. He leaves Doddington with only 'a few words' to the children. Maybe he found it hard to say goodbye, embarrassing to be the centre of attention.

Physically, he is a tough man. He can bike fifty miles to the coast, watch birds for six hours, and ride back. He can go out in freezing temperatures, with merely a footnote about them in his records. He won prizes for running and jumping at school and again at Oxford (27). 'He was an active explorer of the countryside on foot and cycle' throughout his life (28). In his Lincoln years he skated, played golf and went fishing. We have advanced a tentative theory that he may have suffered some problem (such as arthritis) in the hands, as his writing sometimes deteriorated markedly. He was often out late (to see nightjars) or up early.

F.L. is the epitome of the Blathwayt motto: through integrity and truth. In his 'listing' activity he is not afraid to exclude the unacceptable record, however great the putative observer. Yet always it is done with a reason and a nod to the other person's feelings. He praises others; yet is tentative in ascribing merit to himself.

There is one theory that has to be interrogated in relation to F.L. and which seems, on the face of it, to have some merit. In a fascinating article for the Rural Theology Association (29) Francis *et al* carry out studies of their own, and review those of others, to test the hypothesis that rural clergy are, in psychological terms, more introvert than urban clergy.

They use, as their subjects, only clergy from 'deeply rural' parishes such as those F.L. served in from 1909-1953. Their definition of introversion is taken from Eysenck's work, and includes these characteristics: that the subject is quiet, retiring, introspective, fond of books, reserved except to intimate friends, tends to plan ahead, takes life with proper seriousness, keeps feelings under close control, is not aggressive, is reliable, may be pessimistic, and places great value on ethical standards.

There can be, from our study, little doubt that F.L. comes closer to the introvert end of any personality continuum than to the extrovert end. Introverts (in the correct sense of the term) can, of course, relate well to people, join in teams, lead and so on – all F.L. characteristics, too. The theory would explain his adherence to the life of a rural parson, and it is consistent with what is known. It has to be stressed, however, that this is pure conjecture. F.L. never took an Eysenck personality test; nor do we know how he would have scored on the 'lie scale' dimension' of this test. This sub-test, buried in the main inventory of scored items, measures social conformity. Francis *et al* maintain, from their work, that rural clergy are also conformists, traditionalists, and likely to maintain the *status quo*. Again, the picture would fit with what we know of F.L. – but he didn't take the test and this is mere speculation.

F.L. Blathwayt – birder

So we come at last to assessing F.L.'s contribution to birding. To explore these issues I want to advance, and then answer, five questions:

- Is the work good science?
- Are the birds well observed?
- Are the articles well written?
- Does the published work add to a) knowledge and b) appreciation of the subject?
- Does the work become authoritative?

I have already hinted at the answers to some of these questions; but it is time to draw these assessments together.

- *Is the work good science?*

The answer is unequivocally: yes. F.L. provided the birding world with the basis for three County Lists: those of Somerset, Lincolnshire and Dorset. There are few people who could claim a third as much! He did this by a rigorous examination and interrogation of written sources, using the living voice of experts, and through his own detailed observations. He broke new ground in finding birds never before seen in particular locations, e.g. the Dorset roseate terns and the marsh warblers. F.L. pioneered the concept of watching a 'patch', and adopted such areas throughout his life, beginning with the Lincoln ballast pits. He asked scientific questions, like those about the distribution of diving birds in the Severn estuary – and he put forward hypotheses to answer them. He made predictions, including some very good ones, about species that might spread into previously unoccupied, but suitable, locations. He solved puzzles such as how snipe drum. He had the foresight to begin a long-term study of herons, something pursued by later generations of birders. He did not take information received at face value: he pursued the detail until he could be certain. When he was not certain, even about his own sightings, he said so. He was aware of the need to study not merely the prestigious and the unusual, but the common-place and over-looked.

- *Are the birds well observed?*

Again, the answer has to be affirmative. Observation is a Blathwayt trade-mark. Wedded from the beginning to his twelve times field-glasses, F.L. is the archetypal observer of nature. Recall, for example, the incident of the crossbills at Hartsholme. His is not the lazy approach of the 'twitcher', turning up to tick the list and moving on to the next thrill. He returns every few days, pursuing issues about: how many are there, are they breeding, and how long do they stay? He collects data from other observers to build a complete picture. The same quiet observation provided the detail we have recorded on the great crested grebes of the ballast pits, the evening evolution of starlings, and even the Washingborough marsh warblers – whose identification F.L. eventually rejected.

- *Are the articles well written?*

He wrote of many of his encounters with birds. This is not the time to rehearse all these encounters. Of course, some of the writing is powerfully scientific, and much of it consists of his favoured 'complete lists'. This kind of writing has stood the test of time, as we have seen. But there are passages that are fine pieces in their own right. His Presidential Address to the LNU and the 'Etiology' article for Dorset are classics of their kind. But birders will be entranced, too, by his descriptions: of his first encounter with shorelarks, of his observation of grasshopper warblers in the Doddington woods, of his approach to the common ternery on the Chesil beach, his first proof of roseates breeding in Dorset. My personal view is that I would have liked to have read even more of these kinds of passage. If they have a fault it is their rarity. So he is a fine writer on occasion, though he did not sustain this style sufficiently to be rated among the greats.

- *Does the published work add to a) knowledge and*
  b) appreciation of the subject?

F.L. wrote a substantial corpus. There is no question that he laid the foundation of knowledge that has stood three counties in good stead, but especially the county of Dorset. His obituary reads at one point:

No one had previously contributed as much [i.e. to Dorset ornithology], and no single person can hope in future to exceed the span and scope of his contribution.

This is a fine legacy for a quarter of a century's work. But my belief is that his contribution to Lincolnshire, though a mere sixteen years in duration, provided an equally impressive basis for that county. For sixteen years, as a very active young man, he toiled in a relatively unappreciative vineyard. It was equally true of his Lincolnshire-based work as of his Dorset-based contributions that (as the *Proceedings* have it):

He was one of the few great local naturalists, close to the Gilbert White tradition.

I believe he would have been accorded his full recognition if his diaries had been edited and published, and if his works had contained just a little more of that descriptive power alongside the listing.

- ● *Does the work become authoritative?*

Now, to the last criterion. How authoritative is the work of F.L. some fifty or a hundred years later?

I conducted an experiment. As someone used to publishing – albeit in a totally different field – one measure of success is citation. How many times, and for how long, is the work one produces used by other authors and quoted either as an exemplar or as a source of knowledge? So I went to my book-shelves and pulled down a few birding texts to see whether F.L. Blathwayt featured in any of them – besides, of course, the county-based literature for Somerset (30), Lincolnshire (31) and Dorset (32). It was a slightly idle gesture: I didn't expect to find much.

I was wrong. Within minutes I found these citations (33):

Marples, G and Marples, A. (1934) *Sea Terns or Sea Swallows* London: Country Life – an acknowledgement for information supplied to this very detailed behavioural study

Smith, S. (1950) *The Yellow Wagtail* London: Collins, New Naturalist Monograph – a well-regarded volume that contains three citations

Campbell. B. (1954) 'The breeding distribution and habitats of the Pied Flycatcher in Britain' *Bird Study* (1) 3, page 98

Doncaster Bird Club (1988) *The Birds of Doncaster* Doncaster: Doncaster Bird Club

Summers-Smith, J.D. (1995) *The Tree Sparrow* Cleveland: published by the author – probably the most revered writer on the species, two citations

Clarke, R. (1996) *Montagu's Harrier* Chelmsford: Arlequin Press, a volume in a series of soaring prestige

Holloway, S. (1996) *Historical Atlas of Breeding Birds in Britain and Ireland* London: Poyser – a reference volume of high calibre, five citations

In addition, a look at the amazon.co.uk web-site produced a roneo copy of F.L.'s article for the LNU: 'The Birds of Lincolnshire'.

To be quoted by such authoritative sources, over such a long period, in such depth, is an achievement of monumental proportions. So one must conclude, with the *Proceedings* obituary:

The results of his work remain as a solid foundation...Its value will be maintained as long as human interest in...natural history.

• *Summary*

F.L. was indefatigable despite being troubled later in life by the arthritis which was signalled in the handwriting of his diaries. He died on 30th June 1953, aged 78. As I was writing this text I went to the churchyard at Dyrham to try to find his grave. Most of the plots were buried under tall grasses and nettles. Maybe he wouldn't have minded, but I did (34).

If the reader will forgive me one final quotation from Dr Rooke's obituary in the *Proceedings,* then it is this, which seems to sum up the man:

With characteristic modesty, he referred to the very great pleasure it had given him to have been allowed to 'keep the flag flying' during [the] difficult years of war and absence from the county...He visited Abbotsbury on 10th June 1953, and wrote a long letter on this and other matters only four days before his unexpected death. He would certainly have wished to extend to all present and future Dorset observers the characteristically encouraging farewell greeting with which he ended his last letter to [me]: 'Good luck among the birds'.

•

In 1977 I promised myself that I would follow in the footsteps of a young clergyman, not only at Hartsholme, Lincoln, but down the path of his life. This story is the result. To write it has been a privilege. I hope it has done him justice, and has been a fitting legacy and tribute to its inspiration,

FRANCIS LINLEY BLATHWAYT

Two photographs of F.L. supplied by Lucy Morrill, his grand-daughter.

The top picture must date from c. 1900 when he was first ordained.

Note the front-buttoned cassock, in the 'Roman' style.

The lower picture shows F.L. in more conventional dog-collar, black stock, and suit jacket.

It probably dates from the 1920s.

The date of this picture is unknown, but probably relates to the Melbury era as it is held at the Dorset County Museum

NOTES TO CHAPTER 12

1.   If this approach offends the more scholarly reader then let me say that much that passes for scholarly detachment will exhibit more bias than the words of this chapter – for opinion can be formed and shaped to a pre-determined view by means more subtle than clear and honest expression of opinion based on facts.

2.   USA President Bill Clinton, Dimbleby Lecture, radio broadcast.

3.   It is possible to calculate the year by deciding in which of the years 1909-1916 the quoted dates fell to Sundays. The Prayer Book table of dates of movable feasts shows that the year was 1911.

4.   Written by Dr K.B. Rooke for the *Proceedings*, being a shortened version of the same author's obituary in British Birds vol XLVII (1953, vol 75, p 33). The latter speaks of the 'wreath of wild flowers gathered from the fields and hedges he knew so well' and laid as a tribute by the children at his burial in Dyrham churchyard. Mr Salmon (pers. comm. 24.08.05) notes that after F.L.'s death the parish was no longer held in singularity and attendances began to decline.

5.   Lincoln Diocesan Magazine vol XXIX no 324 June 1913 pp 90-1. F.L. is not otherwise featured as an author, nor as a preacher at any venue, nor as a member of any committee that is listed. The gulleries article drew correspondence (*LDM* November 1913) from a reader who opined that, despite this piece, the education authorities in Holland, Kesteven and Lindsey did little to promote the RSPB's initiative, a Bird and Tree Competition. By contrast, the church at Doddington does appear: in June 1911 it receives a grant of £35 towards £700 worth of building restoration; in July it closes for work to be carried out and services move to the 'granary above the Hall stables'; and in February 1912 it re-opens having had a new floor, the roof timbers revealed, the East window raised, and the box pews replaced by open ones. The Bishop of Grantham officiated; but Mr Mantle had to accompany the service on the harmonium ' as the walls were not yet dry enough to receive the organ.' In chapter 2 there was a discussion of how 'scientific' clergy rationalised their science with contemporary religious belief. The only other clue we have in F.L.'s case comes from this passage from the All Saints' sermon: 'God the Father...has existed from all time...He is the great Creator...Think of the infinite power of the Creator, and then think what that claim (ie in John 10.30) of Christ's involved - "I and my Father are One"... It is only in the life and teaching of Christ...that we can discover (what no searching into science will ever discover) the great truth, that the splendours of God are the splendours of His moral purity...mercy, truth and love.' So God created the orderly, scientific world, but it does not reveal the higher attributes of God - only the Son can do that. Remembering what was said about John's Gospel in chapter 2 - that it was the 'spiritual' and philosophical gospel - it is perhaps significant that F.L.'s only extant sermon is based on it, and on this rather mystical passage.

6.   Lincolnshire has been my adopted county for thirty years, yet I have to admit that it shares a failing of rural areas: to underplay anything done outside its boundaries or by anyone from without its walls. There is an intensely cruel passage (in C.E.M. Joad's *The English Counties* London: Odhams, undated, pp 218-9) by J. Wentworth-Day: 'The characteristics of the Lincolnshire people are, in fine, like the characteristics of their county – uncompromising, dour in parts, ugly in patches, downright, and of a thorough-going English independence. There is little that is soft about them, least of all their women...Their humour is unsparing but seldom subtle...[with] a box-your-ears defiance of people from other parts...' I would have rejected the notion until I went to teach in a small rural primary school. On the first day, a colleague mentioned the name of the next village, just down the road. I said I didn't know it. 'Don't go there,' was the response, 'they're the

enemy.' Goulding's assessment of F.L., with its sting in the tail, might therefore have been seized on more readily than an open mind would expect. Some of Goulding's resentment stems from the ornithological bias of F.L. However, even this is to some degree a mis-representation. Throughout his years in Lincolnshire F.L. was the secretary of the LNU's Vertebrate Zoology section, compiling its annual reports and, in 1912, one of his favoured and detailed lists - of Lincolnshire mammalia. Throughout 1912-1918 he repeatedly bemoans the fact that there are few ornithologists and fewer students of mammals who send him information. Meanwhile he logs personally both the first and the second sightings ever of the whiskered bat in Lincolnshire; and even as late as 1947 F.L. (who remained a lifelong member of the LNU) writes an extensive note (volume 12, pp 91-93) on 'The Chequered Skipper in Lincolnshire'. F.L. was shown this butterfly by 'my uncle [i.e. his mother's brother] the late Canon W.W.Fowler (of beetle fame)' who lived in Lincoln from 1880-1900, overlapping F.L.'s time there very briefly. Hardly the actions of a man careless of wildlife other than birds. It seems this W.W. was William Weekes Fowler who Armstrong, P. (2000 *The English Parson-Naturalist* pp 57 and 101) seems to confuse with Warde Fowler. Interestingly, little coincidences continue to pop up. In the late 1970s, when I was wardening Burton pits reserve, the manager became very excited by a slide which I had taken, but which – in my ignorance – I had thought nothing of. He heard that it was a shot of a chequered skipper taken on the reserve and, on checking with me, declared it to be first record for the area.

7.   Lorand and Atkin, pp 60-1.

8.   Volume 74 page 135 (cover date 1952).

9.   An example would be: Williamson, K. (1937) *The Sky's Their Highway* London: Putnam.

10.   E.g. White, T.H. (1951) *The Goshawk* Harmondsworth: Penguin, which illustrates the anthropomorphism issue.

11.   E.g. Hosking, E. and Newberry, C. (1940) *Intimate Sketches of Bird Life* London: Country Life; or Simson, C. (1960) *A Bird Overhead* London: Witherby.

12.   E.g. Calvert, W. (1937) *Wild Life on Moor and Fell* London: Hodder & Stoughton.

13.   E.g. Adams, R. (1974) *Watership Down* Harmondsworth: Penguin.

14.   E.g. Allsop, K. (1962 edn) *Adventure Lit Their Star* London: MacDonald.

15.   E.g. Stanford, J. (1954) *A Bewilderment of Birds* London: Rupert Hart-Davies.

16.   E.g. almost any title by W.H. Hudson.

17.   As above, note 16.

18.   E.g. Drake-Brockman, D. (1982) *The Birds of the Air* London: Search Press.

19.   E.g. Calvert op. cit. note 12.

20.   E.g. Hay, J.L. (1991) *The Bird of Light* New York: Norton.

21.   E.g. Badcock, J. (1973) *A Countryman's Calendar* Leicester: Vance Harvey.

22.   E.g. Campbell, B. (1979) *Birdwatcher at Large* London: Dent.

23.   E.g. Mitchell, W. (1983) *Birdwatch Around Scotland* London: Robert Hale.

24.   F.L. is certainly no Edith Holden (1977 *The Country Diary of an Edwardian Lady* London: Michael Joseph). Edith Holden's diary (contemporary with F.L., being for the year 1906) is a charming book: a mish-mash, it is true, of personal observations, exquisite drawings and paintings, other people's poetry, weather notes, reminders of key dates in the Church's calendar, lists of saints' days, and reflections. It does, however, ask some scientific questions: 'I noticed that the white periwinkle blossoms have five petals, while the blue have only four. I wonder if this is always so'; and it is strong on observation (but more wide-ranging in subject-matter being less tied to birding). Holden's diary is also strong on theology, albeit mostly at second-hand from poems and extracts quoted from other authors – something F.L.'s *never* is!

25.   Lincoln Diocesan Magazine vol XXV no 279 p 142 September 1909, Preferments, F.L. Blathwayt to Doddington Rectory 17ᵗʰ September 1909.

26.   Personal communication, Mrs Christiana Poole, 22.06.05. Mrs Poole also notes that the daughters were referred to as Miss Barbara and Miss Jean by their parents and the maid (who was also one of the Guides). Barbara was a member of the Guide International Service that was sent to Europe with a mobile hospital to cater for the needs of the newly liberated people of Holland towards the end of WWII. Jean wrote children's books and dedicated one to her father. Christopher Salmon, 24.08.05, calls Mrs Blathwayt 'a natural leader'.

27.   Notes supplied by his son, Linley Dennys Blathwayt, to the Dorset County Museum, and kindly copied to me.

28.   *Proceedings* vol 75 p 33.

29.   Francis, L., Smith, G. and Robbins, M.. (2004) 'Do introverted clergy prefer rural ministry?' *Rural Theology* 2 (2) pp 127-134. Their work is predicated on Eysenck, H. and Eysenck, S. (1991) *Manual of the Eysenck Personality Scales* London: Hodder and Stoughton. In a piece of research of my own using student teachers as subjects (Kerry, T. 1976 *Discussion Leadership Skills among Student Teachers* Unpublished M Phil thesis, Nottingham University), I found that those with high lie-scale scores on the EPS were the same students who scored highly on anxiety in other tests. Their behaviour as leaders manifested itself as dominant contribution (compared to other leaders) combined with fewer open-ended questions. The modern expression 'control freak' comes to mind!

30.   A. Sutton (1988) *Birds of Somerset,* Somerset Ornithology Society

31.   Smith, A. and Cornwallis, R. (1955) *The Birds of Lincolnshire* Lincoln: LNU; and Lorand, S. and Atkin, K. (1989) *The Birds of Lincolnshire and South Humberside* Hawes: Leading Edge.

32.   Green, G. (2004) *The Birds of Dorset* London: Christopher Helm

33.   This is by no means a complete list. For example, there are many occasions – of various kinds – in *British Birds* alone in which F.L.'s work is mentioned:

Unattributed review (1930): *Report on Somerset Birds 1928* [edited by FLB, BW Tucker and CJ Pring; described as a 'well drawn-out report...carefully put together by the editors'] vol XXIII p 232

Unattributed review (1931): *Report on Somerset Birds 1929* [edited by FLB assisted by BW Tucker; 'special attention has been devoted to duck...this section is valuable for permanent reference'] vol XXIV pp 229,230

Unattributed review (1931) *Report of Somerset Birds 1930* [by FLB and BW Tucker; 'this report, as usual, is well and carefully drawn up ...the willow tit can be added to the County List...blackcaps reported in February'] Vol XXV p 235

Harrison, T. and Hurrell, H. (1931) 'Numerical status of Great Black-backed Gull in Devon vol XXV October

Unattributed review (1933) *Dorset Phenological Report 1932* [by FLB; 'great crested grebe bred in the county for the first time']

Alexander, W. (1934) 'Black-headed gulls nesting in trees at Twigmoor' vol XXVIII [refers to FL's 1909 'Lincolonshire gulleries' paper]

Hollom, P.A.D. (1938) 'Report on the 1938 survey of black-headed gull colonies' vol XXXIII Jan pp 202-221 [FL is listed as an 'informant']

Unattributed review (1944) *Report on Dorset Natural Hitsory 1941* [edited by FLB; 'buzzards now breed regularly in one locality in Dorset'] vol XXXVII p 219 April

Unattributed review (1946) *Revised List of the Birds of Dorset* [by FL; 'very welcome' though the reviewer thinks that single sight record entries should be square-bracketed] vol XXIX p 35

Unattributed review (1948) *Report on Dorset Birds 1945* ['we learn with regret the well-known heronry at Arne...second largest in the country...has been entirely destroyed'] vol XLI Sept p 283

Cox, S. (1949) 'Bittern breeding in Lincolnshire' vol XLII December p 392

34. On a subsequent visit, on a much brighter day, I again searched without success for F.L.'s tombstone. The Dyrham Park guides had been unable to direct me and I had searched in vain in the mid-day heat. I had almost given up the quest and was back on the path when a great spotted woodpecker began calling that urgent 'chack' with which the species greets woodland visitors. I climbed up once more through the graves to get a view of it as it slid elusively through the tree-line on the summit above the church, dodging behind trunks and boughs. When at last I sighted it I found I was standing on the edge of a newly-cleared grave-stone. It was F.L.'s. Mrs E Hitchings tells me that, on F.L.'s death, Marjorie asked - unusually for the era - that no-one should wear mourning clothes to the memorial ceremony, but should make it an occasion of celebration for F.L.'s life. A font cover with a dove marks the event inside the church.

APPENDIX 1
A SELECTED LIST OF ORNITHOLOGICAL ARTICLES BY THE REVD F.L. BLATHWAYT

(1898)   'Birds of the Cairngorms' *The Zoologist* (2)

(1900)   'A visit to Lundy' *The Zoologist* (4), 375-380

(1902)   'The Roseate Tern on the Farne Islands'
The Zoologist (5), 53-54

(1906)   'Notes on the Birds that inhabit Scotton Common'
LNU Transactions (1) 107-113

(1906)   'Birds' in *Victoria History of the County of Somerset*
London: Dawsons of Pall Mall

(1908)   'Notes on the Birds of a Ballast Pit'
LNU Transactions (1), 222-229

(1908)   'Lincolnshire Heronries' *The Zoologist* p 450

(1909)   'Lincolnshire Gulleries' *The Zoologist* pp 139-144

(1909)   'Owls and Hawks of Lincolnshire with special reference
to the collection in the City and County Museum'
Lincoln City and County Museum Publication no. 6

(1911-1918) Sectional Officer's Report: Vertebrate Zoology –
annual reports in *LNU Transactions*

(1915)   'The Birds of Lincolnshire' *LNU Transactions for 1914*
pp 178-211

(1917)   'New Species of Birds Observed in Dorset since the
Publication of Mansel-Pleydell's *Birds of Dorset
1888*' *Proceedings of the Dorset Natural History and
Archaeological Society* (39) 45-52

(1918-1948) 'Reports on Dorset Birds' *Proceedings of the Dorset*

Natural History and Archaeological Society
[annually for 31 years]

(1918-1933) 'Phenological Report on First Appearances'
*Proceedings of the Dorset Natural History and
Archaeological Society* (40-55)

(1918)   'Some Birds of the Chesil Beach from Portland to
Abbotsbury' *Proceedings of the Dorset Natural History
and Archaeological Society* (40), pp 41-47

(1919)   'The Birds of Lincolnshire, Past, Present and Future'
LNU Transactions for 1918 pp 121-133

(1920)   'Dorset Gulleries' *Proceedings of the Dorset Natural
History and Archaeological Society* (42), pp 81-86

(1920-1949) 'Report on Somerset Birds' [annually for 30 years]

(1923)   'Notes on Dorset Heronries' *Proceedings of the Dorset
Natural History and Archaeological Society* (45), pp 75-80

(1932)   'The Etiology of the Occurrence and Dispersal of Birds
in Dorset' *Proceedings of the Dorset Natural History
and Archaeological Society* (54), pp 181-194

(1933)   'A revised list of the Birds of Dorset' *Proceedings of the
Dorset Natural History and Archaeological Society* (55),
pp 165-209

(1934-1943) 'Reports on Dorset Natural History' *Proceedings of the
Dorset Natural History and Archaeological Society* (56-65)

(1939)   'A revised list of the Birds of Dorset' *Proceedings of the
Dorset Natural History and Archaeological Society*
(61), 136-167)

(1945)   'A revised list of the Birds of Dorset' *Proceedings of the
Dorset Natural History and Archaeological Society*
(67), 95-126

Items from British Birds:
[Volume and page number quoted where known]

(1908)   I   pp 386-7 'Stock doves nesting on Lincoln Minster'

(1908)   II p 95 'Inland nesting of sheld-duck and nesting of pochard, shoveler and teal in Lincolnshire'

(1910)   III 'Irruption of crossbills'

(1910)   IV 'Crossbills nesting – probably nesting in Lincolnshire'

(1910)   IV pp 366-7 'Breeding of shoveler, tufted duck and garganey in Somerset'

(1914)   VII p 230 'Black redstarts in Lincolnshire and Northumberland'

(1914)   VII p231 'Ring Ouzel as foster parents of cuckoo'

(1916)   IX p 252 'Rough-legged buzzards and common buzzards in Lincolnshire'

(1916)   IX pp 319-320 'White-tailed eagle and rough-legged buzzard in Lincolnshire'

(1917)   XI p 13 'Nesting of the marsh warbler in Dorset'

(1917)   XI pp 93-4 'Roseate tern in Dorset'

(1920)   XIV p 40 'Wallcreeper in Dorset'

(1920)   XIV p 117 'Woodlark breeding in Somerset and description of nestling'

(1920)   XIV p 141 'Common sandpipers in Dorset'

(1920)   XIV p 167 *Letter: Breeding of the woodlark in Somerset*

(1921)   XV p 46 'Roseate terns breeding in Dorset' [F.L. and two companions prove breeding]

(1921)   XV p 85 'Grasshopper warbler nesting in Lincolnshire'

(1921)   XV p 87 'Breeding of the great spotted woodpecker in Cumberland'

(1922)   XVI p 27 'A breeding record of the spotted crake in Dorset'

(1922)   XV p242 *Letter: Former breeding of the Osprey in Ireland*

(1923)   XV p 242 'Great skua in Dorset'

(1923)   XVI pp 66-7 'Great black-backed gull breeding in Somerset'

(1923)   XVII p 147 'Sandwich tern breeding in Somerset'

(1923)   XVII p 147 *Letter: A habit of the lesser redpoll*

(1924)   XXVII p 89 'Sandwich tern breeding in Dorset'

(1925)   XVIII pp 301-2 (with B.W.Tucker) 'Ferruginous and Long-tailed ducks in Somerset'

(1925)   XIX p 22 'Water pipit in Dorset'

(1925)   XIX p 52 'Alpine swift in Dorset'

(1926)   XIX p 313 'Spoonbill in Dorset'

(1926)   XXI 'Water Pipit in Dorset'

(1930)   XXIV p 344 'Iceland gull in Somerset'

(1931)   XXV 'Iceland Gull in Devon'

(1932)   XXV p 334 'Drumming period of lesser spotted woodpecker'

(1936)   XXIX p 183 'The American Pectoral Sandpiper in Somerset'

(1938)   XXXI pp 267-8 'Some records of the calls and cries of British waders'

(1942)   XXXV pp 18,19 'Old record of Tengmalm's Owl in Somerset an error'

(1945)   XXXVIII p 119 'Breeding of kittiwake and lesser black-backed gull in Dorset'

(1945)   XXXVIII p 373 'Rose-coloured starling in Somerset' [part of a composite note from several observers]

(1950)   XLII p 386 'Wallcreeper in Jersey'

(1950)   XLII p 393 'Green-winged teal in Dorset' [includes correspondence with Peter Scott]

APPENDIX 2
A SPECIES LIST OF THE BIRDS OF
HARTSHOLME PARK 1975-1980

As recorded by EMBSC on the British Trust for Ornithology's Register of Ornithological Sites. [Grid Reference SK9446. Nomenclature follows the BTO's list as issued at the time. *indicates breeding. Refer to Chapter 4 for details.]

1. Great Crested Grebe*
2. Little Grebe
3. Cormorant
4. Grey Heron
5. Bittern (Sp)*
6. Mallard*
7. Teal
8. Gadwall
9. Wigeon
10. Pintail
11. Shovelor
12. Tufted Duck*
13. Pochard
14. Goldeneye
15. Goosander
16. Pink-footed Goose
17. Dark-bellied Brent Goose
18. Canada Goose
19. Mute Swan*
20. Whooper Swan
21. Buzzard
22. Sparrowhawk
23. Marsh Harrier
24. Kestrel
25. Red-legged Partridge
26. Grey Partridge*
27. Pheasant*
28. Water Rail
29. Moorhen*

30. Coot*
31. Lapwing
32. Golden Plover
33. Snipe
34. Woodcock
35. Green Sandpiper
36. Common Sandpiper
37. Great Black-back
38. Lesser Black-back
39. Herring Gull
40. Common Gull
41. Black-headed Gull
42. Common Tern*
43. Stock Dove*
44. Woodpigeon*
45. Turtle Dove
46. Collared Dove
47. Cuckoo
48. Barn Owl*
49. Little Owl
50. Tawny Owl
51. Nightjar
52. Swift
53. Kingfisher*
54. Green Woodpecker*
55. Great Spotted Woodpecker
56. Lesser Spotted Woodpecker
57. Skylark
58. Swallow*
59. House Martin
60. Sand Martin
61. Raven
62. Carrion Crow*
63. Rook
64. Jackdaw
65. Magpie
66. Jay*
67. Great Tit*
68. Blue Tit*
69. Cole Tit*
70. Marsh Tit*
71. Willow Tit
72. Long-tailed Tit*
73. Nuthatch

74. Treecreeper*
75. Wren*
76. Mistle Thrush*
77. Fieldfare
78. Song Thrush*
79. Redwing
80. Blackbird*
81. Stonechat
82. Nightingale*
83. Robin*
84. Grasshopper Warbler
85. Sedge Warbler*
86. Blackcap*
87. Garden Warbler*
88. Common Whitethroat*
89. Lesser Whitethroat*
90. Willow Warbler*
91. Chiffchaff*
92. Goldcrest*
93. Spotted Flycatcher*
94. Pied Flycatcher
95. Dunnock*
96. Meadow Pipit
97. Tree Pipit
98. Pied Wagtail*
99. White Wagtail
100. Grey Wagtail
101. Yellow Wagtail
102. Great Grey Shrike
103. Red-backed Shrike
104. Starling*
105. Greenfinch*
106. Goldfinch*
107. Siskin
108. Linnet*
109. Redpoll*
110. Bullfinch*
111. Chaffinch*
112. Brambling
113. Yellowhammer*
114. Reed Bunting*
115. House Sparrow*
116. Tree Sparrow*

APPENDIX 3
F.L.'s BIRDING EXCURSIONS AROUND
LINCOLNSHIRE 1901-1904

The intention of this Table is to indicate two main facets of F.L.'s birding in Lincolnshire with data taken from his birding diaries. The first is to give a taste of the frequency of birding expeditions, in particular to places about which he wrote or which contributed to the County List data. The second is to identify the range and geographical spread of his personal birding activity within the county.

The survey would have become very extensive if applied to the diary data for the whole period 1900-1916 when Francis was based in Lincoln city and then at Doddington. For this reason the period 7 November 1901 (the start of a new volume in his diary) until the close of 1904 has been sampled. This represents roughly 20% of his stay Lincolnshire, though all of it while domiciled in the city itself. By the end of 1901 he knows his way around the area and has had time to form some patterns. He often watches late morning (about 11a.m.) or in the late afternoon, which presumably relates to his availability after his clergy duties. He clearly has free days which he devotes entirely to either birding or some form of sport (golf, skating), though the two activities are not mutually exclusive.

Lincoln city locations are listed first, then those in the county – roughly in order of distance from Lincoln, the furthest being listed last.

The emergent data give a flavour of F.L.'s massive birding activity, carried out largely on foot and by bicycle, and sometimes in company with dogs, men and women (the last perhaps quite daring for a clergyman of that era). Many of the entries consist only of lists of species seen, of more or less significance; but a few add some detail (see Notes column for a selection of these items).

No.	Location	Dates	Notes
1	Ballast pit, Lincoln	<u>1901:</u> 7/11;21/11; 28/11	Location of the article 'Birds of a Ballast Pit'
		<u>1902:</u> 24,30/1; 13,22/2; 10,22/3; 11/7; 19,30/8; 6,20/9; 20,30/10; 17/11; 27/12	Some visits are made in company e.g 24,30/1 1902 'with WTL' On some occasions he skated on the frozen pit: e.g. 13/2 1902 & 26/11 1904
		<u>1903:</u> 14/1; 7,20/2; 21/3; 6/4; 26/6; 6/8; 5,17/10; 23/11	10/3 1902 was the source of his description of grebe behaviour
		<u>1904:</u> 9,26/1; 9,16/2; 15/3; 30/4; 16/8; 3,26/11	30/8 1902 was the date of his first black tern
2	Lincoln Arboretum, Monks Road	<u>1902:</u> 5,22/1; 17,19, 20,21/2; 16/3; 21/8; 15,23/9; 7/10; 1,6/11; 22/12	F.L.'s 'nearest' birding location when he lived in Monks Road and Monks Ley Terrace
		<u>1903:</u> 7,27/2; 5/3; 4, 8/4; 23/5; 20,27/7; 6/8; 3,30/9; 3,17, 21,	17/2 1902 he records a chaffinch singing which had no 'finish' to the song
		22/10	23/5 1903 six young swans hatched on the pond
		<u>1904:</u> 7,11/2; 19/4; 8/5; 5, 16/8; 22/12	17/10 1903 twenty geese in chevron
3	Bunkers Hill	<u>1904:</u> 5/2; 2/12	5/2 back via Greetwell Hollow
4	Greetwell Withy Beds	<u>1902:</u> 1/2	
5	Pyewipe	<u>1902:</u> 17/11	
6	Washingborough	<u>1902:</u> 17/3; 10/5; 6/12	17/3 records 'many' hooded crows
7	Washingborough Withy Beds	<u>1901:</u> 11/11 <u>1902:</u> 28/1; 19,22/3	

8	Wragby Road	<u>1904:</u> 25/5	Biked to hear nightingales
9	Harmston	<u>1904:</u> 17/3	Talked to the keeper, Mr Steward
10	Sudbrooke Park	<u>1904:</u> 10/3; 23/4; 24/5; 1/6	
11	Branston	<u>1904:</u> 26/4	
12	Eagle	<u>1903:</u> 1/1	
13	Hackthorn	<u>1902:</u> 1/3 <u>1904:</u> 18/5	
14	Brigg Road to Welton	<u>1901:</u> 7/12	By bicycle via Spridlington
15	Fiskerton and River Witham	<u>1901:</u> 5/12 <u>1902:</u> 27/6	5/12 1901 'very cold' 27/6 1902 'with Bill' to Aubourn
16	Newark	<u>1902:</u> 23/1	
17	Newbold Woods, Langworth	<u>1902:</u> 6/2; 31/3 <u>1903:</u> 5,8/6 <u>1904:</u> 18/2	6/2 1902 'walked' 31/3 1902 'with Harry'
18	Blankney	<u>1902:</u> 20/11	
19	Market Rasen to South Willingham	<u>1903:</u> 5/2	'walked with FFB'
20	Southrey	<u>1904:</u> 8/4	This is a rare occasion when F.L. takes eggs from a nest, one imagines for the museum collection in Lincoln. The nest was that of a long eared owl, in an old sparrowhawk nest; there were 5 eggs and he took three. He records that the female sat 'pretty close' and the male drew himself up with 'ear tufts sticking up'

21	Woodhall	1902: 3/3	
		1903: 17/2; 13/4	13/4 1903 he played 36 holes of golf in a location still renowned for its golf courses
22	Fulnetby Woods	1904: 25/5	
23	Donington-on-Bain	1904: 9/5	'a day's fishing' 'landed only six'
24	Spital & Hibalstow	1904: 31/3; 1/4; 6/12	On 1st April he visited the vicarage where there were nests of blackbird, song thrush and hedge sparrow in the garden; on 6/12 he cycled there
25	Walesby	1903: 14/12	'with TES [see item 27] to meet Burton hounds'; he saw a fox
26	Claxby	1902: 4/9; 4/12	4/12 1902 'went with FFB'
		1904: 20/12	20/12 1904 'went with Bill and Jack' – Jack being a dog
27	Caistor	1904: 20/10	'rode with T E Swangy'
28	Scotton	1902: 13/3; 6/5; 17, 24/7; 26/9	13/3 1902 walked from Gainsborough (?station) 'the keeper tells me he sees small parties of golden plover but they don't stay long'
		1903: 25,29/1; 5,26/3 16,25/4; 12,22/6; 4/8; 3/9	24/7 1902 'biked from Scotton Common and back through Corringham – 21 miles'
		1904: 22/3; 21,28/4; 17/5; 10/8	5/3 1903 told by keeper's wife that black-headed gulls had arrived this week
			25/4 1903 accompanied by Charles Branwell
			12,22/6 and 4/8 1903 all visits with friends
			All the 1904 visits were with friends

29	Skegness	1902: 8/7; 13/9 1903: 6/10	13/9 1902 F.L. records 'enormous numbers of gulls' of 'several species' near Gibraltar Point
30	Mablethorpe	1902: 3/4	'with ASB'
31	Saltfleet	1902: 9/1; 1/5; 9,21/10 1903: 20/11	9/1 1902 'rode via Louth' and recorded hooded crows, dunlin, little stint among others 1/5 1902 'went with Allison' 9/10 1902 'went with two Allisons' 21/10 1902 'with HWB', and on 20/11 1903 with the same companion and two dogs
32	Sutton-on-Sea	1903: 19/3	

Analysis:

Locations	32
Furthest from Lincoln	Saltfleet
Furthest north	Scotton Common
Furthest south	Blankney
Furthest east	Skegness
Furthest west	Scotton Common; (out of county, Newark)
Number of visits/total	147
Average visits per month	3.76
Most visited locations	Lincoln Ballast Pits (37); Lincoln Arboretum (36); Scotton Common (20)
Area covered	A line forming the rectangle of land marked by joining Scotton to Newark, across to Blankney, then up to Skegness and Saltfleet and back to Scotton covers approximately 925 square miles (2400 sq. kms)

NB On moving
to Doddington

a number of changes of pattern occur: F.L. is more free to watch at times of his own choosing, and this is often very early in the morning. There are sometimes more entries simply because he recorded on a daily basis birds seen in the Rectory or the adjacent land. He continues his frequent trips to far-flung areas. But there are a few occasions when, for a time, numbers of entries drop off or individual entries become rushed and minimalist.